Praise for

OF DICE AND MEN

"Dungeons & Dragons has been a huge part of my life. The book sheds light on the world of [D&D cocreator] Gary Gygax, and it also lets the reader into the mind of somebody who's questioning how cool this game is."

—Vin Diesel

"David Ewalt's wit, insight, and infectious love of D&D make him the perfect guide to the most significant game of the twentieth century. The book is a joy to read."

—Tim Harford, author of *The Undercover Economist*

"It's almost impossible to explain how Dungeons & Dragons works, and harder still to explain how it feels. This book comes as close as any I've ever read."

—Chuck Klosterman, author of *Sex, Drugs, and Cocoa Puffs* and *I Wear the Black Hat*

"David Ewalt writes about the world of fantasy role-playing junkies with intelligence, dexterity, and even wisdom. (I am unable to speak to his strength, constitution, or charisma.)"

—Ken Jennings, author of *Maphead* and *Because I Said So!*

"Long before I made my mark in software, I was a pretty good Dungeon Master, and D&D has played a significant part in my life. In addition to covering much of the deep history of the game that I never knew, *Of Dice and Men* brought back tons of fond memories, and damned if it didn't make me pull some dusty old rulebooks off the shelf at home."

—John Carmack, cofounder of Id Software

"A fascinating history of D&D written by an author who authentically loves the game. Whether you know what d20 means or not, you will love this book!"

—Felicia Day, actress, producer, creator of *The Guild* and Geek & Sundry

"The best book I've read since the *Monster Manual*."

—David X. Cohen, executive producer of *Futurama*

"A fascinating window into the storied history of fantasy pen-and-paper gaming. A must-read for anyone curious about the genre."

—Dr. Ray Muzyka, cofounder of BioWare

"Even audiences normally indifferent to D&D's charms will find Ewalt's overview witty and absorbing, and the game's devotees will discover much here to revel in and quibble with."

—*Booklist*

"The author's devotion to the game does much to illuminate role-playing's enduring power over mortal men and women."

—*Kirkus Reviews*

"David Ewalt offers a genial history of Dungeons & Dragons and its impact on his own geek life. . . . A highly readable account of a game that seized the imagination of a generation and maintains its grip three decades later."

—*Publishers Weekly*

"The core of Ewalt's story is his experience of role-playing games. He explains it about as well as anyone could, short of experiencing it yourself."

—*The Seattle Times*

"An engaging book that fuses history and memoir. [Ewalt] tracks D&D's turbulent rise, fall, and survival, from its heyday in the 1980s . . . to the twenty-first century."

—*The Wall Street Journal*

OF DICE AND MEN

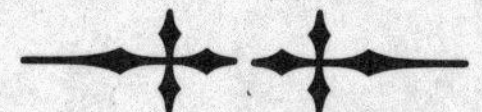

THE STORY OF DUNGEONS & DRAGONS AND THE PEOPLE WHO PLAY IT

David M. Ewalt

SCRIBNER

New York London Toronto Sydney New Delhi

Scribner
An Imprint of Simon & Schuster, LLC
1230 Avenue of the Americas
New York, NY 10020

This Scribner trade paperback edition March 2024

SCRIBNER and design are trademarks of Simon & Schuster, LLC

Simon & Schuster: Celebrating 100 Years of Publishing in 2024

For information about special discounts for bulk purchases, please contact Simon & Schuster Special Sales at 1-866-506-1949 or business@simonandschuster.com.

The Simon & Schuster Speakers Bureau can bring authors to your live event. For more information or to book an event, contact the Simon & Schuster Speakers Bureau at 1-866-248-3049 or visit our website at www.simonspeakers.com.

Manufactured in the United States of America

1 3 5 7 9 10 8 6 4 2

Library of Congress Control Number: 2013003048

ISBN 978-1-4516-4050-2
ISBN 978-1-4516-4051-9 (pbk)
ISBN 978-1-6680-5010-1 (pbk reissue)
ISBN 978-1-4516-4052-6 (ebook)

For Kara

CONTENTS

FOREWORD

To say that David Ewalt was ahead of the curve when he first published this book in 2013 would be a huge understatement. *Of Dice and Men* came out almost exactly a year before the rollout of Dungeons & Dragons Fifth Edition, which led the way for a global tabletop role-playing game (TTRPG) renaissance. However, even he couldn't have predicted what was in store for a game that had teetered on the verge of fading away several times, amid MMOs and Triple-A video games—entertainment properties that had translated the concepts of D&D into the digital age, garnering a level of popularity the game had never achieved even at the height of its popularity in the 1980s. D&D entered its "dark night of the soul," its absolute lowest point, in 2013, and in that moment, the game was bound for the dusty, fringe nostalgia bin . . . or so we thought.

Jump forward to today—D&D's fiftieth anniversary—and the game is bigger than it's ever been. Tens of millions of people play D&D at the table and online; it's been the subject of and inspiration for some of today's biggest films, TV shows, and actual-play series; its books and video games consistently top the charts; and whether you like it or not, it's spawned hordes of lifestyle products, from apparel and dinnerware to cookbooks and My Little Pony dolls. It's been a strange yet huge decade for a brand pulled back from the absolute brink. D&D has reclaimed, in Arthurian fashion, a throne it never really had, and as a result, the mainstream has been reintroduced to it (in hindsight) as an American art form that influenced everything from the entire video game industry to all your favorite directors, rock stars, and actors.

I was seven years old when I first got my hands on the legendary 1983 *Dungeons & Dragons Set 1: Basic Rules*, aka the "Red Box." I was too young to know it then, but in those days, D&D held the dubious distinction of being the number one hobby for geeks and nerds, and as a result I got into some playground arguments and had to defend it to the parents of some of my friends. It was the era's very definition of nerdiness and the occult. I played the Red Box's introductory module by myself, because at that age, in the pre-Internet era, I couldn't find one kid at my Catholic elementary school who was capable of figuring out what the hell it actually was and how you played it. It wasn't until a few years later that I found some novels on the rack of my local mall bookstore with illustrations that bore a striking resemblance to the one on that Red Box. They were the Dragonlance novels (with cover illustrations by the same D&D artist, Larry Elmore), and because I didn't have the money in my pocket to buy the first book, I shoplifted it. I became obsessed with those books (for the record, I later wrote a check to Waldenbooks to cover the cost of all the Dragonlance books I stole, and I take authors Margaret Weis and Tracy Hickman out to dinner whenever I see them). It was because I carried these novels around that I was identified by a fellow geek whose older brother played D&D, and that's how I finally discovered how the game worked. But nothing lasts forever, and eventually sports and the pursuit of girls took over; it was time for me to stop wasting time on this obsessive hobby and get onto a real career path . . .

. . . That of an actor, playing pretend for a living. I realized somewhere along the way that I had developed all my early characters by playing TTRPGs and Dungeon Mastering. I learned how to write, direct, and produce long-form narrative stories by obsessively playing D&D and other TTRPGs to the point where I was compulsively skipping homework to write my stories. The seeds of the game and the creativity it inspired were certainly apparent in my casting as a werewolf on the HBO fantasy series *True Blood*, but they were also present in everything I produced and wrote as well. I had spent decades away from the game, but because of the "ten thousand hours" I had put into it as a kid, the gift of storytelling had been burned into my DNA. I actually started playing TTRPGs again as an adult while performing as Stanley Kowalski at the Yale Repertory Theatre in a production of *A Streetcar Named Desire*. I was invited to join a group in the Connecticut area made up of people I had actually taught how to play RPGs as kids, meeting with them between rehearsals and shows. I then returned to LA and was roped into a Red Box Basic D&D campaign with a group of industry executives and improv comedians. During that time, fifth edition launched. I had already caught the bug again, as I had been simultaneously pursuing the rights to achieve my lifelong vision of bringing Dragonlance to the screen. I was then hired as a consultant shortly thereafter by Wizards of the Coast and began working out of their office in Seattle, along with the Dragonlance authors Margaret Weis and Tracy Hickman, and began playing in live filmed D&D games like *Force Grey* and *Critical Role*, all while working with D&D's marketing team to destigmatize the game through a series of high-profile talk show appearances. I then grew that little Red Box Basic game in LA into a who's who of entertainment industry titans, who came back to the game in the dungeon I had built in my basement because I had "helped make D&D cool again."

Fast-forward a few years, and I was allowed cowrite a D&D module in which my personal characters appear in official D&D canon as a part of the story for *Baldur's Gate: Descent into Avernus*. I founded Death Saves, my heavy metal/fantasy–themed streetwear company, which allowed me to resurrect and celebrate D&D's dark and edgy past through a licensing agreement that permitted me to redesign scarier and/or more metal versions of their legendary characters. I was hired to direct and produce an official documentary for D&D chronicling the stranger-than-fiction fifty-year story of the game, but most important of all, after years of persistence, I was finally given the green light by D&D to pursue my dream job: last spring, I turned in the script I wrote for the pilot episode of a Dragonlance streaming series based on the first six core novels I fell in love with so long ago. Never as a kid did I foresee being able to play such a big part in the game's development and success, but I've learned to always expect surprises when it comes to D&D, and I'm happy to have had a hand in the rest of the mainstream world's learning that D&D is the ultimate training ground for the imagination and deserves its place as an American art form alongside jazz, comic books, and hip-hop. In the hands of kids like me and the guys in my Friday-night home group, it had the power to change the world and the culture we live in. Viva D&D.

Joe Manganiello

OF DICE AND MEN

I AM NOT A WIZARD

Before we begin, I'd like to take a moment to address the hardcore fantasy role-playing gamers in the audience. If you've ever painted a lead mini, tried to wear the Head of Vecna, or know what happens if you flip a flumph on its back, please continue. Otherwise, feel free to skip straight to the first chapter.

Okay. Now that we've gotten rid of the muggles, there are a few points I want to cover.

First of all, at various points in this tome I quote specific elements of the Dungeons & Dragons rules, including game mechanics, spell effects, and monster descriptions. Unless otherwise noted, these citations refer to version 3.5 of the D&D rules. I default to those books because they're what I use with my friends, and I like them. Gamers who wish to argue the superiority of their own favored edition are advised to write a letter detailing their position, put it in an envelope, and then stick it where the Sunburst spell* don't shine.

Second, when describing in-game action, you may note that I

* "Sunburst causes a globe of searing radiance to explode silently from a point you select. All creatures in the globe are blinded and take 6d6 points of damage." *Player's Handbook*, p. 289. See how I did that?

sometimes break initiative order or skip over a player's turn. This is a conscious decision made to emphasize the drama in an encounter and not get lost in excruciating detail. Rest assured that everything described in-game actually happened in-game, and if I leave out the time Bob the Halfling fired his crossbow and missed, it's because nobody cares.

Finally, while I am confident that even the most grizzled of grognards can learn something from this volume, keep in mind it is largely intended to explain the phenomenon of D&D to a mainstream audience. If you seek a detailed history or obscure arcana, you have just failed your Gather Information check. Fortunately, there is a wealth of scholarship available on the subject, and you'll find a list of some of the best sources in the back of this book.

In short: Read this like you'd play in a friendly campaign. Don't be a rules lawyer, and don't argue with the DM.

1

YOU'RE ALL AT A TAVERN

The day I met Abel, Jhaden, and Ganubi, we got arrested for brawling in a bar.

In our defense, we were fighting for a righteous cause. One of the regulars was six beers past tipsy when he started running his mouth and spouting the worst kind of reactionary politics. Abel and I found it offensive and told him to shut up; Jhaden isn't much for talk, so he hit the guy with a stool. Rhetorical became physical, and the four of us lined up on the same side of the dispute.

The cops must have been nearby, because the next thing I knew they were throwing us in the back of a wagon. We stewed in a cell overnight before Jhaden was able to use some kind of family connection to get us released. I don't know what happened to the drunk guy.

A thing like that will bond a group of young men pretty quickly, and soon we were spending most of our time together—sharing a couple of rooms in a cheap boardinghouse, working together on whatever freelance gigs we could find. The jobs weren't always on the books, but we felt like we were doing good work.

Jhaden was strong as a bull, Ganubi a natural charmer, Abel educated and clever. We got in our share of fights, but I had worked in a hospital, and when anyone got hurt, I'd do my best to patch them up.

I'd like to think I did my part in combat, too—shooting searing rays of light out of my fingers, stunning enemies with thunderclaps of sonic energy. Sometimes I'd summon a giant badger from the celestial planes and command it to do my bidding. Few things end a fight quicker than a magical weasel chewing on your opponent's leg.

I am not a wizard, but I play one every Tuesday night. To be nerdy about it—and trust me, there is no other way to approach this—I am a divine spell caster, a lawful neutral twelfth-level cleric. In the world of Dungeons & Dragons, that makes me a pretty major badass.

Dungeons & Dragons—D&D, to the initiated—is a game played at a table, usually by around half a dozen participants. It's sold in stores and has specific rules, like Monopoly or Scrabble, but is otherwise radically different. D&D is a role-playing game, one where participants control characters in a world that exists largely in their collective imagination.

Even if you've never played D&D, you've probably heard of it, and when I admitted I'm a player, your subconscious mind probably filed me under "Nerds, Hopeless"—unless you happen to be one of us. Role-playing games don't have a great reputation. In movies and TV shows, D&D serves as a signal of outsider status. It's how you know a character's a hopeless geek: A rule book and a bunch of weird-shaped dice is to nerds what a black hat is to the villain in a cowboy movie.

Most people know D&D only as some strange thing the math club did in the corner of the high school cafeteria, or the hobby of the creepy goth kid down the street. Even worse, they have the vague sense it's deviant or satanic—don't D&D players run around in the woods and worship demons, or commit suicide when they lose a game?

Admitting you play Dungeons & Dragons is only slightly less stigmatizing than confessing cruelty to animals or that you wet the bed. It is not to be done in polite company.

But I am immune to your scorn. I know magic.

Jhaden, Abel, Ganubi, and I are freedom fighters. The shared politics that brought us together in that bar are more profound than liberal or conservative; we're all proponents of an active approach to humanity's problems. We want to organize the workers of the world and to strike out against those who would hold us in bondage.

In contrast, our opponents fear change. They don't want to upset their comfortable bourgeois lives or take risks that might overturn the political order. Time is on our side, they say—real progress occurs slowly, over generations. They think we should wait and things will work themselves out.

It's so cowardly and stupid. You can't wait out vampires.

Let's start with a brief overview, for the uninitiated: Dungeons & Dragons takes place within a fantasy world that is invented by its players but inspired by centuries of storytelling and literature. Books like J. R. R. Tolkien's *Lord of the Rings* helped set the tone: heroic knights and wise old magicians battling the forces of evil. A typical D&D session might find a party of adventurers setting off to search an underground cave system for treasure and having to fight all the slobbering monsters lurking in the dark.

But D&D isn't a board game with a preprinted map and randomized game play (roll a die, move four spaces closer to the treasure, pick up a card: "You got scared by a goblin! Go back two spaces"). Instead, each setting is conceived in advance by one of the participants and then actively navigated by the players.

The person who does all the prep work is called the Dungeon

Master, or DM. It's his job to dream up a scenario, something like "Archaeologists have discovered a pharaoh's tomb in the desert, and the players are grave robbers who have to break in and steal the hidden treasure." He also has to sketch out the details, like making a map and deciding where the traps are, where the treasure is, and what monsters are guarding it.

This act of creation gives the players an unknown world to explore and keeps each game session different from the last. It's sort of like sitting down to play Monopoly, except you can't see the names or costs of the properties until you land on them.

An experienced DM takes game design even further. He might decide the players should start out in a Bedouin camp near the tomb and negotiate with the sheik to buy a couple of camels. He could plan for them to be waylaid by desert raiders on the way to the tomb. And once they've found the pharaoh's treasure, he may ask them to make a moral choice: The treasure carries a curse, and if it's removed from the tomb, the region will suffer ten years of famine. The players will have to weigh getting rich and letting thousands die against leaving empty-handed and protecting the innocent.

At this level, setting up a role-playing game becomes something like writing a screenplay or novel. And just as fantasy fiction may include all kinds of different settings and plots, a fantasy role-playing game does not have to be constrained to a standard medieval setting.

Vampires have always hunted man, but we were not always in their thrall. For millennia they hid in the shadows, keeping their numbers small, feeding only on humans who wouldn't be missed. The few stories that betrayed their existence were dismissed as urban legend or lazy fiction.

But at the beginning of the twenty-first century, something changed.

Vampires were tired of hiding, of letting weaker humans ruin the planet. So they gathered, and they plotted, and one dark night, they struck.

Most humans died without ever knowing their enemy. The vampires had magically bound our leaders to their will, and on their command, the armies of the world exploded upon one another. Those who survived the first strike had nowhere to hide: A magically enchanted retrovirus mutated ordinary animals and plants, turning them into monsters that overran both ruined cities and poisoned wilderness.

What few shreds of humankind remained were easily rounded up, brought to a dozen vampire-controlled cities, and locked into pens, like cattle. Our species survived, but only as a food source for Earth's new masters.

We call the time the vampires took over the Nightfall. The Dawn is when humans fought back.

Most people who play Dungeons & Dragons don't just sit down for a single, self-contained session, like they would with a board game. Instead, they join a "campaign," a group that meets on a regular basis and uses the same characters in the same world, building on past actions. One week, the players raid the pharaoh's tomb, and the next, they pick up where they left off, facing the consequences of their decisions.

As these campaigns go on for weeks and months and even years, the successes and failures of past sessions provide history and context and suggest new challenges. If the players stole the pharaoh's treasure and cursed the land with famine, a DM might design a future session where they're hunted by vengeful farmers.

Players are both audience and author in D&D; they consume the DM's fiction but rewrite the story with their actions. And as authors, they're free to make their own decisions. If a troll is trying to eat you, you can hit him with a sword, shoot him with an arrow, or run away—it's up to you. For that matter, you could sing him a song, try to recruit him into Scientology, or lie down for a nap. Your choice might be a dumb one, but it's still yours to make.

Unlike board games, which limit the player to a small set of actions, or video games, which offer a large but finite set of preprogrammed possibilities, role-playing games give the player free will. As long as it doesn't violate the integrity of the fictional universe—proclaiming that up is down or suddenly transmogrifying into Abraham Lincoln—you can do whatever you want.

The resulting game play is rather different than other pastimes. In a game of Clue, you are asked to solve a murder mystery but must do so by moving a token around a board and looking at playing cards. If Clue was played like D&D, you could grab the lead pipe, beat a confession out of Colonel Mustard, and have sex with Miss Scarlet on the desk in the conservatory.

There are rules, of course. Books and books of rules, sold at $19.95 each, which inform a player's decisions and determine their success. Attacking someone with a lead pipe? That's armed combat with an improvised weapon, and page 113 of the *Dungeons & Dragons Player's Handbook* explains how to figure out if you hit your target and how much it hurt. Seducing another character might require a Diplomacy check (page 71), a Will save (page 136), and maybe an opposed Sense Motive roll against your Bluff skill (page 64). It's not romantic, but it works.

All this free will can wreak havoc with the game's continuing story. A DM might spend weeks designing a complex network of caverns to explore, filled with clever traps and new monsters to fight. But if the players stop at the mouth of the cave and decide they'd rather go back to town and get drunk, they are free to do so—and they'll derail the story in the process.

In order to keep freedom of action from leading to chaos, a good DM will usually weave a primary conflict into his story. This often takes the form of a classic heroic quest: a wrong to right, an enemy to destroy, or a world to save.

For a century after the vampires came to power, they imprisoned and fed on what was left of the human race. Stuck in the pens and denied the use of modern technology, humanity lived in fear, never knowing when their masters would descend from the city to feed.

But the undead were arrogant, and humans adapted. They watched the vampires cast spells and copied their actions, developing their own knowledge of magic. These secrets were shared and used to communicate with other pens. Together, humanity planned its escape.

And one day, as dawn swept across the globe, the people of the pens rose up and fought. The vampires were taken by surprise, but their power was still great. Many humans were recaptured, and many more died. But some escaped and returned to their abandoned cities, where they constructed defenses to keep the vampires at bay.

In the generation since the Dawn, both human and vampire have rebuilt. We hold a handful of cities, but they do too, and thousands are still captive in the pens. Beyond the walled cities, there is wilderness, filled with monsters.

But we're not hiding, and we do not rest. We learn, and we prepare, and we plan for the day we can take our planet back.

Frodo Baggins needed the help of three hobbits, two men, an elf, a dwarf, and a wise old wizard to save the world. So nobody expects a role-playing nerd to go it alone. Uniquely among tabletop games—and especially uniquely among activities enjoyed by teenage boys—Dungeons & Dragons is cooperative, not competitive. Players work together to advance the story and solve problems, not to beat each other to a finish line.

This means there's rarely a real "winner" in a D&D game; no

single player comes out on top. In fact, winning is something of an alien concept—most campaigns never last long enough to reach their dramatic conclusion. It's more about the journey than the destination, to invoke that old cliché, and about developing your part in the story.

A player in a game of D&D doesn't just push a premade plastic token around a board. Instead, they create a "player character," or PC, a unique persona to be inhabited like an actor in a role, imbuing it with motivation and will and action. It's like *Avatar,* but with knights instead of weird blue cat people.

Of course, D&D is not a playacting exercise. At the most fundamental level, a PC is defined by a bunch of numbers written down on a piece of paper—the DNA of an imaginary person. (It's no coincidence that so many people who play the game also happen to be keen on math and science.)

At the start of a new game, players roll a handful of dice to determine their PC's basic attributes, following the directions set out in a rule book. Some of these attributes define the character physically: how strong they are, how dexterous, how hardy. Others measure personality traits, like whether they are perceptive or oblivious, strong willed or weak. Each score is recorded by the player and kept for future reference.

Over the course of a game, a player will continually refer to these attributes to measure their success in different actions. Want to pick up a heavy rock and throw it at the barbarians invading your castle? That'll require a high strength score. Trying to dive under the trellis gate before it closes? Sorry, your dexterity is too low.

Next, a player has to select one of about a dozen character classes. This is something like choosing a profession and has a profound effect on the role a PC plays in the game. Classes are best explained within the context of *The Lord of the Rings*—as the most mainstream example of the fantasy genre, *LOTR* references come up all the time in Dungeons & Dragons.

Aragorn, the scruffy hero who turns out to be heir to the kingdom of men, would be a "ranger" in a D&D campaign—at home in the wilderness, an expert tracker, equally comfortable with a bow or a blade. Legolas the elf would be a ranger, too. Boromir and Gimli the dwarf would probably be "fighters"—masters of brute-force combat, emphasizing power rather than a ranger's finesse. Gandalf? They call him a wizard, but D&D "wizards" have to study a lot, write their spells in a book, and use magic ingredients to make anything cool happen. Gandalf's really more like a "sorcerer"—someone who is born with special abilities and doesn't have to learn them. The diminutive hobbits are probably "rogues"—stealthy, agile, and sly. Often, since they're so good at sneaking around, rogues are played as thieves. But our good-hearted hobbits don't have to be pickpockets to play the class properly.*

There are many other classes in the game that aren't represented in Middle-earth. "Clerics" are warrior priests. They can cast spells but frequently do so in order to assist other players, such as to repair a wound. "Paladins" are chivalrous knights who fight evil and follow a strict code of conduct. And "barbarians" are uneducated bruisers, likely to fly into a homicidal rage. They're the anabolic steroid users of the D&D world.

Once they've been assigned a class, PCs are allocated specific skills, as chosen from lists in the rule book. They may learn only a small number, so skills must be chosen wisely: If a player wants their rogue to be a cat burglar, it's best to concentrate on skills like "Open Lock"

---

*That sound you hear right now is thousands of fantasy geeks shouting their dissent. Debating what D&D classes fictional characters or real people would belong to is a contentious sport in nerd society. I once spent hours at work arguing with a colleague about the makeup of our office. At the end of the day, we agreed the boss was a dwarf rogue.

and "Move Silently." Any time the PC tries to perform a related action in the game, their success will depend on it.

Characters are also usually rounded out with a personal history, something that places them in the context of the larger D&D campaign. This is where the process becomes more art than science; each PC is its own work of fiction.

A good backstory can make or break a game. It lends depth to the fictional world, provides the player with motivation for future decision-making, and breathes life into a collection of numbers and rules.

I am Weslocke, a cleric. I was born in Kyoto, one of the few cities reoccupied after the Dawn, and I will not rest until humanity is free.

Generations of my family have dedicated their lives to this cause. My great-great-grandmother, a doctor, practiced her art in secret after the vampires threw her in the pens. Her children learned and did the same, hoping that one day humans would be strong enough to fight back. When that day came, my parents aided in the battle with healing magic, spells that stitch wounds and mend broken bones.

After Kyoto was resettled, my parents pushed to continue the war and destroy the vampires entirely. Few would listen. But they never gave up and raised me in the hope I could finish what they started. I learned to fight, and to heal, and to hate the vampires, and want nothing but their destruction.

When my parents died, I swore to uphold their legacy. I made plans to leave the city, to develop the skills needed to fight the undead, and to find other people who shared my goals. And then, one fateful day, I got arrested for fighting in a bar.

Vampire World is a creation of Morgan Harris-Warrick, a thirty-three-year-old executive for a family-centric marketing agency. By day he runs focus groups, studying how kids are likely to respond to new advertising campaigns. By night he's a Dungeon Master, inventor of the Nightfall and the Dawn.

In any game of Dungeons & Dragons, the Dungeon Master serves as author, director, and referee. A good DM must be creative, designing a world from scratch and spinning it into narrative. But they also must possess an ordered, logical mind, capable of recalling and understanding hundreds of pages' worth of rules.

It's a role that suits Morgan. Tall and rangy, with a shock of short black hair, he dresses in the manner of a nerd artiste, wrapped in a trench coat and topped with a wool felt fedora. He's technical (he once built and programmed his own digital video recorder, instead of just buying a TiVo) but not ignorant of aesthetic pursuits: He's written two unproduced screenplays, including an alternate telling of *Peter Pan* where Tinker Bell dies after a cynical audience refuses to clap.

Morgan started playing D&D when he was in fifth grade. "I was a socially inept little geek when I was a kid," he says. "D&D was a way to socialize that you could be geeky and still do." On Saturdays, he'd walk over to a friend's house and spend the afternoon playing with a small group of like-minded peers.

"It wasn't an ongoing campaign like what I'm running now," he explains. "We had characters, and whoever felt like running an adventure would write something up and we'd throw our characters into it. There weren't big, ongoing stories. There wasn't really even much of a world."

The kids took turns running the game, so Morgan didn't really come into his own as a Dungeon Master until he was a few years older. "In high school we had a D&D club, where we'd meet once a week in a spare room," he says. "I had a separate campaign that I created for that, based on Piers Anthony's *Xanth* books."

In college, a wealth of other social activities beckoned, and Morgan stopped gaming. But when he moved to New York City a couple years after graduation, he started thinking about playing again. "It's a good way to meet people, people with interests similar to mine," he explains. "I had discovered the joys of Craigslist and how you could find people with any specific interest, so I thought, 'Why don't I see if I can find a D&D group?'"

He already knew what kind of game he wanted to play. "I'm a sucker for the postapocalyptic stuff . . . something I recognize, but changed," he says. "I'd seen an anime film called *Vampire Hunter D,* and the premise was that vampires had taken over the world, but it was set after the humans had fought back and won. And I was watching that, and I was thinking, 'You know, this is a fun enough movie, but they skipped the really interesting part, while the humans are just starting to rise up against the vampires. Let's go back and fill in that story.'"

Today our quest was interrupted. We had secured passage aboard a ship sailing to San Francisco, hoping to find new allies in our fight against the vampires. But two days into the journey, the sails went slack and our ship was engulfed in a murky fog. Before we could prepare ourselves, we were set upon by unnatural creatures—bodies like men, but with scaly hides, webbed hands, and the wide-set eyes and gaping mouths of fish.

Taken by surprise, we were captured by the creatures—common pirates, despite their appearance—and imprisoned in the hold of our own ship.

They should have killed us. Within an hour, Ganubi had managed to slip his bonds and untie us. We recovered our gear and headed for the deck—and now, we hide behind the wheelhouse as Ganubi pokes his head around the corner, surveying the scene.

"You see four of the fish-men standing near the mast, about thirty feet away," Morgan says during one of our weekly game nights.

"They carry big, jagged-tipped spears and seem to be having a conversation, though you can't understand their language. It sounds like a bubbling, half-clogged drain."

Ganubi pauses, turns, and grins back at us. I know the look on his face, and it worries me.

"Stay right here," he says. "I've got an idea."

Ganubi is a "bard," one of the more obscure character classes in Dungeons & Dragons. Bards express magic powers through the use of music or performance, sort of like the Pied Piper. Many players avoid the class, preferring to play something more traditional, like a fighter or thief. But there's nothing traditional about Phil.

Phillip Gerba, thirty-one, is a professional clown. He earned a bachelor's degree in theater performance from Northern Arizona University and studied for a year at the Clown Conservatory in San Francisco. After graduation he worked on Royal Caribbean cruise ships as a juggler, and then moved to New York and got a job at the big Disney store in midtown Manhattan. He wore a Goofy suit and did pratfalls to amuse kids.

At the moment, Phil's developing his own stage show, *Onomatopoeia*. It's high-concept vaudeville: Each scene explores an idea, but the only words in the script are onomatopoeias. It's heavy on the slapstick: Bang! Pop! Thud! Sigh.

Phil started playing D&D when he was just a child. "I really wanted to play a lizard man because I liked lizards," he says. "I wanted to be a herpetologist when I grew up." Instead, he went into theater—and now the game table is one more place for him to perform.

D&D players control their characters using a combination of first-person narration and dramatic performance. This is the part of the game that confuses people who've never played. But it's fairly simple, in practice.

Imagine you're playing a character who is locked in a jail cell. The DM describes the room, from his notes: "You're in the corner of a cold, dark room, about ten feet square. The walls are made of stone and are only interrupted by a single wooden door. The door is shut tightly, and a fist-sized window near the top is your only source of light."

As a player, your job is to choose an action and describe it. You might say, "I try to force the door open."

At this, the DM looks up the rules for breaking down a door,* consults your character sheet to see how strong you are, and rolls a couple dice. If you're lucky, he'll say something like "You put all your weight against the door, and a hinge snaps. The door falls out into the hallway with a loud crash."

This narrative technique is useful in most situations. But what if you weren't strong enough to break the door? You might try to talk a guard into releasing you—and your DM might require you to act the scenario out, in character, with him playing the guard. Put on a convincing performance, and he'll open the door.

For players like Phil, this is the best part of the game. He comes to life when our characters are haggling with merchants, negotiating with employers, or trying to talk their way out of a fight.

Ganubi's plans are always dramatic, but not as often successful, so I have my reservations. But he's already turned the corner and pulled out a trinket we obtained in Tokyo: his hat of disguise, a magical item that allows the wearer to change appearance at will.

---

*Table 3–17: Random Door Types, *Dungeon Master's Guide,* page 78.

He puts it on his head, and his features warp and twist, his skin turns scaly, and his face goes flat. In a moment, he looks like one of the pirates.

"Okay, you look like a fish," Morgan says.

Phil flashes a large grin. "I'm going to approach the pirates and see what they do."

Morgan rolls a die, hidden behind the cover of his notebook. "They turn and notice you but don't take any action. You're still about thirty feet away."

"Right." Phil pauses. "When I get about five feet away, I'm going to act surprised, point behind them, and yell in alarm."

"You don't speak their language."

"I know," says Phil. "I make a noise like a panicked fish."

Morgan chuckles and then grimaces. "Okay," he says. "Roll against your performance skill."

Phil picks up a d20—a glittery blue plastic die, twenty-sided—and rolls it across the table. It stops showing a seven.

Morgan checks his notes. "The pirates look confused," he says. "They're just staring at you."

"Okay," says Phil. "Which fish looks the most gullible?"

Alex grunts, exasperated. "To hell with this," he says. "I draw my swords."

Jhaden is the eight-hundred-pound gorilla in our adventuring party, a ranger who fights with one sword in each hand on the front line of battle. He does the majority of damage to enemies and serves as a meat shield for other, less hardy characters.

He's played by Alex Agius, thirty-three. Alex is a graphic designer, working freelance since he was laid off from a full-time job at *Penthouse* magazine. It used to be his job to lay out pictorials, Photoshop blemishes off nude models, and select the proper font for each obscene caption. Now he mostly works for a magazine about investment banking.

Alex was first exposed to D&D when he turned nine years old and a cousin brought the game to his birthday party. "I loved the Conan comic books, so what initially attracted me to D&D was that you could be a barbarian," he says. "But when I realized that I could play a character that was totally my design, instead of a pre-created character like Conan . . . that was really cool."

After his cousin went home, Alex sketched a map of the dungeon they'd explored in the game. When his mom found the drawing, she "thought it was really cool," so she bought him a set of D&D rule books.

Unlike Phil, Alex tends to get restless when there's too much role-playing in a game. He's much more comfortable when the adventure tends toward action.

Combat in D&D is handled as a sequence of narrated actions and lots of dice rolling. If a player decides to hit something with his sword, he may announce the attack, but the DM calculates whether it succeeds. In practice, this amounts to calculating an algebraic equation, something like: (strength of the fighter + skill of the fighter) – (agility of the target + armor worn by the target) + an element of randomness introduced by the dice = whether or not the fighter hits.

Every creature in the game—whether a character controlled by a player or a monster controlled by the DM—has a specific amount of "hit points," a number representing their health. When a fighter hits his target, he rolls dice to see how much it hurts, with higher numbers indicating more damage. The DM subtracts that number from the monster's pool of hit points, and the process repeats. Player after player takes their shots until the monster hits zero hit points and dies.

These rules for combat get incredibly complex. There are specific rules for fighting while blinded, while underwater, and while riding a horse. There are rules that describe how to knock a sword out of someone's hands and how to bash them with a shield. There is even an entire rule book, *Weapons of Legacy,* listing hundreds of different armaments and describing the effect they have upon the game.

Jhaden's sword, Bloodlust, is an epic weapon, magically enchanted to inflict extra damage against vampires and other undead creatures. He wields it in his right hand, and in his left he holds a shorter blade, a foot long and unnaturally sharp. If he comes at you with both, you're going to get hurt.

"I'm charging," Alex says. "This guy." He points at an inch-high plastic figurine on the table, representing one of the fish. Morgan has set them up on our battle mat, a piece of tan vinyl printed with a twenty-by-twenty grid of one-inch squares. Each square corresponds to five feet of space in the game world, and every participant in a battle is represented by a different miniature figurine, or "mini." We don't use it all the time in the game, but it's helpful during combat because it allows us to track each other's location and movement.

"The guards see you, and now it's time for initiative order," says Morgan. Any time players enter combat, they roll a die to determine the order in which they'll take their turns. This time, Alex comes up first.

"Okay, I charge in, and I'm attacking with Bloodlust," he says. He moves his mini—a crouching figure in a brown cloak, holding two swords—across the mat, picks up a d20, and rolls it to determine the success of his attack. It comes up 12. "I get plus two for charging, and plus eight for my melee attack bonus, so my attack roll is a twenty-two."

Jhaden rushes forward, and Bloodlust slashes through the pirate's scales, penetrating deep into its chest. As he pulls the sword from his victim, Jhaden looks back at us and shouts, "Tonight we're eating sushi!"

A Dungeons & Dragons campaign almost always includes a wizard. Abel was our first. He was an "evoker," which denotes a specialization in spells that create something from nothing—like fireballs and lightning bolts. But he was killed just a few weeks ago, when his consciousness was merged with that of an ancient dragon.* Since wizards are so critical to an adventuring party's success, we quickly recruited a new one, Babeal.

Both characters are played by Brandon Bryant. It would be simple to typecast Brandon as a D&D player—he's a big guy with unruly hair who works as an IT manager. But the easy stereotypes end there. At thirty-four, he's on his second marriage, to a recent art school graduate. He's studied karate since he was a kid and regularly travels to competitions around the Northeast. He's also an expert fire dancer—on warm summer nights in Brooklyn, you can sometimes find him on the roof of his apartment building, tossing and catching flaming batons.

Brandon's happy to draw a direct line from his fire dancing to spell casting. "I like the idea of having control over an elemental force," he says. "Here's this primal thing and I'm bending it to my will . . . it's magical but mundane, like having tea with a god."

"The pirate has been badly wounded by Jhaden's attack but is still standing," says Morgan. "Babeal, it's your turn."

---

* It's a long story. Suffice it to say that if we ever manage to rid the earth of vampires, the next world-killing peril we'll have to deal with is a badass flying serpent with a raging case of multiple personality disorder.

The mini representing Babeal is at the far end of the battle mat, where Morgan has drawn a box with a brown dry-erase marker, indicating the walls of the ship's wheelhouse. It's a figure of a man in a forest-green robe, holding a long staff and wearing a bucket-shaped helmet with long antlers curving upward on each side. This mini has always reminded me of the leader of the "Knights who say Ni" from the film *Monty Python and the Holy Grail,* but I have never made this observation aloud. Making a Python reference in a room full of geeks is like bringing brownies to a Weight Watchers meeting. It could take hours to restore order.

Jhaden is across the grid, in a square next to the wounded pirate. The three other fish-men are a few squares away.

"Suck on this, fishies," says Brandon. "Fireball."

Morgan nods. A fireball is a ranged attack spell, so Babeal can cast it from a distance. And since it has a distinct area of effect—a circle forty feet in diameter, or eight squares on the grid—Babeal can target it so as to immolate the pirates but miss his allies.

Morgan draws a red circle on the mat. "You cast and the deck explodes in flame, engulfing the pirates. Roll for damage."

A fireball spell causes worlds of hurt, so Babeal needs to roll ten six-sided dice (in geekspeak, "10d6") to find out how many hit points each pirate loses.

He doesn't have enough dice, though. So he picks 5d6 off the table—three of his own, and two of Alex's—tosses them on the table, scoops them up, and tosses them again. Each affected enemy will take 32 points of damage.

Brandon's fireballs do 10d6 of damage now, but when our game began, he couldn't cast the spell at all. That's changed because of a key element of the D&D rules: Characters don't just persist from session to session, they learn from their experiences.

Anyone who has played a video game in the last twenty years won't find that shocking. But D&D pioneered the idea of characters that become more powerful over time; before its invention, games were almost all static. The rules of Monopoly never change, no matter how many times you go around the board.*

Because D&D characters can grow, like real people, playing the game becomes a uniquely visceral experience. Participants are more motivated to succeed, since victories are accumulative. They experience greater joy from those successes, since they are more emotionally invested. And they know the thrill of real danger, since no one wants to lose a character they've spent years building.

In short, D&D players live vicariously through their characters the way a parent might live through their children—not that any gamer would take the relationship that seriously, unless they're crazy. But more on that later.

Naturally, advancement is measured in terms of a mathematical progression. At various points in an adventure, usually during breaks in the narrative, a DM will review the players' accomplishments and reward them with "experience points." They'll get points for every monster they've defeated, based on their relative threat; killing a rat might earn 100 experience points, while slaying a dragon could be worth 100,000. They'll also, at the DM's discretion, receive points for abstract achievements, like solving a puzzle or successfully role-playing their way out of trouble. When a character has earned enough experience points they advance a level, gain access to new abilities, and become more powerful.

---

*Just imagine if the battleship eventually gained the ability to fire its cannons and blow the thimble to pieces.

The characters aren't the only thing changing over time. Since D&D campaigns can last months, years, or even decades, players will come and go as their personal lives allow more or less opportunity for leisure.

Vampire World has seen its share of personnel changes. Brandon's friend Nick played a barbarian, Taluug, until he moved out of the apartment. A second Alex (we called him "Deuce") had a few characters, including a druid, a magic-user who draws his powers from nature. Deuce was a college student and quit because of school obligations.

R. C. Robbins joined the game well after Abel, Jhaden, Ganubi, and Weslocke met in Kyoto. He plays Graeme, a rogue. They're an essential part of any adventuring party; skills like finding traps and picking locks are frequently useful in the fantasy-adventure genre. But since R. C. didn't make the game tonight, we consider Graeme "in pocket"—he hasn't died or left the party, he's just off in the background until next time. It's a shame, because we could use a little help with these pirates: Babeal's fireball scorched them but didn't take them down.

Now it's my turn. Weslocke is a cleric, and, like Babeal, he's capable of casting powerful spells. Many of them are focused on healing—in any adventuring party, the cleric often plays the role of medic. But I've got a few haymakers as well.

I pick up my mini (a man in silver plate armor, holding a heavy flanged mace) and move it five squares toward the pirates. I'm still allowed to take an action after moving, so I check my character sheet and then pick up a d20.

"I cast Searing Light on this pirate," I tell Morgan, pointing at a figure, and then roll the die: 17, more than high enough to confirm the hit. The spell incurs one eight-sided die's (or 1d8) worth of damage per two caster levels; I'm a twelfth-level cleric, so I scrounge around the table to find six eight-sided dice. I roll and sum the numbers: 41 hit points' worth of damage.

"A blast of light shoots from your palm, like a ray of the sun," says Morgan. "It strikes the pirate and he withers and dies." Alex cackles. I smirk.

I named Weslocke after one of the very first D&D characters I ever played. I was ten years old, in fourth grade, and impossibly nerdy: I wore trousers, black socks, and thick glasses to my magnet school for gifted children.

By that age, I'd already been sucked into many of the classic 1980s nerd interests, including *Star Wars*, computer programming, and listening to Weird Al Yankovic. But I hadn't explored the realms of fantasy literature any deeper than *The Chronicles of Narnia* and was only dimly aware of role-playing games. So when my friend Scott Johnson produced a beat-up copy of the Dungeons & Dragons Basic Set, it was a revelation: In this world, I wasn't a "neo maxi zoom dweebie" in JCPenney slacks. I was an ass-kicking, dungeon-crawling, goblin-slaying epic hero.

I wasn't alone. In the decade following its 1974 debut, D&D grew from an obscure hobby into a worldwide phenomenon—one of the most passionately loved, bestselling, and most controversial games ever made. It dominated my preteen years and became the center of my most important social interactions; my best friends were the guys I played D&D with. When we got together for one of our frequent Saturday-night sleepovers, sometimes we'd watch a movie, sometimes we'd go swimming, sometimes we'd throw firecrackers at each other or ignite pools of lighter fluid in Scott's driveway—but we'd always play D&D.

It's the pirates' turn now, so Morgan takes over the action. After my spell fried their comrade, the pirates decided I'm their biggest threat, so Morgan moves their minis to surround me—one in front, and two on either side. They attack with their spears, and two connect. Suddenly, I'm down to only 55 of my 82 hit points.

Everyone in the fight has made a move, so the initiative order starts again from the top. Jhaden pivots and hacks at one of the pirates but doesn't drop him. Ganubi falls back, draws his bow, and fires an arrow, which misses. Babeal zaps one with a Magic Missile spell, but only for 16 hit points.

I decide to get clever. I announce to the table that I'm casting a spell, Blade Barrier, which summons an immobile curtain of whirling blades into existence. I evoke this barrier, I explain, in a circle directly around Weslocke: the eight squares on the grid bordering my own, three of which are currently occupied by pirates.

Morgan will have to roll high for each pirate to successfully dodge the blades and back out of the curtain. If they don't, they're going to be chum.

He tosses the dice. One dies instantly, shredded by the blades. Another makes his roll and jumps backward, taking no damage. The third also dodges successfully—but instead of pushing his mini away from mine, Morgan picks up the figure and drops it right in my square.

"The pirate jumps forward to escape the blades and crashes into you," he explains. "You both collapse to the ground."

I have trapped myself inside a cage of whirling knives with a raging fish monster.

Playing D&D might be uniquely rewarding, but it's not always easy. Role-playing games carry a lot of baggage, and devotees run the risk of being branded as nerds, weirdos—or even criminals.

To be fair, this prejudice has some root in reality. The game does tend to attract fans of fantasy literature, mythology, mathematics, and puzzles—in other words, nerds. They value the community they find among D&D players and strive to be welcoming to others; the game table becomes a place where outcasts can feel comfortable. It's admirable, but it does the hobby no favors in the PR department.

I don't know if I played D&D because other kids my age thought I was a nerd, or if they thought I was a nerd because I played D&D. Causation and correlation tend to get confused when some hormone-addled thirteen-year-old bully is threatening to sew your ass to your elbow. What I do know is that I had it easy. I played D&D as much as I wanted and put up with only occasional teasing: Other kids were forbidden to play the game and ostracized when they did.

In the 1980s, D&D found itself at the center of a massive hysteria. The game was linked to murders, satanic rituals, and teen suicides. Schools banned it; churches demonized it; courts criminalized it. Law enforcement officials would report that a suspect "was known to play D&D" the same way they might reveal he tortured animals or was a serious drug addict.

I never wavered in my love of D&D, though I did see other games. As we entered our angsty teenage years, my friends and I spent increasing amounts of time with D&D's children: role-playing games that stepped out of the fantasy genre to emulate spy thrillers (Top Secret), science fiction (Star Trek: The Role Playing Game), and whatever it is you'd call Teenage Mutant Ninja Turtles & Other Strangeness.

We were particularly fond of postapocalyptic games like Cyberpunk 2020, which belong to a genre inspired by authors like William Gibson and Bruce Sterling. In high school we spent hundreds of hours playing Shadowrun, a futuristic game that brilliantly combined sci-fi with classic D&D elements. The game imagined an apocalypse caused by the return of magic, instead of warfare or disease: It had trolls on motorbikes, elven computer hackers, and an ancient blue dragon named Dunkelzahn who got elected president.

In practice, Shadowrun played something like *Blade Runner* meets *Conan the Barbarian*. My favorite character was a wizard who could shoot a gun with one hand and cast fireball spells with the other. I sat in a friend's basement and played that character on almost every Saturday night of my high school senior year.

A magic-user controls arcane energies through an act of pure will, so I can dismiss Weslocke's blade barrier just as easily as I summoned it. But not until my next turn. For now, I have to wait, and right now, it's the pirate's turn.

He bites for 11 points of damage, and then Morgan gets a funny look on his face. "Roll against your willpower score," he instructs me. "The pirate has a special attack."

I pick up my favorite d20 and toss it on the mat. Four.

"Sorry," Morgan says, though he is clearly not apologizing. "Weslocke is frozen in fear for the next five turns. You can't take any actions, including casting or dismissing spells."

I lie inside my magic cage, cowering, while the monster tears at me with his claws. He digs under my armor and rips through my clothes, slashing my skin in dozens of places. Outside, Babeal, Ganubi, and Jhaden dispatch the other pirates, but reinforcements arrive from belowdecks.

And even if they weren't occupied, they couldn't help me without being shredded by the barrier.

I can feel my life force bleeding out of me. I'm going to die.

By the time I reached college I had become conflicted about my identity as a role-playing geek. Sure, the games were awesome, but I worried about ghettoizing myself in a world of dice and fantasy.

I didn't know anyone at my new school, so my first week on campus I went to two club meetings with hopes of making friends. One was the Science Fiction Forum, a sort of nerd fraternity where members watched videotaped episodes of *The X-Files,* played D&D, and argued about whether the starship *Enterprise* could defeat an Imperial Star Destroyer in a dogfight. The other club was the *Press,* the school's alternative newspaper. It was full of self-styled revolutionaries who smoked clove cigarettes, drank Belgian beer, and thought they were Hunter S. Thompson.

After a few weeks, I quit the Forum and dedicated myself to the *Press*. The women were better looking.

From there I began distancing myself from my nerd heritage. I spent most of my free time in the *Press* office, writing articles and arguing about politics. I only played one game of D&D during my freshman year, at a friend of a friend's off-campus apartment. But I felt embarrassed about it and never returned.

In retrospect, I had merely replaced one geeky habit with another: Only a D&D nerd would think he'd become cool by working on a school newspaper. Still, I managed to cultivate an air of hipster superiority. We were definitely not nerds, oh no; we didn't spend our weekends playing D&D in someone's parents' basement, we spent them arguing about politics in the student union basement.

In the spring of my freshman year, the campus hosted an annual science fiction and gaming convention. I attended under the aegis of a reporter and pretended to look down my nose at the weirdos. When I realized some of the convention's dealers would pay good money for old hardback D&D rule books, I had my parents ship mine to me overnight and sold them for beer money.

I wouldn't play again for more than a decade.

There's one round left until the fear effect wears off, and I've got only 8 hit points. Things look grim for Weslocke the Cleric.

There are three pirates on the deck, including the angry one on top of me. On my turn, I cower. Then the pirate gets his attack. I can barely stand to look as Morgan throws the die.

"He hits," says Morgan. He picks up two six-sided dice to roll the damage. They skitter across the table and come up 3 and 3.

All five guys around the table groan in unison, a sound of relief and disbelief. "All right," says Morgan. "You've got two hit points left, and the fear is gone, so next round, you can take an action."

Jhaden skewers one of the pirates with Bloodlust, killing him. Ganubi finishes off the second with a flurry of arrows. Finally, I feel my courage return. I drop the blade barrier and scramble away from my attacker. He pursues but moves slowly and can't close the distance.

Jhaden's turn. Alex gives me a hard look. "I'm charging," he says, "and declaring a power attack for five points."

Power attacks are one of Jhaden's special abilities, requiring him to subtract points from his roll to hit an opponent. It makes it harder to hit the target—but if the attack is successful, he adds those points to its damage. It's a desperation move. Alex rolls the die.

Jhaden's blades go snicker-snack. The hit connects. The last pirate crumples to the deck.

Morgan shuts his notebook. "And that's it for this week," he says.

I grew up, got a job as a reporter, put on a jacket and tie, and didn't think much about D&D. So did thousands of other gamers: Dungeons & Dragons faded as an object of nerd obsession, replaced by video games and the Internet.

But then something happened. Players started picking up the game again—and this time, they weren't hiding in their parents' basement. In August 2012, more than forty-one thousand men, women, and children descended on Indianapolis for the D&D-heavy Gen Con gaming convention—the biggest crowd in its forty-five-year history. In San Francisco, gamers show up on Market Street and repurpose outdoor chess tables for open-to-the-public D&D sessions. In New York, trendy bars and coffee shops host D&D nights. In London, they play at hundred-year-old pubs.

What happened? People who grew up playing Dungeons & Dragons remembered how much fun they had. D&D offers a unique form of entertainment, a communal storytelling that's more interactive than video games, more engrossing than TV or film, and more social than books. It's hard for people who've experienced that to stay away for too long.

The D&D players of the eighties matured to a point where they recognize, and value, how the game shaped their lives. Above all else, Dungeons & Dragons is a social game, and for many players, it was the tool that helped them form friendships that have lasted a lifetime. It's also a game defined by performance, where players live vicariously through their characters. As such, it's responsible for a kind of resurgent atavism. We fight and win and live or die along with the members of our gaming group. D&D players are our clan.

That's why, after more than a decade clean, I picked up my dice bag and responded to a Craigslist ad seeking players for a new D&D campaign. It will make a good story, I told myself. I hoped to justify the lost hours of my youth by approaching the game as a journalist and reporting on the phenomenon with the advantage of insider experience. And I didn't worry about getting sucked back into the world of swords and sorcerers, even if my friends and girlfriend did: I'm an editor at *Forbes* now, I bragged, an award-winning journalist, not an impressionable kid in a *Conan the Barbarian* T-shirt.

I was wrong. Before long, I was in over my head. Sure, I did witness the revival of the game and met lots of normal people who play D&D the same way they might join a weekly poker game. But I didn't expect the game to change my life. I didn't anticipate making new friends—good ones—and coming to terms with the way I relate to other people. Returning to D&D forced me to redefine my self-image, reexamine my childhood, and change the way I look at the world. And after a while, I wasn't just a reporter writing about people who play Dungeons & Dragons. I was one of them.

Now I know magic.

2

LITTLE WARS

The current publisher of Dungeons & Dragons, Renton, Washington–based Wizards of the Coast, estimates that over thirty million people have played the game since 1974. I'm willing to bet that twenty-nine million of them had their first adventure begin in a tavern.

It's easy to imagine why. Bars are a dramatically convenient place to bring together a cast of characters—where better for strangers to meet and decide to do something dangerous? As a result, "You're all at a tavern . . ." has become the D&D equivalent of "Once upon a time." In a section on establishing a campaign, *The Dungeon Master's Guide* actually refers to this as "The Cliché." Still, you can't argue with tradition. Even Geoffrey Chaucer gathered his pilgrims in a tavern before they set out for Canterbury.

My adventure into the origins of Dungeons & Dragons began at Bemelmans Bar on East Seventy-Sixth Street in Manhattan. It's an upscale Art Deco cocktail lounge: brown leather banquettes, black granite bar, twenty-four-karat-gold-leaf-covered ceiling, and a mural painted by Ludwig Bemelmans, author of the classic *Madeline* children's books. It is, in other words, almost entirely unlike Chaucer's Tabard Inn or Tolkien's Prancing Pony. But it's also just a few blocks from the Metropolitan Museum of Art, and the perfect place for a drink before seeing some of the primitive progenitors of Dungeons & Dragons.

Fantasy role-playing games were born in the 1970s, but you might trace their family tree back half a billion years. At some point in the Paleozoic era, a frisky invertebrate picked up a shell and passed it idly from tentacle to tentacle, thus becoming the first living creature on earth to engage in voluntary recreational activity, or play. (To be fair, definitions of "play" vary wildly, but I'm crediting its invention to the cephalopods, because octopuses are cool. Besides, scientists have pretty clearly documented them playing catch.)

Several hundred million years later, *Homo sapiens* appeared on the family tree. At this point, some prehistoric proto-geek decided that while play was all well and good, what it really needed was *rules.* He formalized play, mixing recreation with ritual and symbolism; the result was the world's very first game.

It's impossible for us to know the rules of that game. It might have involved pantomime or acting, something like caveman charades; if so, it left no physical record, nothing for an archaeologist to dig up and study. The same is true for hand games—perhaps rock-paper-scissors without the paper or scissors.

What we do know is that eventually people started making board games. In 1989, archaeologist Gary O. Rollefson found a curious slab of limestone in the remains of 'Ain Ghazal, a prehistoric settlement in Jordan. Sometime around 5870 B.C., it was carved to roughly the size and thickness of a legal pad, with two rows of six circular depressions on its surface. Rollefson supposed it could be an example of mancala, a board game where players move stones or seeds through a series of cavities; other scientists dispute that conclusion.

Still, there's solid evidence of board games dating as far back as 3000 B.C. Archaeologists found carved stone dice and an ebony board in Shahr-e Sukhteh, the five-thousand-year-old "Burnt City" in southeast Iran; it's believed to be an ancestor of backgammon. The evidence shows that games were common in antiquity, not a rare luxury. The Bronze Age settlement of Mohenjo-daro boasted a full-blown gaming culture. Founded around 2500 B.C. in what is now southern Pakistan, it was one of the world's first big cities, with a peak population of over thirty-five thousand people. When archaeologists discovered the site in the 1920s, they recovered numerous small objects that appeared to be board game pieces, including six-sided and four-sided dice, and a variety of carved stone "gamemen"—playing pieces quite similar to the tokens you'd find in a box of Parcheesi or Clue.

All considered, nearly one out of every ten artifacts recovered from the site is related to gaming, according to archaeologist Elke Rogersdotter, proving games were already an important part of people's everyday lives more than four thousand years ago.*

My trip to the Metropolitan Museum of Art was to see one of the most famous games in antiquity. In a long gallery in the Egyptian wing, just steps from the Great Hall, there's a modern facsimile of a painting discovered in the tomb of Nefertari, the wife of Ramesses the Great. It depicts the queen seated in front of a table, upon which rests an assortment of carved game pieces. Hieroglyphic captions identify her opponent as Fate.

---

*Games are also a frequent subject of ancient scriptures: In one Indian story, Shiva and his consort Parvati are playing a game of dice and ask the divine bull Nandi to officiate. Shiva loses, but Nandi declares that he's the winner anyway. This may be the world's earliest example of a bad Dungeon Master.

Nefertari is playing a popular Egyptian board game known as senet, which set two players to race their playing pieces around thirty squares on a rectangular board. Senet was known as the "game of passing" and came to symbolize the journey of the dead into the afterlife. It was often placed in the graves of pharaohs and their families; Howard Carter found an elaborately carved senet board in the tomb of King Tutankhamen, dating to around 1323 B.C.

Standing in front of the painting, I imagined myself seated at Nefertari's table and that one of the playing pieces was a miniature figure of a man in silver plate armor, holding a heavy flanged mace. Even though we're separated by 3,200 years of history, I knew what she was feeling. The game allowed her to consider her own mortality and vicariously experience the thrill of cheating death.

A key reason why board games spread across the globe is that they're more than simple fun. They teach and tell stories.

Consider the ancient folk tale about a queen who had one son, her only heir. When he died in battle, the queen's counselors could not decide how to break the news to her, so they sought the advice of Qaflan, a great philosopher. He pondered the problem and then summoned a craftsman.

"Take two kinds of wood, one light, one dark," the wise man ordered. "From each, carve identical sets of sixteen small figurines."

When the job was done, he gave more instructions. "Take a square of tanned leather and etch the surface with lines, making sixty-four smaller squares."

When that was finished, the wise man arranged the figurines on the leather. "This is war without bloodshed," he told a disciple, and then explained the rules of a game—one played on a board, with two armies of sixteen figures.

Word spread about the new game, and eventually the queen visited Qaflan, seeking a demonstration. She studied intently as the wise man and his student traded pieces.

When the game was over, the queen understood its meaning and turned to the wise man. "My son is dead," she told him.

That game, of course, was chess, or something like it. The mother of all board games was probably invented in India, though it may have been based on earlier games that made their way west on the Silk Road from China.

While the game's true origin may be lost, the myths surrounding it make one thing clear. "Over and over, chess was said to have been invented to explain the unexplainable, to make visible the purely abstract," David Shenk writes in *The Immortal Game: A History of Chess*. "The Greek warrior Palamades, commander of troops at the siege of Troy, purportedly invented chess as a demonstration of the art of battle positions. Moses, in his posture as Jewish sage, was said to have invented it as part of an all-purpose educational package, along with astronomy, astrology, and the alphabet."

The most ancient ancestor we know of is a game called chaturanga, the Sanskrit word for "army." First played in India during the sixth century A.D., the two-person game replicated an important battle of the Kurukshetra War using carved playing pieces—a raja, his counselor, two elephants, two horses, two chariots, and eight soldiers. It gave birth to chess; D&D is something like a great-great-great-grand-nephew.

Chaturanga is the Genghis Khan of the gaming world. The Mongol emperor sired so many children that seventeen million men alive today are his direct patrilineal descendants; in turn, chaturanga has sired at least two thousand games, ranging from the Japanese variant shogi to Tri-Dimensional Chess, a real game based on a prop that appeared in several episodes of *Star Trek*.

Unfortunately, I stink at all of them. I learned how to play chess when I was a kid but never really understood the game. I could move the pieces and occasionally defeat one of my equally troglodytic* friends, but I had no sense of strategy beyond "Don't lose any pieces" and "Kill all the other guy's pieces."

As a result, I idolized anyone who really knew the game. Chess seemed impossibly erudite, the apex of intellectualism; people who were good at it were smarter and better than the rest of us. I imagined Albert Einstein playing chess with Glenn Gould while Arthur Miller peeked over their shoulders. Even chess players' titles confirmed these assumptions: Call someone "grand master" and I picture an elder wizard with a big white beard, not a pasty teenager with obsessive-compulsive disorder.

My friend and fellow *Forbes* editor Michael Noer is a chess fanatic, and by all accounts quite good at the game. He's not officially ranked, but he's been known to run the table at Johnny's Bar in Greenwich Village, defeating all challengers even while roaring drunk. I asked him to teach me the basics.

The next day, Michael appeared in my office with an old wooden chess clock, a bag of plastic chessmen, and a roll-up vinyl board. "Only posers use fancy chess sets," he said, dumping the lot on my desk. "Do you know how all the pieces move?"

I scoffed, insulted. "I know the moves, Michael."

"Show me."

---

* "Troglodyte: This reptilian creature looks somewhat humanoid . . . It has spindly but muscular arms and walks erect on its squat legs, trailing a long, slender tail. Its head is lizard-like and crowned with a frill that extends from the forehead to the base of the neck. Its eyes are black and beady . . . Hit Dice: 2d8+4 (13 hp) . . . Armor Class: 15 . . . Special Attacks: Stench." *Monster Manual*, page 246.

It turns out I didn't. I understood the basics—a king moves one space in any direction, a bishop moves any number of spaces diagonally, and so on—but had no idea about conditional moves, which allow pieces to behave differently in special circumstances. The pawn, for instance: I knew that on their first move they can advance one or two spaces, on subsequent moves they only advance one, and they can only attack the two spaces diagonally ahead of them. But I didn't know about en passant capture. If a pawn's initial move carries it past an enemy pawn, the enemy can attack backward "in passing," taking the piece from behind. I learned this one the hard way, when Michael took my queen's pawn on the sixth move of the game. I was defeated in about two minutes.

We reset the board and tried again. Michael began by moving his king's pawn up two spaces. I selected a pawn at random, the one in front of my queen's bishop, and moved it forward two spaces.

Michael scoffed. "You wanna play Sicilian? You wanna be a little bitch? I was just gonna teach you something, but if you really want to play . . ."

"I don't know what Sicilian is."

"The Sicilian Defense. It's actually a great opening, but you don't know that."

I'd heard of openings, but I imagined them as complex battle scenarios requiring the memorization of dozens of moves. Openings are why I'd been intimidated by chess: When I hear "Sicilian Defense" I think of the scene in the movie *WarGames* when a military supercomputer simulates hundreds of variations of global thermonuclear war. Their names flash across the huge NORAD monitors: CZECH OPTION. MONGOLIAN THRUST. DENMARK MASSIVE. SUDAN SURPRISE.

But it turns out the Sicilian Defense is as simple as it gets: Two pawns, two moves, two spaces. It's not a heavily choreographed war plan, it's just a smart way to begin a match—the equivalent of choosing the center square in a game of tic-tac-toe.

Of course, there are lots of openings, some of them much more complex. But none of them require rote execution. "The reason why you learn them is not to play the same way every time," Michael said. "They teach you how the game develops, to understand the principles. You start a game with an opening, but you don't have to memorize every possible response. Ideally, it's just you and me and a battle of wits, and there's nothing you can memorize."

He picked up one of his knights and hopped it forward over a pawn. "See these four squares?" he asked, pointing to the center of the grid. "The board is a mountain. This is the peak of the mountain. You are always going for these four squares." He took one of my knights and mirrored his move, and then took his own bishop and slashed it across the board.

"That's the Spanish Game. For the next hundred years or until you get good, whichever comes first, play that opening. With this, I can teach you how to beat ninety-five percent of all chess players."

Over the next four days Michael gave me a dozen ten-minute lessons, popping in my office whenever he felt the need to procrastinate. I spent my free time browsing YouTube videos of common openings—the Giuoco Piano, the King's Gambit, the Dragon Variation. And before long, I reached a critical realization: Despite its origins, chess isn't a war game, and the goal isn't to kill all of the other guy's pieces. It's a space game, and the goal is to control the board. War without bloodshed.

Then I got cocky and decided to put my new understanding to the test. I challenged Michael to a real match: No advice, no holding back. I knew I would lose but thought I could put up a respectable fight.

Afterward, I asked Michael for an appraisal. He was blunt. "Your game has improved significantly. But you still fucking suck."

Today's chess players use essentially the same rules as their counterparts in the sixteenth century. But chess didn't stop evolving in the Middle Ages. Over the following centuries, hundreds of chess variants were created in attempts to modernize the game and return it to its roots as a battlefield simulation. In 1664, Christoph Weickhmann of Ulm, Germany, created Königsspiel, the King's Game, boasting that it would "furnish anyone who studied it properly a compendium of the most useful military and political principles." Weikhmann increased the number of pieces on each side to thirty, replacing antiquated knights and bishops with then-modern military units like halberdiers, marshals, and couriers. He also created variant rules for up to eight players, expanding the board to more than five hundred squares.

In 1780, Johann Christian Ludwig Hellwig, "master of pages" in the court of the Duke of Brunswick, went even further. His war game board consisted of more than 1,600 squares, each color-coded to indicate terrain: white for level ground, green for marshes, blue for water, red for mountains. There were hundreds of pieces, each one representing an entire military battalion, including batteries of mortars, pontoon boats, and regiments of hussar cavalry.

In the late eighteenth century, Georg Leopold von Reiswitz, a Prussian civil servant, wanted to play Hellwig's War Chess but couldn't afford a set, so he developed his own version. Published in 1812 as *Tactical Wargame, or instructions for a mechanical device to show realistic tactical maneuvers,* it used a table covered in sand in order to model topography. In 1812, he constructed a luxurious game table using modular wooden tiles instead of sand. He presented it as a gift to King Friedrich Wilhelm III. Kriegsspiel, literally "war game," began to catch on. In the 1820s, von Reiswitz's son, Georg Heinrich

Rudolf, refined the rules further, using dice to simulate the role of luck in battle, and requiring the participation of a neutral third party to direct the game and settle disputes—the nineteenth-century Prussian version of a Dungeon Master. He mass-produced the game in a box the size of a hardcover book—small enough for a soldier to carry in his pack.

In the 1860s, under Otto von Bismarck and Wilhelm I, the game became a standard training exercise for Prussian officers. When two decades of military success followed, Kriegsspiel basked in reflected glory: After the Franco-Prussian War, British generals cited it as a factor in Prussia's decisive victory. Armies around the world copied the game and began using it to train their own officers.

By the twentieth century, war games were commonplace in the military and had begun to spread into the mainstream. In 1913, the British novelist H. G. Wells took his own stab at the genre, publishing *Little Wars: A Game for Boys from Twelve Years of Age to One Hundred and Fifty and for That More Intelligent Sort of Girl Who Likes Boys' Games and Books*. The text amounted to *Kriegsspiel for Kiddies*: a short, simple, accessible set of rules. Wells did away with complicated boards, encouraging play on a kitchen table or bedroom floor. And he ditched the counters and markers that represented military units: *Little Wars* required only a child's own collection of tin soldiers.

It was a seminal moment. Wells stripped away rigid conventions that had built up over centuries and saw into the heart of playing soldier: It's a game, and it's supposed to be fun.

A pacifist, Wells was quick to distance his "diversion" from martial instruments of war. "How much better is this amiable miniature than the Real Thing?" he asked. "Here is the premeditation, the thrill, the strain of accumulating victory or disaster—and no smashed nor sanguinary bodies, no shattered fine buildings nor devastated country sides."

With World War I only a year away, Wells hoped simulated violence might help avoid actual bloodshed. "Great War is at present, I am convinced, not only the most expensive game in the universe, but it is a game out of all proportion," he wrote. "Not only are the masses of men and material and suffering and inconvenience too monstrously big for reason, but—the available heads we have for it, are too small. That, I think, is the most pacific realization conceivable, and Little War brings you to it as nothing else but Great War can do."

3

GROGNARDS

I knew that if I truly wanted to understand Dungeons & Dragons, I had to first understand the games that gave birth to it. But I couldn't just go to a toy store and buy a hundred-year-old war game: today, games like Little Wars and Kriegsspiel are decidedly out of style.* They've been replaced as entertainment by war-themed video games and supplanted in education by incredibly complex simulations. Militaries around the world still use war games for training, but these exercises are usually either computerized or playacted. The U.S. Army employs game designers in the Simulations Division at its Command and General Staff College; their events look like highly moderated role-playing games, a cross between D&D, fantasy football, and high school Model UN.

But dedicated war gamers soldier on. The Historical Miniatures Gaming Society, a nonprofit foundation created to promote the hobby,

*But not extinct: Apple Computer founder Steve Jobs was a Kriegsspiel fan; in the early days of the company, he'd play games with engineer Daniel Kottke, sometimes while they were both tripping on LSD.

has more than two thousand members worldwide and hosts a yearly convention—four days of seminars, socializing, and lots and lots of games. Since I had never actually played a war game, I decided to check the con out—these games are too important to ignore. (In other words: Fear not, ranger. We'll get back to D&D in two shakes of a lamia's* tail.)

Historicon was held over the second weekend in July at the Valley Forge Convention Plaza in King of Prussia, Pennsylvania, an edge city about twenty miles northwest of Philadelphia. The town is best known for its massive mall, the largest in the United States. It's also home to Valley Forge National Historical Park, where George Washington and the Continental Army famously made camp during the American Revolution. But the mall gets way more visitors.

It's easy to find the convention center, an unappealing 1970s concrete bunker connected to dusty and dated hotels at either end; the whole complex rises out of a sea of parking lots like a crashed alien spacecraft. Three thousand attendees walked through the doors that weekend to grab spots at over six hundred games. I got there early on Friday to procure one of twelve tickets for "Napoleon's Battles Boot Camp," a hypothetical skirmish between French and Prussian armies, intended for novice players. With time to kill, I wandered the halls.

There are certain characteristics common to all game conventions, whether they're dedicated to historical minis, role-playing, video games, or board games like chess and Scrabble. The first is gender imbalance. Maybe men are more attracted to competitive games or more likely to obsess about their hobbies; either way, they always constitute a majority of attendees. The second is age imbalance. Convention-goers are more likely to sport gray hair than tattoos and

* "This creature seems to be a cross between a stunningly attractive human and a sleek lion. It looks human from the waist up, with the body of a lion below that." *Monster Manual*, page 165.

ear gauges, probably because of the high cost of attending. Finally, there's racial imbalance. Chalk it up to social differences or economic ones, but crowds inside a game convention are always whiter than the population outside, even in cities like New York and San Francisco.

In other words: The typical game convention attendee is a middle-aged white guy. This will come as a shock to few, but it's worth noting. Appropriately, war gamers refer to themselves as "grognards"—a French term for "old soldiers." The literal translation, "grumbler," was first applied to Napoleon's elite Imperial Guard, veterans so respected they could freely complain about orders and even groan to the emperor himself.

In the main ballroom, a few hundred attendees were setting up games on long folding tables pushed together side by side; sixty or seventy of these surfaces had been set up around the room. A historical-miniatures battle requires significant preparation compared to something like chess; there's no set board or layout of pieces. Instead, participants build scale dioramas, usually representing the location of an actual battle. The simplest of these may be a flat tabletop overlaid with a few pieces of fabric and a handful of plastic soldiers. But many war gamers—particularly the hard-core grognards who go to conventions—strive for the detail and artistry of museum pieces. Their game tables feature tiny plastic trees, realistic hills and valleys, and meticulously painted buildings. And all of it's to scale, usually so that the period-accurate toy soldiers are between ten and twenty-eight millimeters tall.

For one game, simulating the English invasion of a French castle during the Hundred Years' War, the organizers had re-created a medieval village and keep; the plastic resin castle at one end was easily four feet wide and three feet tall. The biggest display, tucked in a far corner of the ballroom, consisted of a fifty-foot-long model of the main street from an Old West village, complete with villagers, horses, stagecoaches, and dozens of buildings, including a saloon, a jail, a market, and a butcher.

In the dealer's room, located in a subbasement of the convention center, row after row of merchants sold the gear required to make these models. To start a game, you need a battlefield. Thrifty players can get away with a tabletop, but wouldn't *you* prefer to cover that surface with a Wargames Terrain Mat? It's a six-by-four-foot chunk of coarse fabric available in "Forest Green" and "Scorched Grass Brown" and costs $29. Of course, once you're simulating grass you've got to decorate the battlefield with details like plastic trees ($7 per thicket), rivers ($8 per ten-inch stretch), and hedgerows ($12 for a pack of four). Get really into the details and you'll want to add buildings like a one-room hut ($17) or a stable ($23). And maybe you'd like a nice old barn ($65), a bombed-out house ($80), or even a church ($120)?

Then there are the actual soldiers. You could buy kits—a set of forty-two twenty-eight-millimeter Napoleonic infantrymen costs $29—but then you'll have to glue them together and paint them. Factory-painted plastic figurines are convenient but costly—eight Roman auxilia troops for $16, or $2.25 each if bought individually. Then there's the top-of-the-line, hand-painted cast metal figurines. They're gorgeous but crazy expensive: twelve "Boxer Rebellion Boxers," $96; twenty late-Roman foot soldiers, $175; twelve French lancers, $220.

The need for all this equipment creates a high barrier for entry and makes it incredibly difficult for a casual gamer to get rolling. All told, a hard-core historical-miniatures gamer could easily spend thousands of dollars on his hobby.

After checking out the dealer's room, I wandered through the corridors of the adjoining hotels, where games were under way in a dozen hot, cramped meeting rooms. As I padded into the deep reaches, I started to feel like the kid in Stanley Kubrick's *The Shining*, my footsteps beating rhythmically on the carpet as strange tableaus flashed by. Through one open door, a guy that looks like Santa Claus waving a yardstick, bellowing about assignment of artillery casualties; through another, a room-sized naval battle, fought with foot-tall model clipper ships; then a Japanese castle, surrounded by a thousand brightly painted samurai; Normandy on D-Day; William Wallace at Falkirk; the Battle of Britain. Finally, it was time to play.

Few of us slept the night before the battle. At sundown, Napoleon's damnable artillery began raining death on the center of the Coalition lines. Our position, in the north, was unscathed, but we lay awake listening to the roar of the cannons, a constant rumbling reminder of what was to come.

The sun was high over Saxony when the word finally arrived: The French lines were moving. Our orders were to occupy several small villages in the Bohemian foothills, hold the line, and stop the French advance.

The stakes couldn't have been higher. After Napoleon's Grande Armée was driven from Moscow, Prussia finally drew its sword against the invader; now we fight the Befreiungskriege, *wars of liberation. We will drive the French from our land and finish Napoleon once and for all.*

We checked and rechecked our muskets, sharpened our bayonets, and prepared to fight.

The Napoleon's Battles Boot Camp was staged near the center of the main exhibit hall, on a twelve-foot-by-twelve-foot table. As befitting a beginner's game, the battlefield was simple: a surface covered with green felt, with two long "roads" of balsa wood crossing at the center. Five small plastic houses served as the only ornamentation, each representing a small town—one at the crossroads, and one at the midpoint of each road segment.

Our volunteer game master explained the scenario: Twelve players would fight out a hypothetical engagement between the French and Prussian armies, six to a side. The goal was to force the opposing army to flee from the map. If the game hit its four-hour time limit before that happened, whichever army controlled more towns would win.

The armies consisted of long lines of toy soldiers, arrayed at the edges of opposing sides of the table. At a game scale set to fifteen millimeters, each miniature soldier stood just over half an inch tall. Since each mini represented an entire unit of one hundred twenty soldiers, there were something like thirty thousand men on the table, ready to go to war.

Each player was assigned to an army—I randomly drew the Prussians—and given several "stands" of miniature figures representing a specific regiment. I got two stands of line infantry, each one consisting of sixteen little plastic men in blue uniforms, with rifles drawn and bayonets fixed. Since each soldier was so tiny, they were standing in groups, four minis to a single base. I also had a stand of sixteen *Landwehr* infantry, the volunteer troops that proved critical when Prussia and its allies fought to liberate Europe from Napoleon in 1813. My *Landwehr* regiment traveled with a twelve-pound cannon, a piece of artillery on a base about one inch square. When the soldiers moved, they'd need to make sure the cannon moved with them. Finally, I had a single regimental commander, a guy on a gray stallion, perched on his own miniature base. As commander of the First Brigade, he represented my divisional leader—at all times, my regiments needed to be within three inches of him on the table in order to receive instructions.

Major von Lehndorff ordered the regiment into a march column, and we set off for a valley between two villages, about a mile apart. To our left, a division of heavy cavalry would take one town; General von Zastrow himself led the brigade to take the other. Our job was to plug the hole between the two, hold the center, and keep the French at bay.

As we marched to our duty, we made a pretty picture. Like a line of toy soldiers glinting in the sun.

At fifteen-millimeter scale, an inch on our battlefield represented fifty yards of distance. To get my troops into place between the center and northernmost villages, I had to march halfway across the table and change formation into a defensive line. This turns out to be more difficult than it sounds.

Under the Napoleon's Battles rules, each military unit has a different movement rate, and the rate varies depending on the unit's formation. In their starting configuration, a four-man-wide-by-four-man-deep column, my line infantry could move ten inches per turn. But change them into a long marching column—two men by eight—and they could move sixteen inches. *Landwehr* infantry move eight inches in column, a cannon nine inches, and so on.

As such, the first few moves of our Napoleonic battle—the first hour of the game, really—consisted of little more than moving pieces around the board. On my turn, I'd lean over the table with a tape measure, mark ten inches' distance from the front of my line, and then carefully move each mini to traverse the gap. At the same time, I'd have to measure the distance from my commander to each regiment, making sure nothing was too far away.

By the time we could see the French they were half a mile distant. They had stopped their advance and formed lines; directly ahead of us, light infantry chasseurs made a wall of green coats a hundred yards wide. On either flank, they were protected by cavalry—four hundred horses pawing at the earth and flicking their tails, their riders leaning back in saddles, muskets at rest.

At that distance, we had little to fear from the infantry, whose muskets barely had the power to hit a target a hundred yards away. But those horsemen could close the distance between us in half a minute and tear through our columns before we had time to defend ourselves. So the major had us stop our march and form a defensive square, twelve men to a row and twelve to a column, muskets bared on all sides. Facing a square, a cavalry charge is useless—all they can do is ride around it in circles. Come too close, and they'll get a half dozen bayonets up the ass.

The disadvantage of forming a square, at least from my position, is that you can't see what the hell is happening. Standing two men back on the left flank, I had a good view of our light artillerymen, who had unlimbered their cannon and were ready to fire. But I couldn't see the Frenchmen and had to guess how they'd respond.

We held position for long minutes before I couldn't stand the tension and turned to my friend Leopold. "What's happening? Why aren't they attacking?" He opened his mouth to speak, then froze—we both heard the answer on the air, faint but coming closer, something like an approaching hailstorm: hundreds of boots beating a rhythm across the dry earth. An infantry charge.

*Behind us the major's bugle sounded three times, and we scrambled back into line. As I fell into place, I could make out the French formation coming toward us—*l'ordre mixte, *a combination of line and column meant to break through enemy infantry. Through my regiment. I raised my musket and waited for orders.*

We didn't fire until we could see the fringe of their woolly epaulettes. Two volleys in quick succession: our front rank, kneeling, then the second, standing behind them. Our muskets belched smoke, and the French line twitched and staggered. A dozen chasseurs pitched forward onto the grass, but the regiment held formation. They stopped, lifted their muskets, and returned fire.

It takes me around twenty seconds to reload my musket, but when someone's shooting at you, twenty seconds feels like an hour. I tried to concentrate on the routine and to tune out the sound of the French guns. Detach the firelock from the shoulder, open the priming pan, open the cartridge box. To my right, I heard a thud and felt my friend Johann stumble. Take a cartridge, bite off the top of the paper, fill the pan with powder. Something whizzed past my ear like a fat, angry bee. Close the pan, swing round the weapon, empty the cartridge into the barrel, tamp it down.

Cock the gun, shoulder it. Return fire.

Fighting in Napoleon's Battles uses a system of modified dice rolls: To attack, both players roll 1d10—one ten-sided die—and then add or subtract based on factors like type of soldier, location, and formation. If the attacker ends up with a bigger number, they've killed a few enemies.

A fight is further complicated by rules for morale: If enough soldiers get hurt in a regiment, it will become "disordered" and can't return fire or initiate hand-to-hand combat. Fail to recover from disorder and you could get "routed," forcing your troops to run away from combat. If they happen to run into another regiment as they flee, those guys panic as well.

It's not an easy system. Each player was given a photocopied "training scenario information chart" describing all these modifiers, but it was so complex as to be useless: When you need nineteen footnotes to explain a single page of information, you know you're in trouble.

All this complexity even flummoxes the experts. Tom and Paco, our two volunteer game masters, spent a good portion of the match debating rules between themselves and issuing conflicting instructions—and I don't think they were doing a bad job. It's just the character of the game, complex and confusing. War games are meant to provoke discussion, not stimulate the imagination like D&D.

The fact is that in any historical-miniatures battle, only 10 percent of the match is really spent playing. Half the remaining time is spent arguing about history, and the other half arguing about the game's rules. War is hell.

Around us, I could hear panic and pain. On our left, the cavalry was being routed, falling back and exposing our flank. But my regiment held its position. We traded three volleys with the French infantry. They kept advancing. They were only forty paces away when our cannon finally opened fire.

The explosion took me by surprise, and I nearly dropped my ramrod. I reflexively turned to look but caught only an instant of motion—the big gun rolling back and digging into the earth—before it was enveloped in a huge cloud of thick gray smoke.

Then I heard the screams. The gunners had loaded the cannon with canister, a mix of scrap iron and musket balls—ineffective at long distances, but murderous up close. The shot tore into the French line and shredded its front ranks. The shocked soldiers who remained panicked and were routed, turning heel and fighting back through their own men—anything to get away from the big brass gun.

At this point, I was ready to declare Prussian victory. But one of the peculiarities of Napoleon's Battles is that soldiers get routed all the time. Just as a player manages formations, he must also manage morale, rallying troops and reimposing order to keep as much of his army fighting as possible. The idea is that everyone gets their butt kicked, but good players know how to take a beating. A successful general advances like the tide, surging and breaking, losing ground one moment but gaining the next.

The French learned this lesson quickly. When their light infantry was routed and fell back, I marched my *Landwehr* regiment forward into the hole, hoping to pursue and destroy. But on their very next turn, the French commander was able to rally the unit and stop their retreat.

At the same time, he moved two more infantry units toward my position. I needed a turn just to change formation from march column back into a line. So by the time I was ready to fight, I had exposed myself to fire from three separate French units. When the French attacked, their commander would roll 3d10 and add them together; my only way to avoid slaughter was to roll higher, but I'd get only a single d10.

He picked up the dice and tossed them on the table. One, one, and four.

I rolled a ten. Somehow, my troops not only avoided destruction but also took no casualties. My infantry was immune to bullets.

Game master Tom leaned across the table and smiled. "What's the difference between a fairy tale and a war story?" he asked. "A fairy tale begins 'Once upon a time,' and a war story begins 'No shit, this really happened.'"

The victory was short-lived. When our game hit the four-hour time limit, the French army held three out of five towns on the map. Napoleon took the day.

I thanked the game masters and left the table, the ballroom, and the conference center. I traced a march column across the parking lot, unlimbered my car, and sent two hundred horses down the left flank of the Pennsylvania Turnpike. Four hours of little war was enough for the weekend—or for a lifetime, really.

Historical-miniatures battles aren't for me. It's not just that there are too many rules—I can handle rules; I love rules. It's that these rules are too complicated, and they're the absolute focus of the game; it's not about telling a story and having an adventure but about accurate simulation. For me, at least, historical-miniatures war games have too much regimentation and not enough imagination.

It's interesting, but it's no Dungeons & Dragons.

4

DRUIDS WITH PHASER GUNS

Ridiculously complicated rules and hand-painted miniatures are not a recipe for success. Despite H. G. Wells's efforts to take war games mainstream, the hobby remained obscure into the mid-twentieth century. The general public proved more interested in simple, self-contained board games like Monopoly, which debuted in the 1930s, and Scrabble, first published in 1948. Kriegsspiel and its brethren continued to have their fans, but they were few in number, almost exclusively older men, and usually veterans who wanted to relive a bit of the thrill of the world wars.

In 1952 someone finally figured out how to make war into a family pastime. By the age of twenty-two, Charles Roberts had already worked at two newspapers, completed a four-year stint in the army, and then enlisted in the Maryland National Guard. Hoping to be assigned to combat duty in Korea, he decided to study up on military strategy. "To be conversant with the Principles of War is to a soldier what the Bible is to a clergyman," Roberts wrote in a 1983 article. "The Bible, however, may be readily perused . . . wars are somewhat harder to come by. Thus I decided that I would practice war on a board as well as the training field . . . Since there were no such war games available, I had to design my own."

Roberts's game, Tactics, used the tools of mass-market board games to simulate war. It had a simple preprinted board with a hand-drawn map; it used cardboard chits to represent units, instead of metal miniatures; and it did away with all historical baggage, imagining a hypothetical conflict between two imaginary countries.

In 1954, "almost as a lark," Roberts decided to manufacture and sell the game to the public. It sold only two thousand copies in the next five years, but Roberts saw an untapped market for adult board games and pressed on. In 1958, he designed and published Gettysburg, which simulated the American Civil War battle; it was a hit, and by 1962 Roberts's Avalon Hill game company was the fourth-largest producer of board games in the United States.

Around the country, small groups began to coalesce in community centers, hobby stores, and private homes for weekly sessions of Gettysburg and other war games. These gatherings were inevitably all-male; while the mainstreaming of the pastime broadened the player base enough so that teens might face off against crusty World War II vets, women were still nowhere to be seen. This likely had as much to do with the hobby's martial subject matter as it did with the bellicose tone of the gatherings: Players would spend hours arguing about rules and fighting over results. (It also probably had something to do with the presence of certain nerdy, poorly socialized males—there is good reason why a group of gamers has come to be known as a "stink.")

One of the most important war-gaming communities in the U.S. developed around the Twin Cities of Minneapolis and Saint Paul, where a motley crew of amateur historians, miniature modelers, and gamers rediscovered a solution to the problem of bickering over rules.

It came in the form of an eighty-year-old army training manual, *Strategos: A Series of American Games of War,* published in 1880 by Charles A. L. Totten, a lieutenant in the Fourth United States Artillery. Dave Wesely, an undergraduate physics student at Saint Paul's Hamline University, was one of the gamers who unearthed the book in the University of Minnesota library and learned about the centuries-old idea of an all-powerful referee. It quickly became standard practice.

By the mid-1960s, the young war-gamer crowd was meeting regularly to play out traditional Kriegsspiel-style Napoleonic battles and board games including Avalon Hill's Gettysburg, Parker Brothers' war game Conflict, Milton Bradley's Cold War simulator Summit, and a French game called La Conquête du Monde, or "The Conquest of the World," known in the U.S. as Risk.

In the fall of 1967, Wesely left the Twin Cities to attend graduate school in Kansas, and in 1970 he reported for active duty in the U.S. Army. Sometime during that period, while separated from his gaming friends, he started to plan something memorable for when he returned home on break. What he came up with was one of the first modern role-playing games.

The scenario was set during the Napoleonic Wars, in the fictional town of Braunstein, Germany, surrounded by opposing armies. But Wesely didn't simply put armies on the board—he also assigned each player an individual character to control within the scenario. Some players controlled local military officials, and others took nonmilitary roles, like the town's mayor, school chancellor, or banker. Wesely then gave each player their own unique objective, forcing them to consider motivations for their actions and to think beyond battlefield strategy.

The game quickly spun out of control. Players wanted to do things Wesely hadn't planned for, like duel each other, so he had to make up rules on the spot. They also wandered away from the table in small groups to hold secret negotiations—a supposedly all-powerful referee's nightmare. Wesely returned to school thinking the game had flopped.

But the players felt otherwise. Before long, they were begging Wesely for "another Braunstein." He obliged by designing new scenarios, like one that explored a Latin American dictatorship through the eyes of student revolutionaries, secret policemen, and corrupt government functionaries.

Wesely's friend David Megarry was one of the players in the second "Braunstein" game, set in the fictional country of Piedras Morenas. "It was sort of a banana republic," Megarry says. "I was a revolutionary and trying to blow up something." The players were intrigued by the freedom of the game and excited for the opportunity to play more. "It was a new dimension," he says. "It was really quite electrifying."

David Wesely's innovations—using a referee, assigning players individual characters with unique objectives, and giving them the freedom to do whatever they wanted—lit a fire in the Twin Cities gaming community. His Braunstein role-playing adventures appealed to players and got them thinking about where the games could go next. It wasn't long before others began to follow his example.

David Arneson* was born in 1947 and grew up in Saint Paul, Minnesota. When he was a teenager, his parents bought him a copy of Avalon Hill's Gettysburg, and he got hooked; later, he moved on

* There are a lot of people named David involved in this game, aren't there?

to the hard-core stuff, including Civil War simulations and Napoleonic naval battles. After enrolling at the University of Minnesota to study history, he joined the Castle & Crusade Society, a chapter of the International Federation of Wargaming focused on the medieval period; when its members began collectively designing a fictional "Great Kingdom" as a setting for new games, Arneson was inspired to contribute.

Seated on a cushy couch "throne" at the head of a Ping-Pong table in his basement game room, Arneson ran his friends through a series of role-playing games set in the Great Kingdom, and began to make his own refinements to traditional war-game rules—mostly by breaking them. One (possibly apocryphal) story recounts how he got bored during a battle set amid the Roman conquest of Britain, and decided to spice up the action.

"I'd given the defending brigands a druid high priest," Arneson explained years later in an interview. "In the middle of the battle, the *dull* battle, when the Roman war elephant charged the Britons and looked like he was going to trample half their army flat, the druidic high priest waved his hands and pointed this funny little box out of one hand and turned the elephant into so much barbecue meat." Arneson removed the war elephant from the game, explaining that the druid had killed it with a *Star Trek*–style phaser gun. "That was absolutely the only thing in the game that was out of the ordinary, but they weren't expecting it," he said.

The players were nonplussed—save for the delighted commander of the British druid. But Arneson wasn't put off from sneaking elements of fantasy into his war games. In April 1971, after a two-day binge of watching monster movies and reading Robert E. Howard's Conan the Barbarian books, Arneson invited his friends over for "a medieval Braunstein . . . [featuring] mythical creatures." When they arrived, he introduced them to the city of Blackmoor.

"They came down to the basement and there was a medieval castle in the middle of the table," says Megarry. The players, Arneson explained, had been sent through time and space to a medieval city and had to control original heroic characters, each with their own attributes, powers, and goals.

"My very first character was a thief," says Megarry, "and my nemesis was Dan Nicholson, the merchant. His role was to try to get stuff into town and then sell it. And my role was to try to steal his stuff and make my money that way. It gave us a framework of how to operate in this world."

In subsequent Blackmoor games, Arneson sent the players to explore the dungeons beneath the castle and town. Inside, he hit them with another twist: The subterranean passages weren't defended by human soldiers but inhabited by fantastic monsters—like a dragon, which Arneson represented on the table using a plastic toy brontosaurus with a fanged clay head.

"Frankly, the boys in my club were bored," Arneson said. "They wanted to try something new. To me, it was a logical extension to go into fantasy. It was less restrictive than history."

Much of the appeal of the game came from the excitement of exploring the winding corridors underneath Blackmoor. "There was that thrill of discovery," says Megarry. "You have to make a decision . . . left or right, or staircase in front of you going down?" The game was so popular, people wanted to play even when they couldn't make it to Arneson's house and would call him on the phone to lead them on solo adventures through the dungeons.

Over the following months, Arneson and his players obsessed over the new game—although it did have its critics. One local Napoleonic-miniatures fan campaigned loudly against Blackmoor after watching his gaming buddies abandon traditional war games in favor of newfangled dungeon crawls; he insulted the game and its players, and even played a nasty practical joke on Arneson. But the Dungeon Master had his revenge. Not long after, Arneson introduced a new villain in the game: the "Egg of Coot," a riff on the disgruntled player's name and temperament, described as an "all consuming personality [that] lives off the egos of others to support his own . . . a huge mass of jointly operating cells, a huge mass of jelly . . . the physique of this creature is too horrible for any mortal to behold."

Arneson wasn't the first person to introduce elements of fantasy into role-playing; Blackmoor relied upon the rules of a medieval-miniatures war game called Chainmail. The "Man-to-Man Combat" section of the forty-seven-page booklet explained how to manage individual heroes amongst your army; another section, the "Fantasy Supplement," included rules for casting magical spells and fighting hideous monsters.

Chainmail—and other works based on it for the Castle & Crusade Society's Great Kingdom—provided a framework that helped Blackmoor develop from a novelty into a consistent, ongoing game. But ultimately the system proved too limited for Arneson's growing fantasy world. He began adding his own innovations, including new classes, dungeons, magical artifacts, and provisions for improving a character over time.

Like any passionate hobbyist, Arneson was excited to share his work with others. So he decided to show off Blackmoor to Chainmail's author.

Ernest Gary Gygax grew up playing games. Born in Chicago in 1938, he knew pinochle by age five and chess by six. His grandfather would challenge him to matches, checkmate him, start the game over at the point where "Gary" had made his biggest mistake, and then repeat the process until the boy's play was perfect. When he was eight, the family moved out of the city—in part because mischievous Gary had been involved in a forty-kid rumble—to the quiet resort town of Lake Geneva, Wisconsin. Gary passed his time there playing board games and cards. As a young adult, he discovered Avalon Hill's Gettysburg. "That sealed my fate," he'd later write, "for thereafter I was a wargamer." Later he got hooked on military miniatures battles and built his own sand table.

He also loved fantasy. When Gygax was a boy, his father, a Swiss immigrant, put him to bed every night with tales of wizards and warriors. He picked up the Brothers Grimm as soon as he could read, mastered Poe before he was ten, and devoured the amazing stories in pulp digests like the *Magazine of Fantasy*. Gygax found a favorite in the works of Robert E. Howard: "Even now I vividly recall my first perusal of *Conan the Conqueror*," he wrote in 1985. "After I finished reading that piece of sword and sorcery literature for the first time, my concepts of adventure were never quite the same again." Maybe the thirst for adventure was in his blood: Gygax family tradition holds that they are descendants of the giant Goliath, whose progeny fled the Holy Land after the future king of Israel played a trick with his sling.*

Bright and highly literate, Gygax had little interest in formal education and dropped out of high school in his junior year. Later, he attended junior college classes and toyed with the idea of becoming an anthropologist. But his childhood interests had instilled an undeniable ambition to write and design games. He took a job as an insurance underwriter to support his gaming habit, and then a growing family: In 1958, he married an attractive redhead, Mary Jo Powell, and they eventually had five kids.

---

* Eventually, they made their way north; Gygax is a Swiss name, properly pronounced "GEE-gox." After Gary's father immigrated to the United States, the family Americanized the name to "GUY-gacks."

In 1966, Gygax became a member of the United States Continental Army Command, a club whose impressive name belied the fact that its members were engaged in play-by-mail campaigns of war games. A year later, the group changed its name to the International Federation of Wargaming and broadened its focus to include promoting the hobby.

To that end, Gygax agreed to host a war-gaming convention. He rented out the Lake Geneva Horticultural Hall for fifty dollars, and on August 24, 1968, he welcomed friends and IFW members to the "Lake Geneva Wargames Convention," or, as it would later become known, "Gen Con"—a double pun referring to both the rules of war and the event's location. Admission cost a dollar, and the show made just enough money to cover the rental.

In August of 1969, Gygax held the event again. This time, Dave Arneson drove from Saint Paul to check out the action, and the two gamers spent a lot of time together. "Since we're only talking a couple hundred people at that point, we pretty much ran into each other all the time," Arneson said. "We were both interested in sailing-ship games." Arneson had developed new rules for naval warfare simulations and showed Gygax his system; after the convention was over, they stayed in touch via phone and letters, and shared ideas about how to make the game better.

In 1970, Gygax cofounded the Castle & Crusade Society and helped kick off its efforts to create the Great Kingdom. When he lost his job as an insurance underwriter, he found work writing and editing rule books for Guidon Games, a tiny publisher based in Evansville, Indiana. To supplement the meager income from a profit-sharing deal, he learned how to repair shoes and practiced cobblery out of his basement.

Guidon Games barely lasted as long as a new pair of leather soles. But before it folded, it produced two games of particular importance:

1971's Chainmail, written by Gygax and his friend Jeff Perren, which provided a starting rule set for Dave Arneson's Blackmoor campaign; and 1972's Don't Give Up the Ship, authored by Gygax, Arneson, and war-gaming friend Mike Carr, the result of their ongoing discussion about naval warfare.

Based on his use of Chainmail, the successful collaboration of Don't Give Up the Ship, and a mutual involvement in the collectively designed Great Kingdom, Dave Arneson knew what to do after he created the fantasy role-playing game Blackmoor: He shared it with Gary Gygax.

In the four decades that have passed since Dave Arneson and Gary Gygax began their most important collaboration, various geek pundits have attempted to describe, by way of analogy, the nature of their momentous and fateful partnership. I've heard them described as Paul McCartney and John Lennon, James Watson and Francis Crick, even John the Baptist and Jesus. I enjoy a bit of careless sacrilege as much as the next guy, but these comparisons make me cross.

Here's my attempt: Two young men meet in the late 1960s and bond over a shared love of a nerdy pastime. They both belong to the same hobbyist's club and start making things to share with the other members. Before long, they're working together on something new and exciting. One of them is the engineer; he invents new ways of doing things. The other is the visionary; he realizes the potential. The product they create could not have existed without both of them. When it's released, it launches a brand-new industry and changes the world.

The story's the same whether you base it in the International Federation of Wargaming or the Homebrew Computer Club, where Steve Wozniak and Steve Jobs jump-started the personal computer industry by founding Apple Computer. Wozniak, the engineer, designed the hardware and made the computer function; Jobs, the visionary, made it user-friendly and something people wanted.

Arneson visited Lake Geneva in the fall of 1972 to show off his Blackmoor game, but what he really delivered was innovations: Fantasy heroes seek adventure in a dungeon setting, and by doing so, they gain experience and become more powerful.

Gary Gygax took those ideas and turned them into a commodity. "I asked Dave to please send me his rules additions, for I thought a whole new system should be developed," he wrote. "A few weeks after his visit I received 18 or so handwritten pages of rules and notes pertaining to his campaign, and I immediately began work on a brand new manuscript."

Over the next two months, Gygax labored at a portable Royal typewriter crafting the rules for a new kind of game, where players roll dice to create a hero, fight monsters, and find treasure. By the end of 1972, he'd finished a fifty-page first draft. He called it the Fantasy Game.

The first people to play it, Gygax later remembered, were his eleven-year-old son, Ernie, and nine-year-old daughter Elise. Gygax had created a counterpart to Arneson's Blackmoor, which he called Castle Greyhawk, and designed a single level of its dungeons; one night after dinner, he invited the kids to roll up characters and start exploring. Ernie created a wizard and named him Tenser—an anagram for his full name, Ernest.* Elise played a cleric called Ahlissa. They wrote down the details of their characters on index cards and entered the dungeon. In the very first room, they discovered and

* Like several other characters from the original Greyhawk campaign, Tenser ended up becoming something of a D&D celebrity. Gygax borrowed his name for several spells that appeared in the game, including "Tenser's Floating Disc," an evocation that creates "a slightly concave, circular plane of force that follows you about and carries loads." The character also appeared in a number of Greyhawk campaign sourcebooks.

defeated a nest of scorpions; in the second, they fought a gang of kobolds—short subterranean lizard-men. They also found their first treasure, a chest full of copper coins, but it was too heavy to carry. The two adventurers pressed on until nine o'clock, when the Dungeon Master put them to bed. Fatherly duties completed, Gygax returned to his office and designed another level of the dungeons.

The next day the play tests continued, and Ernie and Elise were joined by three players plucked from Gygax's regular war-gaming group: his childhood friend Don Kaye (Murlynd) and local teenagers Rob Kuntz (Robilar) and his brother Terry (Terik). He also sent the manuscript to a few dozen war-gaming friends around the country, requesting feedback. "The reaction . . . was instant enthusiasm," wrote Gygax. "They demanded publication of the rules as soon as possible."

The local gamers also clamored for more. As they got farther into the depths of Castle Greyhawk, they faced greater challenges and began to feel like they were a part of a legend: Thanks to Dave Arneson's innovation of persistent characters, the dungeons had a living history. If Tenser killed a pack of kobolds on Tuesday, Robilar might find the corpses on Thursday. It was a brand-new way to create a story.

Gygax began running regular sessions of the Fantasy Game for a growing group of players; simultaneously, David Arneson tried out the rules with his Blackmoor players in Saint Paul. Arneson and Gygax spent a year testing the Fantasy Game with their respective gaming clubs and then discussing what did and didn't work.

"I don't know if any game ever has been play-tested as much as this game," says Michael Mornard, the only person to play a regular character in both Gygax's Greyhawk campaign and Arneson's Blackmoor. Mornard grew up in Lake Geneva and was sixteen when he met Gygax, through his classmate and fellow war-gaming enthusiast Rob Kuntz. Mornard recalls that he was playing a miniatures battle with Kuntz and Don Kaye at Kaye's Lake Geneva home when he heard about the Fantasy Game.

"Either after or between turns of the battle," says Mornard, "Rob tells us, 'Gary's got this new game he's working on. You're a bunch of guys exploring an old abandoned castle full of monsters and treasure.' And Don says, 'That doesn't sound very interesting.'" Mornard felt otherwise. "I was like, 'What do I have to do to get in?'"

A few days later, Mornard went over to Gygax's house for his first foray into the depths of Castle Greyhawk. He rolled up a character with 15 strength and 15 intelligence, and decided to make him a fighter (or, as the class was known at the time, a "fighting-man") named Gronan of Simmerya, an "obvious parody" of Robert E. Howard's barbarian hero.* Mornard's memories of the game are a blur, but Gronan lived to fight another day. "At the end of it, I was like, 'I don't know what this game is, but that was really freakin' great,'" he says. "It was kind of like a war game, only not . . . it was really different."

Gary Gygax's early Greyhawk sessions were understandably surprising to players like Mike Mornard, who'd never seen this brand-new thing called a fantasy role-playing game. But they'd also look different to today's experienced D&D players.

There was no common gaming table; the players sat together, and Gygax sat alone at his desk. "The way Gary's study was arranged, he had a desk with a filing cabinet next to it, and he pulled out the drawers on the filing cabinet so we couldn't see him," says Mornard. "What you did was listen. You heard his voice. All the action took

---

*Many character names of this era were puns or corny jokes; later, when Mornard rolled up a magic-user, Gygax named it "Lessnard."

place entirely inside our heads . . . If you wanted a map, you drew one yourself."

There wasn't much talking. Each party had a "caller" who spoke for the group. Players quietly discussed their actions and then told the caller, who told Gygax. If anyone talked too much, they risked missing an important announcement from behind the filing cabinet. "The tension in the room was palpable," says Mornard.

There were no set adventuring parties, nothing like Frodo's Fellowship of the Ring. During early play-testing, Gygax ran the game for three to five players each time, drawn from a pool of about twenty people. "We were adventurers who occasionally banded together," says Mornard. "He ran several games at several times during the week, and you got invites for certain times. I was usually on Thursday nights, but not invariably."

And there were no piles of rule books—and not just because they hadn't been written. Gygax wanted his players to learn the game through experience. "For about the first year we played we didn't see the rules at all," says Mornard. "That's an interesting way to play. It requires a certain amount of common sense." Some players didn't have it. Mornard recalls one adventure where a younger player opened a door in the depths of a dungeon to find a room where the floor was covered with piles of jewels:

"He says to Gary, 'I'm going to run in the room and start scooping them up.' Gary says, 'Okay, you're standing in gems and jewelry up to your ankles.' And the kid says, 'I'm going to throw them up in the air and dance around.' 'Okay, now you're standing in jewels halfway up your calves.' And the kid keeps going on about how he's dancing and throwing money around, while Gary says, 'You're standing in jewels up to your knees,' and then 'You're standing in jewels up to your armpits.' There was three inches of jewelry on top of quicksand. And the kid just didn't get it. It wasn't a trap where you take one step in and you're gone. About the time you're in to your knees, you're supposed to start noticing something is going on. You've got to pay attention."

Because the game was so new, players never knew what to expect from their Dungeon Master, or from their cohorts. Gygax was learning the game alongside his players and changing the rules based on their actions. Night after night, small groups of players pushed the boundaries of what was possible. Their actions shaped Gygax and Arneson's work, and decades of games that followed.

Mornard remembers a small action that had a very big effect: When one of Arneson's players decided he wanted his character to be a vampire, another said he would like to play a vampire hunter. "They had to figure out what a vampire hunter would be like in the game," says Mornard. "So, to counter the vampire, they gave him healing powers. That sort of became the template for the cleric. It was a counterpoint to the vampire." Today, clerics aren't just one of the core D&D character classes—they're a full-blown fantasy archetype, appearing in countless novels, films, and video games. Some random guy in Minnesota decided to screw with his buddy, and forty years later two hundred million gamers are playing with the result.*

After the better part of a year spent playing in Gary Gygax's Fantasy Game play tests, Mornard moved to Minneapolis to start college at the University of Minnesota. Naturally, he made friends with the local gamers—and soon found himself in Dave Arneson's basement.

---

* Other character classes had odder origins: Mornard says the martial artist class of monk was created "because Jim Ward liked the song 'Kung Fu Fighting.'"

Perhaps because the Blackmoor players were more often college-aged, and less often neighborhood children, Arneson's games were less playful than Gygax's. "Blackmoor was a much grimmer, grittier place than Greyhawk," says Mornard. "In Greyhawk, if you were killed, the other players would drag your body home. But in Blackmoor there was no honor amongst thieves. You'd be looted before your body hit the ground."

The game played a little differently too. "It was a different way of interacting," says Mornard. Arneson liked to use miniatures, while Gygax rarely did so. Arneson used to draw maps for his players instead of insisting they do so themselves. And he made people write up their moves instead of shouting them out and talking over each other.

Based on feedback from play tests in Blackmoor and Greyhawk and from war-gamer friends across the country, Gygax completed a 150-page revision of the Fantasy Game in the spring of 1973 and sent it out to more friends for testing. "The reaction was so intense that I was sure we had a winning game," he wrote. "I thought we would sell at least 50,000 copies to wargamers and fantasy fans. I underestimated the audience a little."

The demand was there, the game worked . . . the only thing missing was a name. "Fantasy Game" was a fine working title but too bland for the final product. So Gygax created a list of words that related to the game and wrote them in two columns on a sheet of paper—words like "castles," "magic," "monsters," "treasure," "trolls," "mazes," "sorcery," "spells," and "swords."

He read them aloud to his players, including Ernie and youngest daughter Cindy, to gauge their reactions. The girl's delight at two of the words, an alliterative pair, confirmed the choice: the game would be called Dungeons & Dragons.

Now they only had to print it. In the summer of 1973, Gygax called Avalon Hill and asked if they were interested in publishing his game.

"They laughed at the idea, turned it down," Gygax wrote.* Most of the gaming establishment wanted nothing to do with Arneson and Gygax's weird little idea. "One fellow had gone so far as to say that not only was fantasy gaming 'up a creek,'" wrote Gygax, "but if I had any intelligence whatsoever, I would direct my interest to something fascinating and unique; the Balkan Wars, for example."

No matter; the Dungeon Master wanted to choose his own adventure. Gygax had aspirations to run his own company—he just didn't have the money to start one. At the time he was ready to start printing game books, Gygax's income came from repairing shoes in his basement, and Arneson was "a security guard who couldn't afford shoes."

The solution was found in the place where the whole project started. In August, the annual Gen Con convention—now in its sixth year, and bigger than ever—was held in several buildings in Lake Geneva, including the Horticultural Hall and the Legion Hall. Members of Gygax's ever-growing D&D play test flocked to the con and caught the eye of one of Gygax's old friends. "Don Kaye saw the turnout, noted the interest in the fans," wrote Gygax, "and after the event was over, asked, 'Do you really think you can make a success of a game publishing company?'"

Kaye didn't have cash to invest, either. But after seeing the crowds at Gen Con, he was convinced D&D was a salable product. So he borrowed $1,000 against his life insurance, and that October he and Gygax became equal partners in a new company called Tactical Studies Rules. It was based out of Kaye's dining room.

There were still problems. A thousand dollars wouldn't print enough copies of D&D to meet anticipated demand. So Kaye and

* According to Gygax, Avalon Hill would come to regret that decision. Years later, noting D&D's success, the company tried to buy the game after all; "It was my turn to laugh," Gygax wrote.

Gygax decided to publish a different game first: Cavaliers and Roundheads, a set of rules for English Civil War–miniatures battles cowritten by Gygax and his Chainmail partner, Jeff Perren.

"We published Cavaliers and Roundheads . . . hoping the sales of the booklet would generate sufficient income to afford to publish the D&D game soon thereafter," wrote Gygax. "We both knew [D&D] would be the horse to pull the company." The game raised only $700 in sales.

Then the last piece fell into place. Another local gamer, Brian Blume, had also been to Gen Con, seen the crowds of people, and "badgered Gary into letting [him] in at the ground-floor." Blume was twenty-three, divorced, and worked as a tool-and-die maker's apprentice at a company owned by his dad, Melvin Blume. In December, he borrowed $2,000 from his father and became a full partner in Gygax and Kaye's company.

A few weeks later, Gygax sent his manuscript—now broken into three small booklets called *Men & Magic, Monsters & Treasure,* and *Underworld & Wilderness Adventures*—to Graphic Printing in Lake Geneva. He paid $2,300 to print a thousand sets.

In January 1974, Tactical Studies Rules made its creation public. It cost $10 and came in a hand-assembled cardboard box covered in wood-grain paper. A flyer pasted to the top lid featured a drawing of a Viking warrior on a rearing horse—art copied from a Doctor Strange comic book. Gygax and Arneson's names were also on the cover, and above that was the title:

DUNGEONS & DRAGONS

Rules for Fantastic Medieval Wargames
Campaigns Playable with Paper and Pencil
and Miniature Figures

5

STRENGTH OF CHARACTER

When I decided to end my decade-plus retreat from the world of Dungeons & Dragons, I did so with great trepidation. I wasn't worried about getting obsessed with role-playing games like when I was in high school—I thought I was far too sophisticated to fall into that trap again. But I was embarrassed.

Every Tuesday, I left my tiny studio apartment in Brooklyn and slinked to Brandon's third-floor walk-up like I was doing something illicit. From the shame on my face, an observer might have guessed I was off to buy drugs or had developed an addiction to strip clubs. My fear was that they might prefer a junkie or lech to what I was really becoming: a grown man who liked rolling dice and talking about wizards.

I didn't tell any of my friends. I wasn't eager to explain my motives or defend the pastime. Since I grew up playing D&D, I knew all too well that the game has a poor reputation. Like many nerdy pursuits, Dungeons & Dragons imparts a sense of undesirability. If you're a kid who plays D&D, people assume you're a nerd with no social skills. If you're an adult who plays, the stereotype is worse: You're a loser, you're a freak, you live in your parents' basement.

It's strange, because I am unquestionably a giant nerd, and it's hardly a secret. My friends would have been no more shocked if I told them I played Dungeons & Dragons than if I said I had chicken for dinner. But the desire to keep the hobby secret was burned deep into my psyche—a self-defense mechanism that came from years of teasing, bullying, and living on the fringes of schoolyard society. Geeky kids learn to hide their passions and play their cards close to their chest, lest they surrender more fodder for mockery.

The one person I did tell was my girlfriend Kara.* She had never tried D&D and didn't know anything about it; Kara played sports and went to parties in high school instead of fighting trolls and hiding from reality. She was supportive but a little confused. "Are you going to wear a costume?" she asked.

I took care to explain the game in detail and reassure her I wouldn't be dressing up like an elf or doing anything deviant—just sitting down at a table with a couple of normal guys. "It's no different than playing cards," I told her. "Just think of it like I'm going to a weekly poker game."

That satisfied her, for a while. But as weeks passed and it became clear that I wasn't on a temporary flight of fancy, she started to get more concerned. "Why are you still doing this?" she asked me one night. "Are you okay with me telling people you're going out and playing Dungeons & Dragons?"

I had no answer.

My new D&D companions had their own problems. When we started playing, Alex Agius, who plays Jhaden, was living with a girl who had strong negative feelings toward the game, thanks to a D&D-

* She's now my wife. Spoiler alert: This story has a happy ending.

playing brother. "He was a pothead, a dropout, kind of a fuckup," Alex told me. "She had always associated D&D with that. When I started playing with you guys it really stuck in her craw. It was a sticking point between us until the day we broke up."

Later, when Alex met Jennifer, the girl who eventually became his wife, he hid his D&D habit until the relationship started getting serious. "I was very hesitant to tell her," he said. "I don't remember how it finally came up, but I told her that I was playing D&D, and she was just like, 'That's cool.'"

Despite any reservations held by certain players and girlfriends, our D&D group continued to meet, and our adventuring party prospered. After Weslocke, Jhaden, Babeal, and Ganubi fought off the fish-monster pirates, we managed to free our ship and sail to San Francisco, the only human city left on North America's Pacific coast—Los Angeles, of course, is full of vampires. We spent a few sessions knocking around the Bay Area, killing random monsters, and eventually earned enough experience points for our characters to advance a level.

Leveling up a Dungeons & Dragons character is serious business. Level isn't just a badge of honor indicating how long a character's gone without dying; it's a way to quantify the heroic journey and allow characters to become more powerful over time. The process is detailed in the *Player's Handbook,* with tables that cross-reference statistics like base attack bonus with level, and instructions that tell players when they can add a point to one of their ability scores or skills. This time, as Weslocke advanced from a level-twelve to a level-thirteen cleric, the transition was simple. But advancement can get really complicated if you want it to—particularly if you start pulling abilities, spells, and powers from one of the dozens of supplemental D&D rule books.

The next time we met, Morgan asked us if we'd completed the leveling process.

"I did," Phil said. "I'm now a fourth-level rogue, fourth-level bard, and fourth-level shadowdancer." D&D characters aren't limited to a single class, even though most players stick to one. Phil has taken this to extremes, stacking levels first in bard, then in rogue, and then adopting an advanced "prestige class" available only to higher-level characters, the super-stealthy shadowdancer.

"And I'm going to take another prestige class at next level," he said. "The Evangelist from the *Complete Divine* sourcebook.* I'm going to try to start a religion."

Morgan laughed. "The Church of Ganubi."

After a long day traveling through the mountain foothills south of San Francisco, we made camp at the top of a ridge, a few hundred yards from a primal oak forest. Jhaden caught a rabbit, built a fire and a spit. When the cooking was done, Ganubi told one of his stories while we feasted.

"Hark to the tale of Ganubi and his gallivanters," he began, "brave heroes on a righteous quest. One night, while sailing across the great ocean, their ship was overtaken in an unnatural fog . . ."

I usually enjoy Ganubi's accounts of our adventures, even if he does make himself out to be the hero and the rest us become mere grooms and squires. But on this night, exhausted from our travel, I skipped the stories and bedded down for the night. I drifted to sleep with the sound of Ganubi's voice on the wind.

A few hours later, I awoke to his screaming.

For a moment, lost in the dark, I clutched my bedroll in panic. But

* "Evangelists travel the world proclaiming their devotion to a particular deity, pantheon, or religious doctrine. . . . While clerics and even druids can make powerful evangelists, few trade in their spellcasting abilities for the power this prestige class offers. Bards, naturally charismatic, may find religion and become evangelists." *The Complete Divine,* page 39.

a warrior's instincts are strong, and I gathered myself quickly. Ganubi was on watch, and something was attacking the camp. I sat up and, peering into the darkness, tried to identify the threat.

There seemed to be nothing there. Jhaden was already standing and scanning the landscape, sword in hand. On the other side of the camp I could see Ganubi, his back to me, rapidly disappearing into the night. He was fleeing our camp and some unseen enemy, all the while screaming: "Run away! Run away! Run away!"

Ganubi is an interesting character. Phil's a performer, so he plays the part with zest and gusto, and will frequently make decisions based on "what Ganubi would do," even when that's not the best course of action. This devotion to role-playing sometimes makes the game more difficult—Ganubi is overly trusting and not that bright—but it always makes the story more compelling.

Characters are the heart of any D&D game. As a player, the character is your avatar; you see through its eyes and make it do as you wish. But the act of inhabiting an avatar goes two ways. The more you play with a particular character, the more you identify with it and it controls *your* actions.

As a player, I knew what happened before Weslocke woke up. The party was attacked by a pack of invisible demon dogs, and Ganubi fell prey to one of their magical abilities, a fear effect that forces him to flee for 1d6 rounds. I understood that, from a tactical standpoint, the smartest thing to do on my turn would be to get up, chase Ganubi, and cast a Remove Fear spell, allowing him to rejoin the battle. But I also understood Weslocke, and I knew he had just woken up, he was startled, and his instinct was to protect himself. So instead I cast Blade Barrier, putting a whirling curtain of magical knives between me and the dogs.

D&D players invest a lot of time and emotion in their characters, so it's not surprising that they want to protect them. This impulse even spills out of the game into the real world; I may have sold my rule books back in college, but I still preserve the character sheets from my childhood role-playing games. From fourth grade to my high school graduation, I kept all my characters in a red vinyl document organizer, an off-brand version of the Trapper Keepers that were popular in the seventies and eighties. It was my constant companion to games for a better part of a decade, and even during the long years when I avoided role-playing, I kept it safe—rarely consciously, but always carefully.

In recent years, the character keeper slumbered, forgotten, at the back of a cabinet in my living room. But once I started playing D&D again, it awoke and called to me. Like the One Ring trying to get back to its master, it wanted to be found. So on a quiet spring morning I went to it, shoving aside piles of old tax returns and pay stubs, and held it in my hands for the first time in ages.

It looked old, and its vinyl cover was peeling along the edges, revealing a tatty cardboard core. But it felt vital in my hands, solid and reassuring. The wraparound flap was secured with a small Velcro closure, and when I peeled it open the ripping noise made me shiver—a sound, like a bugle call before a battle, that heralded action and adventure. Inside the organizer there were three expanding folders, all stuffed to bursting, and a half-empty pocket on the inside cover. I reached into the pocket and pulled out a small stack of paper.

It was a pile of possibility . . . or a few dozen blank character records, if you want to be literal about it. Most role-playing game rule books provide one of these fill-in-the-blanks forms for players to photocopy and use when they make a new character. To devoted players, each sheet represents a chance to be a different person, a new and exciting escape. As a child I fetishized them, and constantly searched new game books and magazines for better layouts. I even made my own on the Brother LW-20 word processor I was stuck with in the days before our home had a computer and a printer. I remember the hours of painstaking work—counting presses of the space bar to ensure that attributes on one line would align perfectly with those below, and holding down "shift" and the hyphen key to produce long underscores where I'd later pencil in each character's details. After dozens of imperfect drafts, I'd have a pile of crumpled-up pages next to my desk, like a frustrated novelist in an old black-and-white movie . . . and a single perfect sheet, tabula rasa, which I'd protect between the flaps of a stiff manila folder and carefully place in my father's briefcase. The next day he'd use his office photocopier to make me a few dozen copies, and when he came home from work I'd tear down the stairs to our front door, give him a grateful hug, then grab the prize and bolt back to my bedroom. I'd extract the original character sheet from the folder, archive it between the pages of an oversized children's illustrated dictionary, and then place the copies into my red vinyl organizer. There they'd stay, safe and secure, until I needed a hero.

I loved the process of character creation so much that I'd spend hours designing characters with no intention of using them. When you're making a new character, you may have to record anywhere from a dozen to a hundred personal details, depending on the game. Some parts of the process are simple, like when you roll four six-sided dice to determine a D&D character's starting ability scores.* But you're also required to dig deeper, imagining a character's personal

* "Disregard the lowest die roll and total the three highest ones. The result is a number between 3 (horrible) and 18 (tremendous). The average ability score for the typical commoner is 10 or 11, but your character is not typical. The most common ability scores for player characters are 12 and 13." *Player's Handbook*, page 7.

history and motivations. I enjoyed it as an analytic exercise (How can I exploit the rules to my advantage?) and as an act of creativity (Who is this person, and what drives them?).

The three expanding folders inside my organizer contained hundreds of characters, and each said something about who I was when I made it. The first pocket was full of D&D characters, most of them created when I was in elementary school. They're goofy, sweet, and naïve.

On top of the pile was Wizzrobe, an elf wizard I based on an enemy in one of my favorite video games, The Legend of Zelda. My grandparents gave me a Nintendo Entertainment System for Christmas in 1986, so I was probably ten or eleven years old when I made the character. Looking at it years later, I couldn't help but be impressed by the way I replicated powers I saw in the video game: Wizzrobe wears a ring of teleportation and carries a magic wand that casts the spell Telekinesis.* Farther down the pile I found Aries, an eleventh-level human cleric. In the upper left-hand corner of the character record, in a space labeled "Player's Name," I'd written "Dr. Dave," and below that, after "Character Began," the date: 2/19/88. I was eleven years old. Aries carries a Bag of Tricks, one of my favorite magical items: It's full of small fuzzy objects, and when a character pulls one out and throws it, it balloons into a full-sized, living animal. Rolling 1d8 determines the species, and, depending on your luck, you could get anything from a weasel to a lion.

As I flipped through the sheets, each character reminded me who they were and what I wanted them to be. Leaf, a rogue, was

* "By means of this spell the magic-user is able to move objects by will force, by concentrating on moving them mentally. The telekinesis spell causes the desired object to move vertically or horizontally. Movement is 2″ the first round, 4″ the second, 8″ the third, 16″ the fourth, and so on, doubling each round until a maximum telekinetic movement of 1,024″ per round is reached." *Advanced Dungeons & Dragons Players Handbook*, page 82.

inspired by Matthew Broderick's role in the 1985 fantasy film *Ladyhawke.* Robin, a swashbuckling fighter, was my attempt to emulate C. S. Lewis's Prince Caspian. Another character, written in pencil on a faded piece of graph paper, wasn't mine, but I remembered it all the same: Nightwind, a level-fifteen human ninja, carried a distinctive +3 wakizashi.* He belonged to my friend Michael Bagnulo and was used in a campaign we played all summer long before we started sixth grade. When school was out, role-playing game campaigns could stretch to a truly epic length and complexity; this one drew to a close in a marathon thirty-hour session at a beach house owned (and barely supervised) by our friend Scott Johnson's parents.

Not long after that, Michael transitioned from player to Dungeon Master and eventually ran the games that captivated me throughout high school. The next character sheet in the pile, a tenth-level human magic-user with the goofy name Alka the Seltzer, hinted at the beginnings of that storytelling skill: In the character description area of the sheet, under "Fears/Dislikes," I wrote "sharks and anything else Mike thinks up."

Next I found Sir Howland the Wolf Knight, a level-fifteen human ranger. This character was a great example of a game gone wrong—an inexperienced Dungeon Master who has allowed his players to build ridiculously powerful characters and then showered them with money and treasure.** Sir Howland carries a +6 vorpal sword, a +4 dagger, and a +5 lance; in the section of the character sheet labeled "Special Abilities," my younger self wrote "incredible senses, great speed, immune to disease, detect evil, summon ethereal sword,

---

* "This is a short sword, similar in design and construction to the katana. Like the katana, the wakizashi may be named for some past deed or event. It holds almost as important a place in the samurai's honor as his katana." *Advanced Dungeons & Dragons Oriental Adventures,* page 48.

** This is known in gaming circles as a "Monty Haul" campaign.

black belt in karate and ninjitsu, use technology, time/dimension travel."

Deeper in the red vinyl organizer, I found character sheets from other pursuits, like Star Trek: The Role-Playing Game. Instead of controlling wizards and warriors in a medieval fantasy setting, players of this 1982 game took the roles of crew members aboard a Federation starship. It bored the hell out of me, but I sure did like imagining new *Star Trek* heroes like the ones on these official "Starfleet character data records." There's Charles Adams, captain of the USS *Achilles*; T'Pec, his Vulcan helmsman; Lieutenant Commander John Martin, first officer of the USS *Lexington*; even Lieutenant David Ewalt, chief security officer of the USS *Enterprise*.

The final pocket contained characters I created when I was in high school and devoted to bleak dystopian games like Cyberpunk 2020 and Shadowrun. Their *Blade Runner*–style settings were the perfect places for nihilistic teenage boys to run rampant, and the futuristic weapons and gear echoed my growing interest in computers. My characters from this era tended to be high-tech savants or streetwise urban brawlers. There's Leonard Collins, a scientist who goes by the code name of Doc; most of his skill points are allocated to genetics, engineering, and parazoology. Then Columbo, a detective; his list of gear includes a microrecorder and "stogies." Lurch, a bodyguard, belongs to one of Shadowrun's unique races; he's a sasquatch, eight feet tall and strong enough to rip a man's arm off. King Sun, a soldier of fortune, was named after an obscure rapper affiliated with Afrika Bambaataa's Universal Zulu Nation; I'd deserve street cred for that reference if I hadn't dropped it in the most uncool context possible. Then a computer hacker named Keystroke, and another named Technomancer. David Walters, a cop who fights with two pistols, John Woo–style. A soldier called Blackjack. A mercenary named Elvis.

My blade barrier protected me from getting bitten by the invisible attackers, but my companions were still easy targets. I watched Graeme scramble up a tree to get above the danger; Jhaden, swords at the ready, was still looking for something to fight.

The problem, of course, is that while Alex knew the enemy was out there, he couldn't see them. He had to attack at random and hope he connected with something solid. "Jhaden's going to swing his longsword here," he said, pointing at an empty square on the battle mat, next to the mini that represented Jhaden. "This is plus-twelve to hit," he said, rolling a die, "for a total of twenty."

"Okay, that's enough to hit," Morgan said. "Now roll percentile dice."

Alex picked up two ten-sided dice. "The red one is tens," he said, tossing the dice on the table. They came up 7 and 5. "Seventy-five!"

"You hit nothing."

"What?"

"You would have hit something if there was anything there."

"Goddamn it!"

Brandon waves his hand. "Hey, guys? I can't hear." His voice had an unusual echo. He was smaller than usual, too. "Can you move the microphone closer?" Brandon moved to Los Angeles two weeks ago, but we wanted to keep him in the game, so he dialed into Alex's computer using videoconferencing software. We saw him in a tiny window on the monitor and heard him through speakers; he watched us through a webcam pointed at the game table.

Alex moved over to the computer, grabbed the mouse, and adjusted a few controls. "Can you hear better now?"

Brandon's lips moved, but no sound emerged.

Alex clicked at the controls. "Oops, sorry, man. I turned off your audio."

Morgan laughed. "You can mute Brandon! Now, if only we could mute Phil . . ."

It was novel having Brandon virtually present at the table, but not a long-term solution. He couldn't follow the action or participate fully, so it's wasn't a satisfying experience. Since wizards are such a critical part of any D&D party, we really needed one at the table, and that meant finding a new player to join our weekly game.

We'd had mixed luck with this sort of thing before. R. C. Robbins, who plays our group's rogue, Graeme, joined the campaign well after it was under way, and he turned out to be a great addition. R. C. is thirty-six years old, married for four of those, and works as a business technology consultant for a big corporation based in Manhattan. He's the kind of guy who always has some crazy story at hand, whether it's about a confrontation he just had on the subway or a wild party he went to a decade ago. We tease him about it, but he's a good guy and well liked.

Other additions didn't go as well. Before R. C. came on board we recruited Jonathan, a local grad student, through a post on a website where interested players hook up with regular weekly games. Jonathan was welcomed into the group but immediately started ruffling feathers. He was obsessed with the rules of the game and seemed to view each session as an opportunity to demonstrate his mastery of obscure details rather than, as Brandon described it, "a chance to get together with friends and have fun . . . a break from the 'real world' where things like rules give me a headache."

But the real issue was personality. Jonathan was just difficult to get along with. He was loud, he talked over people, he lectured, he insulted anyone who disagreed with him, and yet he was easily offended. Even outside of the game he was a lot to take, frequently clogging our e-mail in-boxes with thousand-word essays on topics like the merits of using an off-hand weapon to defend against melee attacks instead of carrying a heavy shield.

And frankly, he was kind of creepy, with a strange, often misogynistic sense of humor. Once he e-mailed everyone in the group to ask our opinion on whether a wizard could reassign people's gender using the Polymorph spell:* "I'm wondering if I could set up a spell casting side business during down time between adventures. I'd bet rich men would pay big bucks to experience multiple orgasms."

Jonathan meant well, and we wanted to integrate him into the group. But his behavior at our weekly games was disruptive, and none of us were interested in spending what little free time we had being annoyed. When friendly attempts to talk to him about it went nowhere, the rest of the group started to discuss telling Jonathan he was no longer welcome.

It hurt to even consider such a thing. Dungeons & Dragons is supposed to be a safe haven for people like Jonathan. Many of us gravitated to the hobby precisely because we had difficulty integrating into traditional social groups. We were the nerdy kids, the outcasts, and we found a welcome at the game table. Dismissing someone from a D&D group because they're too socially awkward seemed like hypocrisy at best, a rejection of everything we are supposed to stand for at worst. High sacrilege.

Besides, we all understood Jonathan too well. A lack of social grace and argumentative behavior are not uncommon traits among

* "This spell functions like 'alter self,' except that you change the willing subject into another form of living creature. The new form may be of the same type as the subject or any of the following types: aberration, animal, dragon, fey, giant, humanoid, magical beast, monstrous humanoid, ooze, plant, or vermin." *Player's Handbook,* page 263.

my people. Jonathan seemed to suffer from a terminal case of what's sometimes known as Arrogant Nerd syndrome, a disorder where smart people hide their insecurities and fear through intellectual bullying, and seek to preempt condemnation by judging other people first and finding them inferior.

Thankfully, Jonathan quit coming to games on his own when his schoolwork demanded more attention, so we never had to make a decision about booting him. But now we're acutely aware of what can go wrong with the introduction of a new player and a little gun-shy about recruiting.

It doesn't help that sometimes even people you really like can become problem players. One of my friends from college, Jamie Polichak, is a terrifically smart guy who delights in wrecking role-playing campaigns. "In gaming, many people play a kind of idealized version of what they would like to be in real life," he says. "I was the albatross around their necks. Excessively vicious, entirely useless, or completely insane."

In one game, he played a cleric of Cthulhu, a malevolent alien god first introduced in an H. P. Lovecraft horror story. Jamie decided the cleric suffered from multiple personality disorder and that one of his personalities actually believed he *was* Cthulhu. He would summon himself and try to eat the other characters' faces.

Another time he played a fighter who refused to reveal his character class to the other players or to enter battle directly. "He insisted he was a chef and was adventuring to raise money to build his restaurant," Jamie says.

At one point, Jamie's friends banned him from playing the *Star Wars* role-playing game because he wanted to play two particularly annoying characters: a one-armed Wookiee who could speak and understand only his own native language, and an intelligent robot built into the Wookiee's prosthetic arm, who acted as translator.

"They did not get along with each other," Jamie says, "thus bringing up the question: An angry Wookiee will rip the arms off of a person, but will he rip off his own arm?"

Jamie was also banned from playing the gothic horror role-playing game Vampire: The Masquerade. "No chimpanzee vampires allowed."

Some people approach conflict as a chance to wreak havoc. I think of it as a puzzle to be solved. For instance: How do you fight creatures that you cannot see?

As a cleric, my greatest asset is my magical ability. So as soon as I realized we were under attack, I ran down a mental checklist of spells I was prepared to cast, looking for something to give us an advantage. Dispel Magic cancels out spells that have been cast by another wizard or cleric, so it would have made our attackers visible if they had been hidden by an Invisibility spell. But I figured our attackers were some kind of wild magical animals and their invisibility was an innate ability, like a chameleon's color-changing skin. The True Seeing spell would work, since it allows someone to see through any kind of invisibility. But I can cast it on only one person, and I have to touch them to make it work. With our party so scattered, I'd just end up casting it on myself and then have to watch helplessly as a pack of animals chewed up my friends. A Darkness spell would even out the odds, since our attackers wouldn't be able to see us either. Of course, being animals, they could still smell and hear us, so they would just eat us in the dark.

And that was the key. Our enemy couldn't be seen, but they could be smelled and heard. Human senses aren't strong enough to do the job, but if I cast the Summon Monster spell, I could cause a magical animal to pop into existence and command it to find our attackers for me.

I put down my character sheet, picked up a copy of the *Player's Handbook* that was lying on the game table, and flipped to the 108-page-long section that describes all the basic D&D spells in detail. There are actually nine different Summon Monster spells, each one available to progressively higher-level characters and each with its own table listing summonable monsters that the spell caster must choose from. At level one, you can summon tiny stuff like a rat or a raven; at level two, a poisonous viper or an eagle. The most powerful version of the spell that Weslocke can manage is Summon Monster VI, so I jumped to that list. A rhinoceros would have been pretty badass, but I needed something that could sense invisible creatures. Polar bears were an option. Do they have a strong sense of smell?

I put down the *Player's Handbook,* yoinked a copy of the *Monster Manual* out from under Morgan's notes, and flipped through the pages. Chapter 2: "Animals" . . . Bear, Polar . . . 68 hit points . . . claw attack for 1d8+8 damage . . . special qualities include low-light vision and scent. I jumped to the back of the book and consulted the glossary. "Scent" means that creatures can sniff out hidden foes, but it would take the bear a few rounds to zero in on a single target. If there was a whole pack of invisible dogs, they'd tear us to pieces while Yogi was just sniffing at dirt.

I returned to the *Player's Handbook* and reviewed the long spell description for Summon Monster VI. "This spell functions like Summon Monster I," it said, "except that you can summon one creature from the 6th-level list, 1d3 creatures of the same kind from the 5th-level list, or 1d4+1 creatures of the same kind from a lower level list." Five relatively weak creatures might not kill the invisible dogs, but if they could find them all, the boys and I could step in to finish the deed. So it was back to the creature tables, and the *Monster Manual* again, before I finally solved the puzzle.

"I'm going to cast Summon Monster Six," I announced. "But instead of summoning one monster from the Summon Monster Six list, I'm going to summon a whole pack of yeth hounds.* They're going to fan out and use their scent ability to find the invisible creatures."

"That's smart," Morgan said. I tried not to blush.

The plan worked perfectly. The yeth hounds quickly zoned in on the invisible enemies, and we targeted our own attacks where we saw them scratching and biting.

A little later, Ganubi finally stopped running away in panic. He turned and ran back toward camp, but by the time he returned, we had just finished off the final invisible foe.

I wonder how he'll tell this story.

D&D players treasure their characters' successes and tell stories about them like a new parent brags about their baby. Ask Alex, and he might tell you about the time he fought and killed Si, a vampire who was our primary antagonist in the early days of Morgan's campaign. It was our first big victory and gave us hope that we could eventually free our fellow humans from the pens. In contrast, my favorite Jhaden story is slightly less heroic. We were trying to pass through an underground complex full of angry, man-sized ants when Jhaden came up with a plan: He killed one of the insects, glued its legs and antennae to his body, smeared himself with its guts, and tried to bluff his way past the creatures in the hope that they'd think he was just another ant. It didn't work.

Phil might remember the time we were hiding in another vampire's cellar, planning an ambush; when the villain started down the

* "These fearsome flying hounds glide low over the countryside at night, seeking likely prey. A yeth hound stands 5 feet tall at the shoulder and weighs about 400 pounds," *Monster Manual*, page 261.

stairs, Ganubi surprised us all by jumping out of the shadows and singing "Happy Birthday." The vampire bought it and walked, smiling, right into the middle of a trap.

Mike Mornard told me about a character he played in the Greyhawk campaign who was a balrog—a kind of demon most recognizable to nongeeks as the creature Gandalf fights on a bridge in *The Fellowship of the Ring.** "We had to distract this wizard in his tower," Mornard says. "So I asked Rob [Kuntz] if it was possible for a balrog to make a little jet of flame come out the tip of his finger. He looked at me. 'Okay, sure.' So I got a hat with a little card in it that said 'PRESS,' and I got a wooden box, attached a can to it, glued in a piece of glass, and knocked on the wizard's door. When he answered, I told him that I was doing a feature article for *Balrog Times Magazine*; held up the box; said, 'Watch the birdie!'; and then stuck my finger up and made a little puff of flame." The flattered wizard spent the rest of the night showing off his workshop, answering questions, and posing for pictures.

When gamers share our war stories, we're really sharing something about ourselves. "It doesn't matter how radically different that character is from you," says Rodney Thompson, a designer at Wizards of the Coast who works on the Dungeons & Dragons line. "You're still investing it with some shred of your personality. That's something that D&D does like no other game."

* "I am a servant of the Secret Fire, wielder of the flame of Anor. The dark fire will not avail you, flame of Udun. Go back to the shadow! You shall not pass!" It gives me a nerdgasm every time.

6

TEMPLE OF THE FROG

Like a sleeping dragon, D&D was slow to get on its feet. Tactical Studies Rules sold the first "brown box" set of rule books at the end of January 1974, via mail order; the rest sat next to the furnace in Gary Gygax's basement, on the side of his shoemaker's bench. Michael Mornard remembers returning to Lake Geneva during his university's winter break, spotting the pallet of boxes, and asking Gygax about them: "He said they'd printed a thousand copies," says Mornard. "We thought he was out of his mind."

D&D was the first and only fantasy role-playing game on the market, and Gygax's hometown players loved it. But printing a thousand copies was a risky move, since it wasn't entirely clear there were that many people in the game's core customer base. "War-gaming was a very fringe hobby," says Mornard. "Gen Con would attract three hundred guys . . . you could literally know almost all of the war gamers in the world."

The quality of the product didn't speak well for the game's sales prospects, either. The printed text was rough and hard to read, and when you could make out the instructions, they were confusing and contradictory. "With all due respect to Gary and Dave, the original rules were incomprehensible," says Mornard. "Unless you were an experienced miniatures wargame player—essentially, one of the three hundred—you would have no idea how to play it."

Still, by the summer of 1974, TSR had sold around four hundred copies of Dungeons & Dragons, and Gygax was increasingly optimistic about its prospects. "Sales are really quite good and we hope to do even better once we get some ads going," he wrote that June in a letter to his friend Dave Megarry. "At the present, TSR has three partners and the company worth is about $6,000 or so. I'd say in a couple of years we should have that tripled at least."

Initial sales came mostly via mail order and through a handful of specialty retailers, including game shops and hobby stores. But Gygax was convinced that his receipts didn't represent the game's true market. "Counting all of the illicit photocopies that were floating around, and the players who didn't own their own set, it is a safe bet that no fewer than ten thousand persons then knew of and were enthralled by the D&D game," he said. By November, TSR had sold out its first run of one thousand copies and ordered one thousand more.

D&D wasn't TSR's only product, but it was clearly its most promising. Tricolor, a book of rules for Napoleonic miniatures battles, proved about as popular as a grenadier at a garden party. Warriors of Mars, a war game set in the fantasy world of Barsoom, fared better—but the fifty-six-page rule book, written by Gygax and Brian Blume, was printed without permission from the estate of Edgar Rice Burroughs, whose John Carter novels had been plundered for the game's setting. It was available for less than a year before TSR received a cease-and-desist letter and stopped selling it.

By the end of 1974, the company had generated about $12,000 in sales, mainly from Dungeons & Dragons and Warriors of Mars. "Although this was not exactly a 'hot' reception, we were satisfied, for it was a start," Gygax said. "Wargamers were not exactly flocking to fantasy role playing, but a few came into the fold, and we were recruiting players from outside the hobby." Revenues were expected to triple in 1975. Tactical Studies Rules was ready to bloom.

TSR suffered its first major setback on January 31, 1975, when cofounder Don Kaye died of a heart attack. He was thirty-seven. Kaye's wife, Donna, inherited his shares in the company and took over some of his duties, so the business kept moving; in the first quarter of 1975 TSR shipped several new products, including Star Probe, a space exploration game, and two tank-centric World War II war games, Panzer Warfare and the punnily spelled Tractics. But the loss of Kaye was deeply felt within the small company, particularly by Gygax, who'd lost both a childhood friend and his closest business partner.

In a letter to Dave Megarry, Gygax promised to uphold Kaye's legacy by keeping TSR for gamers, by gamers: "We will never allow TSR to become a company which is run by any outside group," he wrote. "We may take others in as partners eventually, but we will never seek any non-wargamer capitalization. We will not grow as fast this way, but we will do very well nonetheless."

It seemed at first that Gygax was right: By March, revenues were over $2,000 a month, and TSR had developed wholesale relationships with retailers across the country. But while sales of Dungeons & Dragons were accelerating, they weren't living up to the promise of the game's hugely successful play test. When new players had walked into Gary Gygax or Dave Arneson's basement, they had walked out addicted: At one point, Gygax hosted D&D games several nights a week, sometimes with more than twenty players, and had to deputize Rob Kuntz as co–Dungeon Master in order to meet demand. Why weren't gamers around the country embracing the game as rabidly as they had in Lake Geneva?

The problem was that a mail-order purchase of the D&D box set didn't ship with Gary Gygax or Dave Arneson. The rules taught a mechanism for play but did a poor job conveying the experience of role-playing. Without seeing the game in action, war gamers had a hard time making the mental leap from precise simulations of historical battles to creative fantasy adventures—and even if they did, they suffered from a lack of access to worlds as compelling as Greyhawk and Blackmoor.

The first step toward solving that problem came with the debut of *The Strategic Review,* a newsletter edited by Gygax and Blume and published by TSR. Available by subscription at the rate of $1.50 per year, or 50¢ per copy, the slim pamphlet primarily served as a marketing vehicle, listing games for sale and touting future releases. But each issue also included a few articles that fleshed out existing games and taught customers how to play them. The *Review* clarified D&D's confusing rules ("A magic-user can use a given spell but once during any given day, even if he is carrying his books with him . . ."), added new weapons and character classes (Jhaden can trace his ancestry to an article titled "Rangers: An Exciting New Dungeons & Dragons Class"), and shared more of the color that made Arneson and Gygax's fantasy worlds compelling to their players. The very first issue introduced one of D&D's most popular monsters, the mind flayer, in a section called "Creature Features": "This is a super-intelligent, man-shaped creature with four tentacles by its mouth which it uses to strike its prey. If a tentacle hits it will then penetrate to the brain, draw it forth, and the monster will devour it. It will take one to four turns for the tentacle to reach the brain, at which time the victim is dead."

Still, the fantasy game of Dungeons & Dragons was incomplete until the publication of its first fantasy world. In the spring of 1975 TSR released *Dungeons & Dragons Supplement I: Greyhawk,* a fifty-six-page book full of rules and details from Gygax's home campaign. The expansion included improved rules for managing combat, replacing a wonky system adopted from Chainmail; added a variety of spells, creatures, and magical items; and introduced two character classes, the paladin and the thief.

It also taught, by example, how to create your own adventures. You might, the book suggested, include a magical source of monsters ("Greyhawk had a fountain on its second level which issued endless numbers of snakes," Gygax explains in the text) or a trapped room where all the furniture has been enchanted to attack the players—chairs that kick, stools that trip, and rugs that smother ("Ours is known as the 'Living Room'"). These details helped bridge the gap between players who learned the game at Gary's table and those who picked it up in a hobby store. Instead of just explaining how to play a game, *Greyhawk* showed its readers they could make their own world.

Greyhawk's impact didn't stop there: Its most important innovation may have been that it was published in the first place. By releasing an optional expansion to Dungeons & Dragons, Gygax encouraged the idea that the game should evolve and grow. It suggested that players add, remove, and personalize, and made it okay for different groups to use different rules. You can't open up a Monopoly box, throw out all the money, invent rules for military conquest of properties, and still call it Monopoly. But D&D players are encouraged to change the game, expand it, and mold it in their own image.

As a result, the game offers infinite playability. If I get tired of fighting vampires in Morgan's postapocalyptic world, I can find another group running a traditional adventure in the world of Greyhawk. If that game has too much combat for my taste and not enough role-playing, I can move on again. The system encourages long-term engagement, and it's one reason why D&D fans are particularly devoted to their hobby.

It also suggests a solution to a problem that's plagued game makers for centuries: You can only sell a game once. I bought a Monopoly set fourteen years ago, and I'll probably still be using it fourteen years from now—barring a house fire or theft, or, more likely, that I destroy the board in a bankruptcy-induced fit of bad sportsmanship. Parker Brothers got twenty bucks from me, and that's it. But D&D is different. With the publication of *Greyhawk*, it became clear that if you kept adding on to the rules, you could keep selling stuff to players. The key to TSR's success would be found not in a single set of rules but in a whole universe of stories, settings, and color.

By the summer of 1975, sales of Dungeons & Dragons were rapidly accelerating. It took eleven months to sell the first thousand D&D box sets, but the second thousand flew off the shelves in half that time. When TSR ordered a third printing—either two or three thousand sets, depending on the source—the company was low on cash, so the printer took payment by manufacturing a few hundred extra copies and selling them directly to stores.

In its first year, D&D had sold mostly through mail order and direct sales to game shops. TSR did very little wholesale business and only had relationships with three ersatz distributors—small companies who made the lead miniature soldiers used in war games, so they had existing relationships with hobby stores. But now that D&D was really starting to move, Gygax and Blume were able to secure deals with several major distributors.

They also started thinking about selling products overseas. Historical war-gaming had deep roots in Europe, and there were lots of small hobby groups and newsletters. So Gygax pitched D&D to all the influential European gamers he could find.

Before long, Dungeons & Dragons made its way to a small flat on Bolingbroke Road in West London, headquarters (and home to the founders) of a tiny company called Games Workshop. War-gaming buddies Ian Livingstone, Steve Jackson, and John Peake started the company in early 1975, selling handmade wooden games like Go and backgammon. They printed up a newsletter, *Owl & Weasel*, to promote the company and sent it to everyone they knew in the game business—including Gary Gygax, who sent back a copy of Dungeons & Dragons, hoping for a positive review.

"John thought it was horrendous," says Livingstone. "It had quite unintelligible rules . . . you had to interpret them, and ad-lib a lot. But Steve and I were immediately hooked, from day one . . . it unlocked worlds of the imagination."

Livingstone and Jackson loved the game so much, they decided to change the focus of Games Workshop away from handmade board games to concentrate on role-playing and war games. Peake left the company, and Livingstone called Gary Gygax. He ordered six copies of D&D and signed a three-year agreement to exclusively distribute the game in Europe.

"These milestones in games don't come along very often," says Livingstone. "There's Monopoly, there's Scrabble, then there's a long gap, and there's D&D. It was such an amazing fundamental shift in how you play games . . . making it more theater rather than just being fixed to a board. It was just fantastic."

The more TSR grew, the more its founders worried about staying true to their gamer roots. The summer edition of *The Strategic Review* included an editorial explaining the company's goals to customers, but that probably served more as reassurance for Gygax and Blume themselves: "Tactical Studies Rules is not a giant company; it is not even a large one. But we are growing now, and in the future we might attain substantial size. While we must make a profit in order to remain in business, TSR is not around solely to make money. The members of TSR are longtime gamers who have found that there is a great deal of satisfaction in creating and/or publishing a good set of game rules."

Part of the tension over "keeping it real" was due to the continued involvement of Don Kaye's widow, Donna. Don had grown up playing games with Gary and shared his passions, but Donna wasn't part of the war-gaming crowd, and Gygax found her "impossible to work with." So in July 1975, Gygax and Blume used what little cash they had to buy out Kaye's interest, dissolve Tactical Studies Rules Inc., and reform the company without her as TSR Hobbies Inc.

The new company began life as Gary Gygax's baby. Operations moved out of the Kayes' house and into Gygax's basement, and he took a controlling interest in the corporation, with 60 percent of the shares; assumed the title of president; and became the company's only salaried employee, at a rate of $85 a week.

But instead of solidifying the company under Gygaxian rule and securing its future by gamers, for gamers, the shakeup did the opposite. Because he'd spent so much money buying Kaye out of the company, Gygax threw TSR off balance at a critical point in its growth. Within a few months, the company was out of cash. In order to raise the capital needed to print, ship, and develop new products, TSR issued more shares of stock. Brian Blume bought some, as did his father, Melvin (later, Melvin transferred his shares to his other son, Kevin). By the fall, the Blumes controlled the company, and Gygax owned just 35 percent of its stock.

Even decades later, Gygax clearly regretted losing control. In 2005, he told an interviewer that TSR's ultimate fate may have been sealed in that very first year of operations: "There is no question in my mind that had Don Kaye lived, the whole course of later events at TSR would have been altered radically. Don was not only a very intelligent guy, a gamer, but he was also one who was not given to allowing the prospect of greater profits to cloud his judgment."

Back in 1975, the future looked bright. TSR published several more war games, including Classic Warfare, a set of Gygax-authored rules for reenacting battles "from the Pharaohs to Charlemagne." Gygax and Blume penned the company's second role-playing game, Boot Hill; it was set in the Old West and focused mostly on gun-fighting. Dave Megarry contributed Dungeon!, a Blackmoor-inspired board game that represented TSR's most ambitious production to date: a color game map, customized cards, tokens, dice, and a rules booklet all packaged in an attractive box.

University of Minnesota professor M. A. R. Barker also made his game-design debut at TSR. A scholar of ancient languages,* Barker had spent decades crafting a fantasy world called Tékumel, writing thousands of pages of histories, describing its culture, and even constructing its languages.** He served as adviser to the university's war-gaming club, and after Michael Mornard showed him Dungeons & Dragons, Barker wrote two games based in Tékumel: a role-playing game, Empire of the Petal Throne; and a combat-oriented board

* Like Tolkien.

** Like Tolkien.

game, War of Wizards. Barker died in March 2012, leaving behind an epic body of work describing Tékumel.*

Even with so many new products, Dungeons & Dragons continued to pay TSR's bills: the third printing of D&D sold out in about five months. In November, faced with surging demand, the company ordered a new printing of five thousand copies, more than all the previous print runs combined. TSR also issued a second expansion to their less-than-two-year-old game: *Blackmoor,* written by Dave Arneson.

Like *Greyhawk,* the *Blackmoor* supplement added new rules to the game, including instructions for players wishing to move, fight, and cast spells underwater, and two new character classes, the monk and the assassin. But the sixty-page booklet said almost nothing about Arneson's actual campaign—there were no descriptions of the inside of Blackmoor Castle or anecdotes about clever player-killing traps. Instead, more than half of the slim volume was dedicated to an equally important innovation: the first prewritten D&D scenario, a do-it-yourself adventure called *Temple of the Frog.*

D&D scenarios are the microwave dinners of the role-playing world.** Every time players sit down at the game table, they consume an adventure that's been prepared by their Dungeon Master. If they're lucky, a talented storyteller like Morgan is doing the cooking, and he's constructed a narrative from scratch—not just a "fight these monsters" conflict but also plot, character, setting, and theme. Less-experienced DMs are sometimes more comfortable heating up a story that's been prepared and packaged by an outside expert. A

---

* His admirers sometimes call him "the forgotten Tolkien."

** This is not to say they are all of low quality. They're often quite good—but while I can appreciate good frozen pizza, I know it's not the same as the brick-oven pie at Juliana's in Brooklyn Heights.

scenario like *Temple of the Frog* gives them everything they need to tell a story; all they have to do is follow directions.

Prewritten adventures read like a Lonely Planet guide compiled by a madman. Typically, they begin in the same manner as *Temple of the Frog,* providing background information about the region the players will visit and setting up the central conflict of the plot:

> Deep in the primaeval [*sic*] swamps of Lake Gloomey, shrouded in perpetual mist, lies the city of The Brothers of the Swamp. For years past this "religious" order has delved into the forbidden areas of study and determined that animals have more potential to populate the world than man, who was, after all, a biological abomination which would ultimately threaten the existence of all life. Therefore the good Brothers began developing a strain of amphibian that would combine the worst ferocity and killer instincts of larger mammals with the ability to move through swamps with great swiftness to strike and avoid retaliation.

From there, scenarios resemble more typical travel guides, providing maps of the area and describing points of interest:

> Pool of the Frog: A downward sloping area, very slippery, leading to the next level down. Entrance into the area marked DOWN will cause the party to slide down the ramp to the next level, only persons of an 18 dexterity having a 50% chance of not falling, being able to slow his descent.

Some scenarios, like *Temple of the Frog,* simply describe an area and its residents and leave it to the DM and players to decide what to do—rob the temple, join it, or burn it to the ground. Others are tightly written stories that push the players down a specific narrative path. Sometimes they even come with prerolled characters, so all you have to do is sit down and play; I took the name Weslocke from an elven fighter/magic-user in Gygax's 1982 D&D module *The Lost Caverns of Tsojcanth.** All this serves to make it easier for a DM to do their job and provide an easy point of entry into the world of fantasy role-playing. Without prewritten scenarios and modules, Dungeons & Dragons would probably have remained a wonky hobby just for war gamers and not a worldwide phenomenon.

Blackmoor also marked the debut of Tim Kask, an Illinois war gamer and friend of Gygax who became TSR's first full-time hire. Kask's first assignment at the company was to edit the *Blackmoor* supplement; afterward, he took over as editor of *The Strategic Review.* Gygax's co-DM Rob Kuntz and his older brother Terry also joined the staff in 1975, to help write and edit game materials. And as winter rolled into Lake Geneva, Dungeons & Dragons coauthor Dave Arneson made the move from Saint Paul to start work as TSR's full-time research director, responsible for coordinating with freelance designers and producing material "like a grist mill."

For the first time, Dungeons & Dragons's two creators were in the same place, working on games full-time. But the true promise of their longtime partnership would never be realized. "It started out being fun," Arneson said later. "But as the money increased, the fun decreased."

---

*Gygax had a true gift for inventing character names. In 1981's *Against the Giants,* you could play as Gleep Wurp the Eyebiter, Beek Gwenders, Redmod Dumple, or Faffle Dwe'o-mercraeft. *Descent into the Depths of the Earth* featured Fnast Dringle, Fage the Kexy, Keak Breedbate, and Philotomy Jurament.

7

THE BREAKING OF THE FELLOWSHIP

An elf wizard, a dwarf fighter, and a human thief walk into a bar. The bartender looks up and asks, "What is this, a joke?"

It's a corny gag, but it illustrates a truth about most D&D campaigns: Successful parties tend to exhibit a range of character classes, races, and backgrounds that borders on the absurd. Diversity may be admirable, but it doesn't make much sense that a book-smart wizard (in our world, the equivalent might be a computer programmer) would team up with a battle-hardened warrior (army drill sergeant) and a self-interested rogue (cat burglar).*

Like so many things in modern geekdom, the origins of this convention trace back to a crusty English philologist. When J. R. R. Tolkien published *The Lord of the Rings* back in 1954, he didn't build his fellowship from equals, like the Knights of the Round Table; he con-

* I'm imagining Michael Cera, Channing Tatum, and Kristen Stewart as the respective leads in the buddy flick based on this paragraph, working title *Cognitive Dissonance*. Hollywood, you're welcome.

structed a diverse group with individual strengths and weaknesses. There's nothing in the D&D rules that says adventuring parties have to strike the same balance, but players tend to hew close to the archetype. You won't often find a party consisting entirely of bards, and not just because it would be the most annoying group ever.

There are tactical reasons to mix things up, too. In combat, it's advantageous to have a diverse set of skills in your group: a fighter who attacks hand-to-hand and soaks up damage, a thief who hides behind a tree and fires off arrows, a cleric who casts spells to aid his companions. Constructing a successful adventuring party requires good human-resources management, just like hiring for a successful business. Paladins might make great CEOs, but you're better off with a wizard in accounting, a couple of rogues on the sales team, and a bard handling marketing.

This truth may help explain one of the biggest mysteries in the history of Dungeons & Dragons: Why did Dave Arneson leave TSR after less than a year at the company?

In January 1976, D&D was at a tipping point. TSR had sold several thousand copies of the basic rules, but the game had easily ten times as many players, thanks to sharing and unauthorized photocopying. D&D had two supplements, distributors across the U.S. and on three continents, and a growing company behind it that finally included both of its cocreators. As Arneson settled down to work on new material, the company was blooming.

Several buds appeared in April's *Strategic Review.* "This is the last issue," Tim Kask warned in his editor's note, "but harken well, better things are in the offing!" A new periodicals division of TSR Hobbies was set to launch two different magazines: *The Dragon,* devoted to "fantasy . . . sci-fi and roleplaying games," and *Little Wars,* "to deal with the established types and periods of wargaming." The hobby business was growing too: Game designer Mike Carr joined the staff as an editor, and Dave Megarry took over as a bookkeeper.

To house its new employees (and increasingly large amounts of inventory), TSR moved out of Gygax's basement and into its own space about half a mile away in Lake Geneva. The gray house at 723 Williams Street had once been a family residence; now rezoned for business, its second-floor bedrooms were converted into offices, and the ground-floor parlor rooms were turned into TSR's first retail outlet—a hobby shop called the Dungeon.

Skip Williams, a local high school kid who played in Gygax's D&D campaign, landed a part-time job working as a clerk at the store. "The Dungeon had everything that TSR published, which was D&D and all of the miniatures rules, and a couple of board games," he says. "It also sold miniatures, scale tanks, scale ships . . . all the things that Gary liked to play with." A few tables were set up for miniatures battles, and players could rent the space for a few hours if they paid a small fee. Before long, the store became a destination for gamers. "There were people coming literally from all over the country," says Williams. "It was pretty cool."

While TSR was certainly happy to sell more product, the proliferation of D&D rule books did have its drawbacks. Tim Kask described the problem in the foreword of *Eldritch Wizardry,* a new rule supplement published that May: "Somewhere along the line, D&D lost some of its flavor, and began to become predictable . . . When all the players had all of the rules in front of them, it became next to impossible to beguile them into danger or mischief." *Eldritch Wizardry* tried to fix things by adding even more rules to the game—new powers, new monsters, new magic, and treasure—in the hope that players couldn't possibly keep track. "These pages should go a long way toward putting back in some of the mystery, uncertainty and danger that make D&D

the unparalleled challenge it was meant to be," Kask wrote. "No more will some foolhardy adventurer run down into a dungeon, find something and immediately know how it works, or even what it does."

It didn't work, of course, as generations of players with encyclopedic knowledge of D&D's rules can attest. But the supplement did introduce a number of important concepts to the game, including the druid character class, a kind of cleric who worships nature rather than a deity. New monsters included denizens of the underworld like succubi and the demon princes Orcus and Demogorgon—an editorial decision that would lead to quite a bit of trouble a few years later. And a set of rules governing psychic powers (known therein as "psionics") attempted to address a frequent criticism of D&D's system of magic—that wizards and clerics must memorize a fixed list of spells from a book instead of possessing the innate ability to cast whatever they want.*

In June, even more new rules arrived inside the first issue of *The Dragon*. "The Magazine of Fantasy, Swords & Sorcery and Science Fiction Gaming" was thirty-two pages long and cost $1.50, or $9 for a six-issue, one-year subscription. The cover art was a trippy illustration of an emerald-skinned dragon sitting on a pile of rocks in front of a riotously airbrushed background of hot pink, crimson, and yellow—and the contents of the magazine were no less chaotic. There were stats for new D&D monsters, descriptions of new spells, advice for Dungeon Masters, supplemental rules for several war games, and press releases for upcoming TSR products. The features ranged from the nerdy ("Magic and Science: Are They Compatible in D&D?") to

---

* Game systems where players memorize a fixed list of spells are described as using "Vancian" magic, because that's the way magic works in a series of books by author Jack Vance. *Eldritch Wizardry*'s psionics (and countless modern video games) use a point-based system, where players have a flat amount of magic available, and each spell has its own cost. The debate over Vancian vs. points is one of the most enduring and annoying arguments in modern geek culture, right up there with Kirk vs. Picard and Marvel vs. DC Comics.

the extremely nerdy ("How to Use Non-Prime-Requisite Character Attributes"). There was even some fiction, the first installment of a fantasy novel called *The Gnome Cache,* which was serialized over the next few issues. It was written by Garrison Ernst—a pseudonym for Gary Gygax.

Gygax and his TSR crew didn't pen the entire magazine by themselves. Fantasy author Fritz Leiber contributed an article, and several D&D players contributed features inspired by their own campaigns. In his editor's note, Tim Kask solicited more help from the community: "gaming, variants, discussion, fiction by authors both known and unknown, reviews of interest to our readers and anything else." Through *The Dragon,* TSR hoped to rally its fans, cement their loyalty, and exploit their energy—lest they follow Gygax's example and start making their own games. The threat was obvious: Dungeons & Dragons was conceived out of Guidon Games's Chainmail rules and quickly eclipsed it in both popularity and sales. No one at TSR wanted to see the same thing happen to them.

A few companies had already launched competing products. In early 1975 Illinois-based Game Designers' Workshop released Frank Chadwick's En Garde!, a role-playing game set in seventeenth-century France that emphasized man-to-man sword fighting. Players responded to the *Three Musketeers*–style setting, but they didn't care for the rules. War game publisher Fantasy Games Unlimited pushed setting even farther with 1976's Bunnies & Burrows, a role-playing game inspired by Richard Adams's 1972 novel *Watership Down*: The player characters were intelligent rabbits and had to compete for food, avoid predators, and deal with internal warren politics.

Other designers stuck closer to D&D's swords-and-sorcery setting. Ken St. Andre, a public librarian in Phoenix, Arizona, fell in love with the idea of fantasy role-playing after reading a friend's D&D rule books but found the actual rules confusing, so he wrote his own. Tunnels & Trolls, self-published in June 1975, simplified D&D in a way that emphasized entertainment over simulation: it dropped a lot of the war-game-derived rules for combat and movement; only required six-sided dice instead of hard-to-find polyhedrals; assigned wizards spell points, not spell books; and implemented dozens of other small changes that made the game looser. Arizona publisher Flying Buffalo Inc. released a second edition of the game, and Tunnels & Trolls quickly became one of D&D's biggest competitors.

Gygax was not pleased. When ads and reviews of Tunnels & Trolls started showing up in game magazines, TSR had its lawyers send cease-and-desist letters to Flying Buffalo owner Rick Loomis and magazine publisher Metagaming Concepts. The lawyers claimed that even using the words "Dungeons & Dragons" to help describe Tunnels & Trolls infringed on TSR's rights. Flying Buffalo deleted any such comparisons from future advertisements.

It wasn't the first time TSR had made legal threats against a potential competitor. Earlier in the year, TSR had sent a cease-and-desist to one of its own fans, Boston gamer Robert Ruppert, who made the mistake of typing up a blank form with the header "Dungeons & Dragons Character Sheet" and selling it to fellow war gamers for two cents a copy. The crackdown was especially ironic considering TSR's poor record in regards to other people's copyrights; the company had already been spanked by the estate of Edgar Rice Burroughs for ripping off the John Carter novels in the game Warriors of Mars.

But TSR continued to pay close attention to the rights to its own works. That spring and summer, the company cut its first licensing deals with other companies, first with Miniature Figurines Ltd., a manufacturer of cast metal minis, to make models of D&D monsters, and then with publishing company Judges Guild, to print official D&D accessories like maps and supplements.

Judges Guild released their first licensed product, a game setting called *City State of the Invincible Overlord,* at Gen Con IX in August 1976. During the three-day event, over 1,300 people from around the country visited three different venues in Lake Geneva (the Horticultural Hall, the Guild Hall, and the Legion Hall) to play, buy, and talk about games. TSR had a special interest in showing off new products at the convention, since they'd taken control of the show from the Lake Geneva Tactical Studies Association. So in a bid to dominate their attention, TSR showed off two new D&D rule books, billed as the final additions to Dungeons & Dragons.

Swords & Spells, written by Gygax, is the odd man out in the original D&D rule set. Rather than adding new details to the fantasy role-playing game, it takes a glance backward and provides rules for large-scale miniature war games that are merely *based* on Dungeons & Dragons. In his foreword, editor Tim Kask describes it as "the grandson of Chainmail."

The other book, identified as "Supplement IV" on its cover, put the final touches on the original rule set for Dungeons & Dragons. *Gods, Demi-Gods & Heroes* (coauthored by TSR's Rob Kuntz and James M. Ward, a gamer and junior high teacher from Prairie du Chien, Wisconsin*) introduces mythology to the game and describes deities in the same manner earlier supplements described men and monsters.

Thor, the Norse thunder god, has 275 hit points, an armor class of 2, and the abilities of a twentieth-level fighter. Hades, Greek god of the underworld and death, is described as "a heavily muscled dark skinned man" who can "shapechange, fight invisibly, has the divine awe power, and his touch or stare acts as a death spell." The holy fig-

---

*In November 1976, TSR released an original game by James Ward called Metamorphosis Alpha, notable as one of the first role-playing games with a science-fiction setting. The game takes place on the starship *Warden,* a vast spaceship built by the player characters' ancestors; in the aftermath of some unknown disaster, their progeny survive on the ship but don't understand its technology and must fight mutated creatures to ensure their survival.

ures of Christianity, Judaism, and Islam don't make the cut, although the "Gods of India" incongruously do: The Hindu deity Vishnu is equipped with "a lotus flower capable of restoring all lost hit points at a touch," as well as "a bow of curses called Sarnge, and a plus 3 sword of demon slaying called Mandaka."

At its heart, *Gods, Demi-Gods & Heroes* represents another attempt to exert control over D&D players. Kask's foreword drips with disdain for Dungeon Masters who allow their players to advance to high levels and explains that the supplement aims to correct their misguided actions: "Perhaps now some of the 'giveaway' campaigns will look as foolish as they truly are," he writes. "When Odin, the All-Father has only . . . 300 hit points, who can take a 44th level Lord seriously?"

With that settled, TSR considered the Dungeons & Dragons rules to be complete. "We've told you just about everything," Kask writes. "From now on, when the circumstances aren't covered somewhere in the books, wing it as best you can."

Of course, the company had no plans to stop making money off the game. Kask advises players to buy TSR's periodicals for new rules and content. "Just don't wait with baited [*sic*] breath for another supplement after this one."

It's possible that some of the resistance against publishing future D&D supplements was caused by Dave Arneson, who, for all his creative genius, was neither a strong nor a disciplined writer. He was slow to produce material, and when he did finish a draft, it required lots of work to get it ready for publication.

This was an issue beginning in the earliest days of Gygax and Arneson's partnership, when Gygax had to work for months to turn Arneson's twenty-page description of the Blackmoor campaign into a fifty-page draft of the Fantasy Game. "Dearly as I love Dave . . . he was not a very good writer," says friend and player Mike Mornard. "What he gave Gary was his handwritten notes for an expanded version of Chainmail, and it looked like shit."

But the problem came to a head when TSR decided that Arneson should pen the second supplement to Dungeons & Dragons. The *Blackmoor* supplement was likely conceived of and added to TSR's publication plan sometime in 1974; in March 1975, Gygax told a wargaming newsletter that Arneson was working on a final draft. TSR began accepting preorders for the product and advertised it in the pages of *The Strategic Review* . . . and then nothing. Months passed and *Blackmoor* wasn't published. The winter 1975 issue of *The Strategic Review* stated the obvious: the supplement was running late. Then the following issue offered an outright apology from editor Tim Kask: "*Blackmoor* is finally done and in the hands of the printers," he wrote. "We know that it's late, but you wouldn't believe me if I listed all the problems we had with it. Suffice it to say that I have been blooded, as an editor, by *Blackmoor*."* Arneson's draft, Kask later explained, was "contradictory, confusing, incomplete, partially incomprehensible, lacking huge bits and pieces and mostly gibberish." The sixty-page booklet took weeks to edit and had to be mostly rewritten before it was completed.

Dave Arneson joined the staff of TSR and moved to Lake Geneva in January 1976, just weeks after *Blackmoor* was finally published. In a *Strategic Review* editorial announcing the hire, Gygax seemed both

---

* A year and a half later, in the foreword to *Gods, Demi-Gods & Heroes,* dated July 4, 1976, Kask still sounds wounded: "My first assignment, fresh out of college, was *Blackmoor*. I came to regard it with a mixture of love and loathing, that has gradually seen the love win out. The loathing grew out of the educational trip that it was for me. They don't teach you in college what to do when the press breaks down, or your manuscript gets mysteriously misplaced; you just have to wing it."

hopeful and anxious that the move might increase Arneson's productivity: "His function will be to help us co-ordinate our efforts with free-lance designers, handle various research projects, and produce material like a grist mill," Gygax wrote. "Crack! Snap! Work faster there, Dave!"

But even when he was in the TSR office, where Gygax could crack that whip, Arneson published very little. In his book *Playing at the World*, author Jon Peterson points out that during all of 1976, Arneson's name appeared in only a few TSR products, including an article for the July issue of *Little Wars* about World War II naval combat; the introduction to *Valley Forge*, a war game written by his friend Dave Wesely; and a credit for "special effort" in Lankhmar, a board game based on Fritz Leiber's novels. Arneson didn't have a single byline related to Dungeons & Dragons, the game he helped invent and was presumably hired to help develop.

In contrast, Gygax published enough material in 1976 to account for both men. He was credited as the designer of Little Big Horn, a war game simulating the "last stand" of George Armstrong Custer; the author of *Swords and Spells*; and the coauthor of *Eldritch Wizardry*. He wrote dozens of articles in *The Strategic Review* and *The Dragon*, including editorials, discussions of war games, new rules for D&D, and his serialized novel. Gygax had six bylines in the February *Strategic Review* alone, filling seven of the newsletter's sixteen pages. He even wrote for a handful of non-TSR newsletters, in order to promote the company's products.

Three decades later, it's unclear why Arneson produced so little during his time at TSR. Perhaps he created lots of material, but it required so much editing, it never got published. Maybe Gygax—anticipating a day when gamers would wonder who truly invented Dungeons & Dragons—killed his projects out of some sense of fratricidal competition.

Or maybe Dave Arneson just wasn't interested. In *Playing at the World,* Jon Peterson asserts that Arneson's limited experience as a writer and editor didn't keep him from finishing non-TSR products: During his time at the company, Arneson published several issues of a newsletter for his Napoleonic miniatures games, and even printed the March 1976 edition on TSR's mimeograph. But he exhibited little interest in Dungeons & Dragons, and "even less in promoting the game," Peterson writes. "Perhaps Arneson simply preferred his nineteenth-century campaigns to fantasy."

In November 1976, after just ten months on staff, Dave Arneson left TSR. The circumstances are again unclear, or vary depending on who's recounting them. Peterson suggests a few: Gygax fired him because of low productivity; Gygax demoted him, so he quit; he quit because he thought his manuscripts didn't need to be edited; he quit because he didn't like making games for profit instead of making them for fun.

Whatever the reason, Arneson's departure was likely, at a fundamental level, related to the issue of party composition. In 1976, TSR was just setting out on a great adventure; its staff was like a new team of heroes gathered in a tavern, brought together largely by convenience and circumstance. But there was a problem with the group's dynamics: Gygax the Barbarian, a competitive brawler, bent on victory and motivated by treasure, was never going to work well with the wizard Arneson, a playful thinker, more interested in theory than practicalities, and motivated by fun. Their differences would always be greater than their similarities.

So as the year drew to a close, Dave Arneson left the party to seek out his own adventure. But he'd be back for his share of the treasure.

8

WHY WE PLAY

At the peak of his fame, the artist Marcel Duchamp developed an obsession with chess, and it quickly took over his life. He played constantly, stopped producing art, and even spent his entire honeymoon studying chess strategies, instead of his wife. "Everything around me takes the shape of the Knight or the Queen," he wrote, "and the exterior world has no other interest for me other than its transformation to winning or losing positions."

I know the feeling. As I threw myself headlong into researching the origins of Dungeons & Dragons, I began to feel an obsession with the game reemerging from deep within my psyche. Every rule book and history I read drew it further out. At work, I read D&D Internet forums; at home, I rolled up sample characters; on the weekends I pored over a library search of every article ever published that included the words "Dungeons & Dragons."

A few months into the project, my girlfriend Kara and I got married. I didn't play D&D on our honeymoon in the Caribbean, but I did bring along a stack of books with names like *The Creation of*

Narrative in Tabletop Role-Playing Games and *The Fantasy Role-Playing Game: A New Performing Art*. "Just beach reading material," I told her.* I told myself it was essential research, but this went far beyond due diligence. I was geeking out.

I needed to play D&D, too—I was dependent on it, like a junkie needs a fix. If my Tuesday-night game was canceled because someone had to work late or Morgan was out of town, I was agitated and restless for the rest of the week. When I was out of town and the game went on without me, that was even worse. Once I had to fly to San Francisco on a Tuesday morning to report a story for *Forbes* and knew I'd be missing a session, so I posted a message in an online "looking for game" forum: "Anyone running a D&D game (any edition) in the Bay Area, preferably within an hour drive of San Francisco International Airport?" It felt dirty, like I was an unfaithful husband trolling for casual sex on Craigslist. It felt worse when I couldn't find any action.

So that Tuesday night, while Jhaden, Ganubi, and Graeme negotiated a job with a group of rich San Francisco merchants, Weslocke stayed home, and I sat in my room at the "real world" San Francisco airport Marriott, reread *A Game of Thrones,* and tried to ignore the irony. I wondered what they were up to and what I was missing—and how I'd gotten to this point again.

We traveled south out of San Francisco, along the edge of the bay, and then east across rolling grasslands and into a great valley. Before long we came across a highway and followed it into the mountains. All that remained of the road were chunks of asphalt, but they were enough to point the way.

The merchants had found the route while studying ancient docu-

---

* Thankfully, Kara was more tolerant of my obsessions than Duchamp's wife, Lydie Sarazin-Levassor, who waited until her new husband was asleep and glued his chess pieces to the board. Three months later they got a divorce.

ments printed in the twentieth century, before the vampires came out of hiding. They also found a description of riches "beyond your wildest dreams"—a treasure, buried beneath a pyramid somewhere in the desert. They hired us to find it and protect them along the way.

It was no easy journey. On the eastern slope of the Sierra Nevada we were caught in a snowstorm and then attacked by walking corpses with icy skin. They fell upon us and tried to consume our flesh, but we fought them off with fire and spells that shattered their frozen bodies. Perhaps they were the remains of some dishonored party—travelers who got lost in the mountain pass and turned upon each other, committing evil deeds that doomed their spirits to an eternity of undeath.

In the desert below, we fought a massive sandworm with a mouth bigger than a man, full of hundreds of tiny teeth. Jhaden charged the beast, tried to jump on its back and ride it—but he missed his mark, and it swallowed him whole. Fortunately, he held on to his sword and managed to cut his way out of the great worm's gullet, killing it in the process.

A few days later, we found the object of our quest: a city, built in an arid basin on the desert floor. At the heart of it stood a huge black pyramid, shining like glass in the midday sun.

In April of 1958, American anthropologists Clifford Geertz and his wife, Hildred, traveled to Bali, Indonesia, to perform an ethnographic study. They found a place to live in the small village of Tihingan, the local chief welcomed them, and the prospects for their research looked good.

The villagers, however, did not care to participate. "As we wandered around, uncertain, wistful, eager to please, people seemed to look right through us, with a gaze focused several yards behind," Clifford wrote. "The indifference, of course, was studied; the villagers were watching every move we made . . . but they acted as if we simply did not exist, which, in fact, as this behavior was designed to inform us, we did not, or anyway not yet."

It's not easy to win the trust of a group of strangers, particularly if your appearance or behavior seems strange. But what broke the ice for Clifford and Hildred Geertz is the same thing that's worked for thousands of geeks over the forty-year history of Dungeons & Dragons: joining the strangers in their favorite game.

Ten days or so after the anthropologist's arrival, a large cockfight—a favorite pastime among the Balinese*—was held in the public square. Clifford and Hildred attended and, in the excitement of the event, found themselves drawn into the crowd, where hundreds of people "fused into a single body around the ring, a superorganism in the literal sense." When the police arrived to break up the match, the Geertzes fled in terror with the villagers, even though they could have easily stayed and simply shown the police their official papers.

The next morning, the village was a completely different world. "Not only were we no longer invisible, we were suddenly the center of all attention, the object of a great outpouring of warmth, interest, and, most especially, amusement," Clifford wrote. "It was the turning point so far as our relationship to the community was concerned."

Author and blogger Cory Doctorow found that games helped him make friends among a different kind of tribe. "I grew up in this very politically lefty household," he says. "Normally when I encountered people from the far right, they'd be shouting 'Get a job!' or 'Go back to Russia, you hippies!' when we were out demonstrating. But when

---

* "As much of America surfaces in a ball park, on a golf links, at a race track, or around a poker table, much of Bali surfaces in a cock ring," Clifford wrote in an essay entitled "Deep Play: Notes on the Balinese Cockfight." It's now considered a classic anthropological text—and how could it not, with deliberate double entendres like this: "To anyone who has been in Bali any length of time, the deep psychological identification of Balinese men with their cocks is unmistakable."

I was eleven or twelve years old, I started going to game stores . . . and there were a ton of military and ex-military guys playing D&D."

As he became a regular at Toronto's gaming hotspots, Doctorow got to see that his political opponents weren't just one-dimensional villains. "These were people who were wearing badges that said 'Nuke 'em all, let God sort 'em out' and 'Better dead than red.' Serious weirdo ultra–right wing nut jobs. But they were nevertheless part of the same thing as me. A whole social group kind of appeared out of nowhere; it was really very interesting."

Humans play games for lots of reasons, but the fact that they so easily bring people together must be near the top of the list. Most of us form our closest relationships through play; it's irrelevant whether that play takes the form of make-believe in the schoolyard, simulated combat on a chessboard, or two angry chickens pecking at each other. They're all games, and they all transport us to a different world.

When a group of people play a game together, they enter a sort of alternate reality where friendships form at an accelerated rate. In part this is due to the structure of the game itself: The players have limited time, so things have to move quickly, and they've got a specific goal, so they focus on winning, not on the normal rules of social interaction. Then, as the game picks up, the players become engrossed in the experience; they stop being anxious scientists and become fighting birds of prey. Lost in the game, behavioral norms are forgotten, and emotional defenses weaken. Players begin to feel—and act upon—unusually strong impulses.* Emotions run high, and they keep getting higher; joy, anger, excitement, fear, even the terror of (simulated) death. In this artificially accelerated and emotionally heightened social environment, bonds are forged quickly and forged strong.

---

*If you've ever flipped a game board over in anger following a loss or performed a little dance to celebrate a victory, you know what I'm talking about.

And even when a game is over, the bonds that have been created persist. "A play community generally tends to become permanent even after the game is over," wrote Johan Huizinga, one of the fathers of academic game studies. "The feeling of being 'apart together' in an exceptional situation, of sharing something important, of mutually withdrawing from the rest of the world and rejecting the usual norms, retains its magic beyond the duration of the original game."

Whether you're a young nerdy kid or a happy adult, this kind of experience can be profound. It's the reason why so many people build their strongest social connections with people like sports teammates or members of a D&D campaign. The people that you play games with become your clan. They share your experiences, know your strengths and weaknesses, and help protect you from a dangerous world.

I knew we were in trouble as soon as I saw the pyramid.

The ancient documents described a desert oasis, a city of fabulous riches. But the vampires destroyed most human cities during the Nightfall, so I'd expected to find the oasis in ruin. Instead, someone—or something—had kept the city standing, and even protected it behind new stone walls. Off in the distance, the glassy black pyramid appeared unmarred and unbroken; dozens of tall buildings surrounded it, sprawling out for miles.

We couldn't see any movement or make out any living creatures, but something had to be there. So we made camp about a mile from the city and waited for dark. Graeme is small and stealthy, so he volunteered to go closer and scout.

"Don't worry," he told us as he slipped into the night. "I'll stay out of trouble."

A few hours later, he returned.

"You're not going to like this." He sat on a pile of rubble and rubbed

his balding head. "I kept my distance at first, at least a quarter of a mile, and worked my way around the walls looking for doors. There's one on the far side from us. But it's closed, and there are guards on the walls. They looked like they could be human, but they were wearing black hooded cloaks, so I couldn't really tell.

"So I decided to sneak in closer. I was sure they hadn't seen me, but when I got about sixty feet from the gate, I heard a voice—well, not heard, exactly, more like felt—a voice in my head. It said, 'Who goes there?' I didn't know what to do. Then one of the guards stepped off the wall, into thin air, and didn't fall . . . it slowly floated toward the ground. So I ran. It didn't follow me, and I wasn't about to go back for a closer look."

We couldn't agree on what we should do. We'd dealt with creatures with psychic powers before and knew we were relatively powerless against their attacks; Jhaden carries a magic amulet that hides his thoughts, but it only protects the person wearing it, not all of us at once. He wanted to find an unguarded section of the city walls, climb over, and scout the city himself. I argued for more caution—I could summon a magical creature, perhaps a hippogriff, and fly high over the city to get a better look. The merchants just wanted us to shut up and get their treasure.

Finally, Ganubi ended the debate. "Listen, it's simple," he said. "When the sun comes up, I'll just walk up and knock on the door."

Games help you make friends. They certainly worked for me when I was a kid. But that doesn't explain why I got addicted to D&D—and not once, but twice. Games, in general, have always been my favorite and most frequently indulged-in pastime, but I usually don't get obsessed with board games or video games. So why is D&D so uniquely powerful?

Part of it, I think, is cultural: In his book *The Evolution of Fantasy Role-Playing Games,* author Michael J. Tresca argues that the game appeals to an American sense of individualism—you build your own world, with your own values and rules. There's a little bit of manifest destiny in the mix, too: "American culture has some nuances that are unique to it, one being the notion of limitless growth for businesses, consumer buying power, and the economy. In Dungeons & Dragons, this ideology is true of dungeon exploration too. There's always a monster with treasure around the next corner, always a new area to explore, always a new frontier to conquer."

But fantasy gaming is popular all over the world, not just in its place of birth. D&D's true appeal goes deeper than international borders, class, or creed: It connects directly to the structure of our psyche.

Because they have a narrative form, role-playing games frequently echo Joseph Campbell's monomyth, the classic hero's journey. Campbell saw that the same basic story kept repeating, across time and cultures: "A hero ventures forth from the world of common day into a region of supernatural wonder: fabulous forces are there encountered and a decisive victory is won: the hero comes back from this mysterious adventure with the power to bestow boons on his fellow man." He believed that variations of this story keep appearing because it springs from the collective unconscious, the deep structures of the mind that are present in all human beings. The classic examples of the hero's journey are the myths of Prometheus, Osiris, and Moses; modern audiences might recognize it in *Star Wars, The Matrix,* and Harry Potter.

Stories that follow the form of the monomyth resonate because they tickle something deep in the unconscious mind. So imagine what happens when you're not watching or reading that adventure—you're experiencing it. That's what D&D does: It doesn't just tell a story, it puts you in it. You become "the hero with a thousand faces." The experience penetrates deep to the core of your being.

And it's therapeutic too. Because the players are active participants in a story, role-playing games produce many of the same benefits as psychodrama, a psychological treatment method that uses dramatic reenactments to provide insight into its actors' lives. "I see role-playing as an opportunity for people to learn more about themselves," physician Leonard H. Kanterman* wrote in a 1979 issue of the game magazine *Different Worlds*. "By exploring the possibilities of different courses of actions, even to the point of different morality systems, through the 'safe' medium of fantasy, people can learn who they are and why they think and act the way they do."

Role-playing games provide a chance for people to work out different aspects of their personality, and no one needs to do that more than an adolescent kid. I think that's a big reason why I spent so much of my childhood addicted to D&D and games like it.

Of course, I was also a big nerd, which doubtless contributed to the attraction. Some research suggests smart kids are drawn to role-playing games like Dungeons & Dragons because they need them the most: In a 2011 study of middle and high school students, education researchers Gregory Harrison and James Van Haneghan reported that gifted children experienced higher levels of insomnia, anxiety, and fear of death than their peers. The researchers also found that encouraging these students "to engage in fantasy game play such as Dungeons & Dragons" could be an effective therapy, allowing them to work out their problems "in stimulating and enjoyable ways."

When morning came, we hid and watched as Ganubi approached the city gates. We sent him alone, wearing the protective magic amulet, because he's the most diplomatic—and charming—member of our group.

---

*Kanterman is a doctor of internal medicine based in Ohio and the author of several games, including 1978's Starships & Spacemen, one of the earliest sci-fi RPGs.

If the creatures in the city were friendly, he'd be the best person to make contact. If they weren't, he's light on his feet and could run like hell.

He approached the gate and, just as Graeme had described, stopped about sixty feet from the city walls. A black-clad figure slowly floated down to greet him. They stood there for some time, not moving . . . perhaps conversing? We couldn't tell.

Several minutes passed. Jhaden nervously palmed the hilt of his sword. Then the city gates opened, and Ganubi and his new friend walked inside. As he entered, he gave us a subtle wave. Friends, not foes.

Still, I couldn't help but worry. Hours passed, and Ganubi did not return. As we hid, roasting in the desert sun, Graeme and I debated our options for entering the city in case we needed to rescue our friend. Jhaden napped, unperturbed.

Finally, as dusk fell, the gates opened, and Ganubi emerged—alone, and smiling.

Dungeons & Dragons players dread facing psychic-powered creatures—probably because they prey on the thing we value the most.

It's obvious why role-playing game fans might respect brains over brawn: D&D is a cerebral game, after all, played almost entirely in your head, and as established, the hobby tends to attract smart people. But the connection between intellect and role-playing goes deeper than the disposition of its audience. Smart people play D&D because D&D makes people smart.

If you think that sounds like an excuse for getting addicted to role-playing, you're not off the mark. When I was in high school, I convinced myself to not feel bad when I didn't get invited to the cool kids' parties, because I was doing something more important: "Sure, they get to drink and have sex, but when the apocalypse comes they'll wish they'd spent more time role-playing disaster scenarios and mastering urban combat strategy. The zombies will eat the jocks while the nerds are busy building fortifications, and *then* we'll have the cheerleaders all to ourselves."

Obviously I was delusional,* but I was right that my hobby had educational value. Games like Dungeons & Dragons require and encourage study; you have to learn the rules, of course, but you also must learn real-world skills in order to understand them—particularly math, statistics, and vocabulary. "I got a perfect score on the SAT verbals in high school in part because of D&D," Morgan told me. "One of the questions involved the word 'comeliness,' and I knew the word because it had turned up in a D&D book, as an optional stat."**

Morgan also says that D&D has helped him advance his career in advertising. "The thing about being a DM is that it forces me to improvise," he says. "It's not possible for me to plan for every contingency. So when you ask me a question about some aspect of the world that I have no idea about, I just have to come up with something. I find myself doing that same sort of thing in business meetings—actually noticing that I had to come up with an answer, on the spur of the moment, based on the narrative that we've created for a business. And I thank my D&D experience for that."

I feel the same way. Every time I had to figure out how to reach a goal in an adventure, it helped me develop real-world problem-solving skills; all the time I spent playing with friends taught me how to collaborate with colleagues at work. And as the games grew more complex, so did the lessons: There have been times in my career when I've

---

*I still believe role-playing games have prepared me to survive the apocalypse, but I have come to accept the value of enjoying the company of cheerleaders while you can.

**"Comeliness reflects physical attractiveness, social grace, and personal beauty of the character. It is used to determine initial reactions to the character, and characters with a high comeliness may affect the wills and actions of others. While charisma deals specifically with leadership and interactions between characters, comeliness deals with attractiveness and first impressions." *Advanced Dungeons & Dragons Unearthed Arcana*, page 6.

been overwhelmed by the size of a project, but then I remember the Shadowrun campaign where Everett Meyer and I spent months perfecting a plan to invade and conquer Seattle. No magazine story will ever require that much work.*

"Doing an adventure for your friends is actually a relatively rigorous undertaking, especially for young people," says Jerry Holkins, writer of the web comic *Penny Arcade.* "You have to essentially give a three-hour extemporaneous speech—and that's in addition to the calculations and the planning and all the narration. There is a ton of work to be done in sustaining a universe."

Holkins started playing D&D regularly when he was a teenager, and tried without success to get his friend Mike Krahulik—now *Penny Arcade's* artist—into the hobby. But years later, after their comic became a hit with gamers, Wizards of the Coast paid the two men to play D&D as part of an advertising campaign, and Krahulik was instantly addicted.

"I had played one game of Dungeons & Dragons, then I started my first game as Dungeon Master," Krahulik says. His games—documented in a series of blog posts on the *Penny Arcade* site—soon reached epic levels of creative effort: In one session, he built a tabletop puzzle that required his players to navigate their miniatures through a maze of actual working laser beams. For another, he constructed and painted a series of 3-D "planets" out of Styrofoam and had the players jump their minis back and forth between the orbs as they "floated" through space.

---

* Of course, role-playing game fans have been known to overstate the value of their hobby. There's a great scene in a 1996 episode of *The X-Files* called "Jose Chung's 'From Outer Space'" where Jose Chung, an author working on a book about alien abductions, interviews Blaine Faulkner, a man who discovered an alien corpse:

Chung: "Aren't you nervous telling me all this?"

Faulkner: "Well, hey, I didn't spend all those years playing Dungeons and Dragons and not learn a little something about courage."

"I joke with my players that the reason we play D&D is so that I can go to Michael's every weekend and buy Styrofoam," Krahulik says. "Some sessions were superelaborate—I spent a month, at least, on one of my games."

Educators caught on to the benefits of role-playing games quickly: During D&D's heyday Gygax was invited to speak at teacher's conventions, and many schools launched extracurricular D&D clubs. Steve Roman, a librarian at the public library in DeKalb, Illinois, has hosted a role-playing game program for teens for over a decade and seen the benefits firsthand. "I use it as a gateway into the reading programs and the book discussions," he says. "I tell them, 'If you really like this, try reading *The Hobbit*.'"

Roman says it can be a challenge getting kids raised on video games to understand open-ended games like D&D, to accept that they can do whatever they want and aren't limited to a set of preprogrammed interactions. But when they get it, the kids blossom. "They challenge each other," he says. "They encourage each other to be creative by example."

*As he is sometimes wont to do, Ganubi described his venture into the desert city with an impromptu bardic song.**

Way down through the mountains past the zombie scene
Way back up in the desert where the worms are mean
There stood a walled city where the fortune's good
Graeme couldn't get inside but Ganubi could
He never ever worried that it wouldn't go well
Just walked up to the door like he was ringing a bell

* Sung to the tune of Chuck Berry's "Johnny B. Goode."

Go go, Ganubi go go
Ganubi go go, Ganubi go go, Ganubi go go
Ganubi did good

The creatures that lived there spoke inside his head
But he had a magic necklace so he felt no dread
Oh, their skin was pink and slimy and their eyes were white
Tentacles round their mouth made them quite a fright
The creatures passing by would stop and say
They'd like to probe his mind, but he said no way

Go go, Ganubi go go
Ganubi go go, Ganubi go go, Ganubi go go
Ganubi did good

His new friend told him they had never seen a man
And took him to the leader of their monster band
The big boss welcomed him to the town
And said Ganubi's friends could all come round
The humans won an ally in their vampire fight
'Cause Ganubi did good that night

Go go, Ganubi go go
Ganubi go go, Ganubi go go, Ganubi go go
Ganubi did good

The tentacled denizens of the desert city—Las Vegas, if you haven't figured that out—were Morgan's variation on the classic D&D creatures known as illithids, or mind flayers. Usually, they're evil beings bent on eating people's brains; in Morgan's world they were friendly, though worryingly interested in "tasting" Ganubi's thoughts.

Because his game is set on postapocalyptic Earth, Morgan had to figure out a way to fill the world with D&D's customary fantastic creatures. I've always admired his solution: Vampires wanted to make the world outside their pens inhospitable to escaped humans, so they released a magically enchanted virus that mutated ordinary flora and fauna. It's a neat trick that lets him use classic D&D tropes but subvert them in interesting ways—like putting mind-reading monsters on the streets of Sin City.*

It's that kind of storytelling that keeps me addicted to Dungeons & Dragons, and it's what attracts my friends too. "Role-playing appealed to me because I always liked to tell stories," Phil says. "Even before I was in kindergarten, I was making stuff up. I always got caught in a lie, because if I told the truth it was kind of boring, but if I told a lie—elephants were stampeding, there's a comet that hit the earth, and didn't you notice it was dark for the last three days?"

Phil says the narrative nature of the game drew him in, but it also reinforced his interest: The more he and his friends played, the more they learned about what makes a good story, and the game got better and better. "They don't teach you until high school about things like rising exposition and falling action . . . but if you're [a role-player], you're familiar with it because you've been creating stories, more than being formally taught."

A good D&D campaign is like a mini storytelling workshop. Novelist Neal Stephenson played D&D in college and it helped him on the path to becoming a writer: "I think it dovetails quite naturally," he says. "Dungeons & Dragons is fundamentally a procedure for collaborative storytelling. You can do it in a purely mechanical way, just rolling the dice and consulting the rules. But the games that people

---

* Morgan has never revealed the mind flayers' previral heritage, but my personal theory is that they're mutated progeny of the dolphins that live in Siegfried and Roy's Secret Garden at the Mirage hotel and casino.

really get involved with and really enjoy are ones that have legitimate narrative—storytelling, good characters, good situations, plot twists, and an interesting world. The better Dungeon Masters are the ones who have legit storytelling and world-building chops and are able to create a fun experience for the players by improvising good narratives in real time."

Pendleton Ward, creator of the animated television series *Adventure Time,* says D&D helped him develop a unique narrative style. "I like seeing characters move through a fantasy world in a realistic way," he says. "I mean, if I was in a dungeon full of gold, I would stop and pick up some of that gold. So whenever [*Adventure Time* protagonists] Finn and Jake are following a story through a dungeon full of treasure, I try to have them stop and pick some up, even if it interrupts the story. Jake loots corpses in an episode . . . but Finn tells him that it's wrong."

After spending a day with the illithids, Ganubi lost his taste for plundering their city. He told us they didn't know about the treasure buried beneath the pyramid, because it was considered a holy place. He said its subterranean passageways were forbidden and that it would be wrong to desecrate a temple. He said if we proceeded, we'd be stealing from friends.

He was outvoted. The next morning, Jhaden and I entered the city and met with their leaders. I proposed that we escort a group of illithids back to San Francisco, accompanied by a wagonload of goods, in order to establish a trade route. They eagerly accepted the offer.

Meanwhile, hidden from sight by an Invisibility spell, and from mind's eye by our magic amulet, Ganubi slipped into the city on his own. He made his way to the temple, sneaked past the guards, and entered its forbidden passageways in search of the ancient treasure.

When our negotiations were completed, Jhaden and I returned to camp to share the news. The merchants were not impressed. "To hell with trade goods," they said. "Where's your friend with the treasure?"

Their question was answered early the next morning, when Ganubi returned to the camp. He was empty-handed, and the merchants demanded to know what he'd found.

"No treasure," he told them. "Just piles and piles of this." He reached into a pocket and pulled out a stack of old paper.

I took a piece off the top. It was old and brittle, but I could still read the words printed on one side.

THIS NOTE IS LEGAL TENDER FOR
ALL DEBTS, PUBLIC AND PRIVATE

ONE HUNDRED DOLLARS

Worthless junk.

Morgan knew that we'd eventually find the "treasure," but he didn't know how. He certainly didn't know that we'd befriend the illithids or that we'd act on behalf of humanity to establish diplomatic relations and interspecies trade. That's the thing I love the most about role-playing games—not that they're social, not that they're creative, but that they combine those things in a totally unique way. They're stories that friends tell together.

"When I tell other people who have never played D&D about the game, I describe it as communal storytelling," says Morgan. "I lay out the broad strokes, but you guys fill in the details, and sometimes set up entirely new plotlines that I wasn't expecting. I love that. We get a much more interesting story that way."

I've been addicted to TV shows. I have favorite books that I reread year after year. If I see even a minute of *The Godfather,* I have to watch the entire film. But I'm just a spectator to those stories. While they may reflect my thoughts and experiences, they're not made from them. Few things can compete with a good story that you actually helped construct. That's why I'm addicted to role-playing games. They grab me at my core.

"I think it goes way back to cavemen sitting around the fire," says Morgan. "We're a storytelling species. Sitting around with a group and telling a story fills a primal urge. It's why I keep playing D&D."

9

ARNESON VS. GYGAX

Whether he caused it or not, Gary Gygax was ready for David Arneson's departure from TSR. He'd already begun work on a new version of Dungeons & Dragons—one that didn't require the game's cocreator.

"Before the third supplement (*Eldritch Wizardry*) was in print, it had been decided that some major steps would have to be taken to unify and clarify the D&D game system," Gygax wrote in *The Dragon*. "Organizational work was in progress when correspondence with J. Eric Holmes . . . disclosed that [he] was interested in undertaking the first stage of the project."

John Eric Holmes, MD, was a neurologist, a writer, and a fan of Dungeons & Dragons. When he contacted TSR with a proposal to clean up the legendarily confusing D&D rule books, Gygax was already at work on his own revision. But where Gygax had planned to rationalize the game by adding more structure and complexity, Holmes proposed the opposite: taking everything that had been published about the game—three original rule books, five supplements, and dozens of articles in *The Strategic Review* and *The Dragon*—and editing it down to a single, simplified rule set.

Gygax decided the two men would work on separate but complementary versions of Dungeons & Dragons. Holmes's mission was to simplify and rewrite the rules until they were accessible to inexperienced players, particularly kids; Gygax worked toward a bigger and better game, meant for existing players and hard-core grognards.

Holmes's game was finished first and released in July 1977. The Dungeons & Dragons Basic Set was packaged in an attractive box, suitable for display in toy stores; on the outside, a full-color illustration of a roaring dragon (drawn by TSR staff artist David Sutherland) beckoned fantasy-minded shoppers into a world of action and adventure.

On the inside, there was treasure. A staple-bound booklet and two piles of loose cardstock sheets provided everything a group of new players needed to start the game—a rule book, a compilation of lists of monsters and treasure, and predesigned map sections meant to be cut out and assembled into unique settings for adventures. And for the first time, a D&D box set included the tools of the trade—five polyhedral dice in a small plastic bag.*

The Basic Set, widely referred to as "the Blue Box," brought much-needed clarity to Dungeons & Dragons. In just forty-eight pages, the rule book explains the concept of fantasy role-playing, provides instructions for creating a character from one of four basic classes (fighting man, magic-user, cleric, and thief), teaches the basics of combat and movement, and demonstrates how to gain experience and level-up a character. Holmes used plain English and assumed his

*TSR quickly overwhelmed its supplier of the cheap polyhedral dice included in each box and had to procure more directly from the Chinese manufacturer. As a result, the fifth and sixth editions of the Basic Set, both printed in 1979, came with two sheets of numbered chits printed on perforated card stock instead of dice.

audience had no war-gaming experience; set at a low price of $9.50 and sold in stores other than hobby shops, the Blue Box brought D&D to the masses. It did to Original D&D what *Calculus for Dummies* did to Isaac Newton's *Principia Mathematica*.

What the Blue Box didn't do was teach players how to advance their characters beyond level three—that was left for Gygax's half of the project. "The 'Basic Set' of D&D is aimed at new players, those persons as yet uninitiated to the wonders of fantasy role playing," Gygax explained in *The Dragon*. "It can lead to either the original game or to the new, as yet unfinished, Advanced D&D . . . AD&D will be a better, cleaner system aimed at improving the understanding of the role playing game system." Gamers had to take his word for it, though, because Gygax's new rules were nowhere near completed.

Meanwhile, TSR's most valuable customers—veteran D&D players who wanted better rules, and new ones who loved the Blue Box and were hungry for more—were anxious to buy but had nothing new to purchase.* So competitors rushed to fill the vacuum. Fantasy Games Unlimited's Chivalry & Sorcery continued the "ampersands & alliterations" trend started by Tunnels & Trolls, but not its sense of humor; the rules, written by Ed Simbalist and Wilf Backhaus, emphasized historical detail and complex simulation. In contrast, Metagaming Concepts' Melee, written by American designer Steve Jackson, was much simpler, focusing on one-on-one combat between heroes and monsters. The fact that both games somewhat resembled Dungeons & Dragons wasn't a coincidence but wasn't cynical imita-

* Gygax's argument that the Blue Box might lead new players into Original D&D made about as much sense as Microsoft saying that fans of the 2012 video game Halo 4 should buy Pong while they wait for the next installment. While TSR did keep selling the original set—in a white box marked "Original Collector's Edition"—through the end of the decade, it's likely that few players moved from Blue Box to White.

tion either; many of the new games had evolved out of D&D home campaigns, as players changed the rules to reflect their own interests.

One of the biggest games of 1977 owed its success to a different kind of swords and sorcery. On May 25, geeks across the U.S. stepped away from the game table to stand in line for George Lucas's *Star Wars*; the film remained in theaters over a year and started a space craze that helped popularize a new science fiction role-playing game. Game Designers' Workshop's Traveller wasn't the first sci-fi RPG, but it was the most complete and most epic. Inspired by tales of galactic empires like Isaac Asimov's *Foundation,* author Marc Miller created a game that let players feel like they were Han Solo or Luke Skywalker. An innovative character-generation system helped draw players into the fantasy: Instead of starting out as inexperienced, mostly useless adventurers, new Traveller characters go through a complex life-development process to determine their background, schooling, career choices, and skills. This helped players identify with their characters and ensured that they were capable of heroics as soon as they hit the table. Traveller was well received and a quick hit—even Gygax had to admit that it was "an imaginative game," and "an imitation by no possible stretch of the imagination."

It's possible Gygax was more concerned with a smaller but more personal threat: new material from Dave Arneson. Now working for himself, Arneson contracted with a small Texas publisher in early 1977 to print the first D&D product he'd authored since *Blackmoor.* The *Dungeonmaster's Index* advertised his former associations proudly: The cover illustration depicted a grinning hooded character standing above a battlefield, controlling wizards and warriors like marionettes, and the credit "By Dave Arneson . . . Co-Author of Dungeons & Dragons." While Arneson still owned a piece of TSR and retained some royalty rights, he didn't control the copyright to publish new content. So the thirty-eight-page book is little more than an index to existing TSR-owned products; it lists various D&D monsters, spells, and magic items, and provides page references for *The Strategic Review* and the original D&D rule books and supplements.

Arneson's second product was a more direct assault against TSR's castle. The cover of *The First Fantasy Campaign*, published by TSR licensee Judges Guild, promises "the history and details of the original fantasy roleplaying game" and invites players to "visit the dread Egg of Coot, Loch Gloomen and the underworld below Blackmoor castle." *The First Fantasy Campaign* is drawn directly from Arneson's notes for his Blackmoor campaign—perhaps the same notes that Gary Gygax used to create Dungeons & Dragons. But where Gygax took those ideas and gave them structure, organizing rough concepts into a game system and salable product, Arneson presented them in the raw, so as to inspire Dungeon Masters to make their own system. A small line of text on the bottom of the front cover half disclaims, half boasted, "Fantasy game system not included."

The book contains rough maps, not to scale, of the Blackmoor environs; random facts about the area's population ("approximately 1,000 Peasants, 100 Soldiers and Nobles, 4 Wizards or Sorcerers, 1 Dragon, several Trolls . . .") and natural resources ("the main livestock consists of an oversized member of the Bison family . . ."); short bios of characters from the game (including the Blue Rider, a warrior unable to remove his magically enchanted armor); tables of figures (like the costs to hire personnel to staff a castle); and descriptions of points of interest, including, of course, a tavern (the "Comeback Inn" offers half-price booze and lodgings, but its doorway is magically enchanted, so that "when you leave you find yourself coming back in").

The First Fantasy Campaign is rough and random but awfully charming. It's meant to be a jumping-off point, and it speaks volumes about Arneson's philosophy, which emphasized inspiration over commodification. It also makes it clear that Dungeons & Dragons could never have happened without Gygax's help—left to his own devices, Arneson publishes notes rather than a fully formed game product.

Surprisingly, TSR let Arneson publish both *The First Fantasy Campaign* and the *Dungeonmaster's Index* without major protest—while there is some evidence that the company considered sending out its usual cease-and-desist letters, the case doesn't appear to have gone to court.

Other competitors weren't so lucky. California gamer Steve Perrin had spent a year compiling fantasy role-playing game monsters from various sources, including home campaigns, game magazines, and rule books, when he received a TSR cease-and-desist letter. But instead of killing the project, Perrin edited out any monsters from official TSR sources and released *All the Worlds' Monsters* through Chaosium Inc., a small game publisher based in Oakland. The bestiary didn't get much attention from fans, but Perrin succeeded at embarrassing Gygax into action: Just weeks after *All the Worlds' Monsters* went up for sale, TSR published its first Advanced D&D book.

The Advanced Dungeons & Dragons *Monster Manual* may have been a rush job, but its quality is undeniable. The 108-page volume was the first role-playing game book printed in hardcover; it had a stitched binding and was clad in the same rough, nearly indestructible material used for schoolbooks in the 1970s. Written entirely by Gygax, the manual compiled over 350 monsters from the original D&D rule books, *The Strategic Review,* and *The Dragon*; each entry included a few statistics for use in the game and a description of the beast's behavior and habitat.

The beholder, a "hateful, aggressive, and avaricious" creature, is described as having a spherical body that's covered in chitinous plates; "atop the sphere are 10 eyestalks, while in its central area are a great eleventh eye and a large mouth filled with pointed teeth."* Displacer beasts look like pumas with thorn-covered tentacles growing out of their shoulders; "the molecular vibrations of the displacer beast are such that it always appears to be 3′ (left, right, ahead, or behind) its actual position. Thus, these monsters always cause opponents to subtract 2 from attack dice rolls." The catoblepas "is loathsome beyond description and has no redeeming features"—picture an overweight buffalo with stumpy legs, a giraffe-like neck, and a warthog's head. "Perhaps its habitat—fetid swamps and miasmal marshes—caused the bizarre combination of genetic characteristics in this monster, or perhaps it was due to some ghastly tinkering with life by a demented godling." The gelatinous cube is a dungeon scavenger, a living mound of transparent jelly that's "ideal for cleaning all living organisms, as well as carrion, from the floor and walls of underground passageways." And woe unto the armor-wearing adventurer who encounters a rust monster deep in some dark subterranean passage: "They roam such places in search of their food—metals of all sorts, but principally ferrous based metals such as iron, steel, and steel alloys."

The *Monster Manual* succeeded not just as a game supplement but by elevating the D&D rule book to fetish object. The solid construction made the book durable and portable, the kind of thing a kid could throw around and take wherever they went; Gygax's short write-ups, paired with hundreds of illustrations by David Sutherland, David Trampier, and Tom Wham, made it perfect for browsing anytime, anywhere. The book became a beloved companion to a generation of gamers, something they came back to again and again. TSR initially printed fifty thousand copies of the *Monster Manual*, selling

* "The various eyes of a beholder each have a different function . . . 1 Charm person spell, 2 Charm monster spell, 3 Sleep spell, 4 Telekinese [*sic*], 5 Flesh-stone ray, 6 Disintegrate ray, 7 Fear, 8 Slow spell, 9 Cause serious wound, 10 Death ray, 11 Anti-magic ray." *Advanced Dungeons & Dragons Monster Manual*, page 10.

each for $9.95; over the next twelve years the company reprinted the book fifteen times. The *Monster Manual* buried *All the Worlds' Monsters* and reminded everyone in the role-playing game business that Gary Gygax was boss.

One fan-made game product had been dealt with, but Gygax was ready for war against the hordes. In a *Dragon* column published in December 1977, he unloaded on what he must have seen as a sea of enemies beating on the gates:

> Imitation is claimed to be the sincerest form of flattery, and D&D has ample reason to be flattered . . . Quite a few individuals and firms have sought to cash in on a good thing by producing material from, or for, D&D. Others have parodied the game. For most of these efforts TSR has only contempt . . .
>
> TSR is quite willing to face competition. We founded our company with a bit of money, a lot of ideas, and no outside help. Our growth has been because we furnished products which gamers found desirable, not because we got any help from anyone else, and possibly in spite of suppression of what we were doing by actively ignoring all we did. These days TSR is too big to be ignored, D&D is too popular to pass by. We feel that competition will only sharpen our collective face, and because of it we will furnish better products which will be more popular still. By no means do we desire suppression of fair and genuine competition! . . .
>
> I cannot resist the analogy of a lion standing over its kill. The vultures scream, and the jackals yap, when the lion drives them off without allowing them to steal bits of the meat. Perhaps a hyena will manage to successfully grab off a mouthful, but that is all. Other lions may also prey upon the same herd and make even bigger kills, but that is the law of the land. Pardon me,

> please, if you find the picture not to your liking. From my end it seems most apropos, for I hear a good deal of screaming and yapping. TSR was the lion which brought down the prey, and we intend to have the benefits derived therefrom. If we share with anyone, it will be on our terms. The hunter which fails to bring down its kill dies itself.

It's a powerful assertion of rights—and powerfully ironic, considering that at around the same time Gygax composed the essay, TSR was once again in hot water for violating someone else's trademarks.

Despite the similarities between the Middle-earth of *The Lord of the Rings* and the fantasy worlds of Dungeons & Dragons, Gygax had always maintained that J. R. R. Tolkien's influence on the game was minimal, and he'd been more directly inspired by Robert E. Howard's Conan stories, Fritz Leiber's tales of Fafhrd and the Gray Mouser, and other authors including Poul Anderson, L. Sprague de Camp, and Michael Moorcock.* "The seeming parallels and inspirations are actually the results of a studied effort to capitalize on the then-current 'craze' for Tolkien's literature," Gygax said. "To attract those readers . . . I used certain names and attributes in a superficial manner, merely to get their attention."

Superficial or not, they did attract attention. Saul Zaentz, an old-school Hollywood mogul who owned some of the rights to Tolkien's works, filed a lawsuit against TSR alleging that D&D improperly used several protected terms, including "dragon," "elf," and "orc." He also took exception to a new TSR product, a war game called

---

* Gygax admitted that he "thoroughly enjoyed" *The Hobbit* but maintained that he disliked the *Lord of the Rings* trilogy: "Gandalf is quite ineffectual, plying a sword at times and casting spells which are quite low powered . . . [Tolkien] drops Tom Bombadil, my personal favorite, like the proverbial hot potato . . . The wicked Sauron is poorly developed, virtually depersonalized, and at the end blows away in a cloud of evil smoke . . . poof!"

Battle of the Five Armies, which simulated an epic clash of goblins, humans, elves, wargs, and dwarves from *The Hobbit.* Zaentz alleged nearly half a million dollars in damages;* though Gygax was usually happy to debate Tolkien's influence, this time he didn't argue. The suit was settled out of court, TSR stopped selling Battle of the Five Armies, and future editions of D&D dropped some of the offending words. Thus the "hobbit" became "halfling," "ent" became "treant," and "balrog" became "balor demon."

With competitors threatened, lawsuits settled, and the *Monster Manual* moving out the door faster than an air elemental** on amphetamines, TSR was growing fast and needed more space. So in the spring of 1978, the editors of *The Dragon* took over the house on Williams Street, and the rest of the staff moved downtown into a former hotel on the corner of Main Street and Broad.

The Hotel Clair was once a landmark. Back in the 1920s, when Lake Geneva was a summer retreat for Chicago's rich and famous, it was the kind of place where Al Capone and William Wrigley Jr. might have shared a cocktail. In 1978, the building was a wreck. "It probably should have been condemned," says Skip Williams, who helped move

---

* Saul Zaentz owns the rights to a lot of creative works he didn't create, and frequently litigates to protect them: In 2011, his company sued a small pub in Southampton, England, that had operated for more than two decades as the Hobbit. Creedence Clearwater Revival front man John Fogerty wrote the song "Zanz Kant Danz" allegedly about Zaentz after they battled over the rights to CCR's music; the chorus of the song is "Zanz can't dance but he'll steal your money / Watch him or he'll rob you blind." After Zaentz sued, Fogarty changed the name of the character in the lyrics and the title to "Vanz."

** "[Elementals] are strong but relatively stupid beings conjured magically from their normal habitat—the elemental planes of air, earth, etc. . . . Upon command an air elemental can form a whirlwind [that] sweeps away and kills all creatures under three hit dice, and causes 2–16 hit points of damage on all non-aerial creatures which it fails to kill outright." *Advanced Dungeons & Dragons Monster Manual,* page 10.

the Dungeon Hobby Shop into a former bar area on the first floor. "The floors were sagging, and in some places . . . had broken away, so they were just sort of hanging there. It had these marvelous tin ceilings, which somebody who didn't appreciate had painted over with four or five layers of paint. It would peel, and you could sit there and shoot rubber bands at it and knock it loose."

On the second and third floors, employees were crammed into small offices, sometimes several people deep. When author and game designer Tracy Hickman started work at TSR in the spring of 1981, he was given desk space in the northwest corner of the building and discovered that the aging building presented some unique challenges to productivity.

"At one point one of the main support beams in the north side of the building had rusted through. They replaced that beam, but by the time they had it in place, the building sagged toward the north, which meant that all of the upper floors slanted northward, just slightly," says Hickman. "I had your typical wheeled office chair, and because of the slant of the building, if I just sat in the chair, it would roll away from the desk toward the windows. So I got in the habit of hooking my foot around the leg of the chair and planting the toe of my right foot against the floorboard, to stop my chair from rolling away from the desk toward the windows. To this day I will occasionally find myself with my toe stuck behind the leg of my chair just to keep me in place, even though I don't have a slanting floor anymore."

Despite its decrepitude, the Hotel Clair buzzed with exuberance. "You had a lot of young people doing creative work, and a lot of them were on their first jobs out of college," says Skip Williams. Employees shot each other with squirt guns, goofed around with toys, and even climbed out the windows onto the fire escape and up to the building's rotting roof. "Somebody fell through a ceiling at one point because they were screwing around in an unused attic space," he says.

While they were having fun, TSR's employees also managed to publish a lot of new games. In early 1978, the company released its first stand-alone adventure module, *Steading of the Hill Giant Chief,* and two sequels, *Glacial Rift of the Frost Giant Jarl* and *Hall of the Fire Giant King.* Unlike *Temple of the Frog,* the loose scenario that appeared in the back of the *Blackmoor* supplement, these three modules provided Dungeon Masters with a tightly written story, setting, and motivation for the players:

> Giants have been raiding the lands of men in large bands, with giants of different sorts in these marauding groups. Death and destruction have been laid heavily upon every place these monsters have visited. This has caused great anger in high places . . . Therefore, a party of the bravest and most powerful adventurers has been assembled and given the charge to punish the miscreant giants. These adventurers must deliver a sharp check, deal a lesson to the clan of hill giants nearby, or else return and put their heads upon the block for the headsman's axe!

Gygax wrote the trilogy after he finished the *Monster Manual* and wanted to take a break from rule books; they're full of vivid detail and descriptions that made the adventures come alive for players.* Later he took another break from AD&D to write a sequel trilogy, *Descent into the Depths of the Earth, Shrine of the Kuo-Toa,* and

* "Topped by a huge mass of yellow orange hair which looks light a fright wig, Queen Frupy's face is a mass of jowls and wrinkles, set in the middle of a very large head which sits squarely upon her shoulders. Her body is lumpy and gross, and her skin is covered with bristles the color of her hair." *Hall of the Fire Giant King,* page 4.

Vault of the Drow, which take the players onward to confront the force behind the rampaging giants—evil subterranean elves called the Drow. These modules are looser, more about exploration, but equally compelling. In 1986, TSR republished all six adventures along with their 1980 finale, *Queen of the Demonweb Pits,* as a single "supermodule" called *Queen of the Spiders*; many gamers consider it the greatest D&D adventure of all time.

Another module published in 1978, *Tomb of Horrors,* has a darker reputation: the deadliest game ever written. Originally created by Gygax for the first Origins Game Fair, a war-gaming convention held in July 1975 in Baltimore, Maryland, the adventure was meant to challenge out-of-control players, putting their outrageously powerful D&D characters to the test—and, hopefully, killing them. Gygax lures the unwitting PCs into the tomb of the evil wizard Acererak with promises of "rich treasures both precious and magical," but then unloads a series of complicated puzzles and nightmarish traps on them, like a hallway where the entire floor is balanced on a fulcrum, so that when players proceed past a certain point it tips and dumps them into a pit of molten lava. Few survive long enough to collect any treasure, and even fewer manage to find their way back through the deadly maze and escape with their spoils. Once the guys in my D&D group decided to take a short break from Vampire World and spend a few sessions testing our mettle against the tomb; not a single player made it out alive. R. C. died in the tomb's very first hallway when he jumped into a hole he thought led deeper into the complex but turned out to be a sphere of annihilation.*

* "A sphere of annihilation is a globe of absolute blackness, a ball of nothingness 2' in diameter. A sphere is actually a hole in the continuity of the multiverse, a void. Any matter which comes in contact with a sphere is instantly sucked into the void, gone, utterly destroyed, wishes and similar magicks notwithstanding." *Advanced Dungeons & Dragons Dungeon Masters Guide,* page 154.

By the summer of 1978, TSR had eighteen full-time employees, several dozen successful products, and at least a hundred thousand devoted fans of its games around the world. A survey published in the June issue of the *Judges Guild Journal* indicated that the average role-playing game fan was a twenty-one-year-old male* college student, with all the free time for games and disposable income that demographic implies.

Finally, just in time for Gen Con XI in August, TSR delivered a new edition of Dungeons & Dragons. While the *Monster Manual* may have been the first book to bear the AD&D moniker, it collected only descriptions of creatures and didn't actually contain much in the way of new and revised rules; in contrast, the *Advanced Dungeons & Dragons Players Handbook* offered 128 pages of detailed instructions. Gygax hadn't just revised D&D—he'd rewritten and expanded it into a whole new game.

Sure, the core was familiar. AD&D preserved all the good stuff from the original D&D rules and supplements: characters had the same ability categories (strength, intelligence, wisdom, constitution, dexterity, and charisma) and were still sorted into a few basic professions. But while the original *Men & Magic* booklet spent less than a thousand words describing the game's main classes (fighting man, magic-user, and cleric), the *Players Handbook* dedicated more than fifteen thousand words to five core classes (cleric, fighter, magic-user, thief, and monk) and five subclasses (druid, paladin, ranger, illusionist, and assassin). Each was fleshed out and detailed: Clerics, for instance, were now required to maintain a relationship with a specific deity,

---

*Only 2.3 percent of respondents to the survey were female. While the hobby is still very male dominated, it's changing fast—as we'll see later.

carrying its holy symbol, showing devotion through daily prayers, and behaving in a manner pleasing to that god. Failure to comply could result in the revocation of magical ability, since a cleric's powers were bestowed in return for "diligent prayers and deeds."

The *Players Handbook* focused heavily on character creation, offering lots of rich detail and opportunities for personalization. In addition to the ten core classes, players chose between seven playable "races"—dwarf, elf, gnome, halfling, human, half-elf, and half-orc. They picked one of nine "alignments" (chaotic evil, chaotic good, chaotic neutral, lawful evil, lawful good, lawful neutral, neutral evil, neutral good, and true neutral) that provided a loose description of their character's moral code.* They determined what languages the character could speak (from a pool including Lizardman, Hobgoblin, Kobold, and Orcish) and what equipment they carried; the handbook describes a monetary system (1,000 copper pieces = 100 silver pieces = 10 electrum pieces = 5 gold pieces = 1 platinum piece) and provides long lists of gear to make each hero unique (low, soft boots cost 8 silver pieces, and a ten-foot pole costs 3 coppers).

For all its detail, the *Players Handbook* doesn't spend much time actually describing how the game is played; the book only covers what a player needs to know to get started, like how to move and fight. Gygax hid much of the game's inner workings behind a curtain, promising those rules in the upcoming *Dungeon Masters Guide*. Until

---

*Broadly speaking, lawful characters respect some kind of authority, chaotic characters follow their conscience, and neutral characters avoid rigid extremes. You could argue that in the original *Star Wars* movies, Darth Vader is lawful evil, Luke Skywalker is lawful good, and Emperor Palpatine is chaotic evil; Han Solo starts out as chaotic neutral but ends the trilogy as neutral good. Debating the alignment of characters in different TV shows, books, and movies is a popular geek pastime and Internet meme; I've seen people deconstruct the casts of everything from *Game of Thrones* to *Downton Abbey*. Violet, the Dowager Countess of Grantham, is apparently true neutral.

that book was published, DMs would have to wing it based on what they could glean from the *Handbook* or default back to the original or Basic D&D set.

One thing was clear about the new rules: The Basic Set didn't really feed into Advanced D&D. Rather, they were two different experiences, parallel universes; AD&D was its own game from level one upward. Before long, most experienced players would come to look down their noses at the Blue Box set: Basic was for kids, AD&D was for men.

AD&D was also Gary Gygax's game, from start to finish. He's listed as the sole author on the cover and on the title page; Dave Arneson only receives a thank-you in the preface, along with twenty other friends, family members, and TSR employees. Gygax even appears on the book itself. The wraparound cover illustration, by David Trampier, shows a group of adventurers looting a temple dominated by a huge statue of a horned devil: "There is one dweeb-like chap on the back cover," Gygax would later admit, "that has a certain resemblance to yours truly."

The *Players Handbook* was another big hit—TSR sold ten thousand copies in the first three months after publication. That kind of success began to attract attention from outside the game world. On November 29, 1978, the Canadian national newspaper *The Globe and Mail* published one of the first long features about D&D to appear in a major media outlet: "Dungeons and Dragons: An Underground Game Is Ready to Surface" features interviews with D&D players at a Toronto hobby shop called Mr. Gameway's Ark and notes that the game "inspires the sort of fanatic devotion usually associated with mind-bending religious cults." Shelley Swallow, a Mr. Gameway's buyer, is quoted describing the game's growth rate as "astonishing" and saying the store sells twenty-five sets a week—twice as many as Scrabble.

Gygax, never shy when it came to publicity, was also interviewed for the article, which describes him as "the J. R. R. Tolkien of the games world" and "the inventor of Dungeons and Dragons." Cocreator Dave Arneson only warrants a misspelled parenthetical: "(The magic ingredient, the labyrinth, was borrowed from another designer, Dave Arnuson.)"

At least he got a mention. Arneson's name didn't appear at all in the *Dungeon Masters Guide* when it finally arrived in the summer of 1979. In his preface to the book, Gygax offers "an alphabetical list of all those persons who in some way contributed to the formation of this work"; the twenty-nine names that follow include his players, his coworkers, and even the novelist Jack Vance, whose fantasy stories helped inspire AD&D's spell-casting rules. Somehow, D&D's cocreator didn't make the cut.

Still, there's no denying Gygax's singular achievement. The *Dungeon Masters Guide* is a mammoth piece of work, written entirely by the man himself—240 pages of rules and tables advising the DM on nearly every matter imaginable. There's a section discussing how to deal with character aging and death, instructions for when your players want to develop new magical spells, even a table specifying the amount of time it takes to mine tunnels through different types of rock. If your players might conceive of doing it, Gygax labors to provide rules for it. The *Dungeon Masters Guide* is comprehensive to a degree that no game before it approached and few that came after attempted.

"Only the most severe critic could point at a minor omission, let alone a serious one," game journalist Don Turnbull wrote in a review of the *Guide* published in the UK magazine *White Dwarf*. "In the end, set to the task of reviewing something to which I know I cannot do justice, all I can say is—can you afford to be without it?"

The initial publication of the *Dungeon Masters Guide* was plagued with technical problems: All forty thousand books in the first printing had to be recalled because they had sixteen pages from the *Monster Manual* mistakenly bound into them; twenty thousand books in the second print run were gouged by a loose wire on a boxing machine, and their covers had to be replaced. But the book was still a critical and commercial success. "Our once lonely pastime has arrived with a vengeance," Tim Kask crowed in the March 1980 issue of *The Dragon*. "Sales of Advanced D&D *DMG* bear this out; it is the best-selling game / gamebook of all time."

Elsewhere in the magazine, Gygax shared in the celebration: "The course of TSR Hobbies' development has been rather like a D&D campaign. When we finished our first fiscal year back in 1975, we were pretty much a low-level-character sort of company, with gross sales of only about $50,000. We had [an] excellent experience the next year, with a $300,000 figure, and in 1977 we doubled that to $600,000. TSR didn't quite double again in fiscal 1978, ending the year at a gross of near $1,000,000, but in '79 we did a bit better, finishing at a gross of well over $2,000,000. From the way 1980 is shaping up, there is no reason to doubt that we'll at least double in size once again. It is possible that we'll be the largest hobby game company—and ready to start toward the really high-level game producers such as Milton Bradley and Parker Brothers—by 1982."

In the four years after Tactical Studies Rules reformed into TSR Hobbies, the company's revenues surged 4,000 percent. By Gygax's reckoning, half a million people around the world were playing D&D, and bringing more of their friends and family into the hobby each day. D&D was competing with Monopoly and Scrabble, not Bunnies & Burrows. The game was practically a license to print money.

None of this had slipped the attention of Dave Arneson.

In April 1975, when Tactical Studies Rules had sales of just $2,000 a month, Dave Arneson and Gary Gygax signed a contract giving the company the rights to Dungeons & Dragons. In return, TSR agreed to pay royalties for each and every copy sold—a total of 10 percent of the cover price, split equally between the two men.

When you're only selling two hundred copies each month, 5 percent of a ten-dollar game doesn't add up to much money.* But D&D grew so quickly that when Dave Arneson left TSR a year and a half later, his royalties were probably around a thousand dollars a month.

Arneson kept collecting his 5 percent after he departed the company, and for years, the checks kept growing. But in the fall of 1977, he noticed his payment was smaller than expected. TSR had started selling the Basic Set, and it was a big hit, but the company wasn't paying royalties on those sales. He protested, but the complaints went nowhere. Then TSR published the *Monster Manual,* and then the *Players Handbook,* and denied payment for those books too. Basic and Advanced Dungeons & Dragons, the company said, were new games and weren't covered under the 1975 agreement, so TSR didn't owe him more royalties.

On February 22, 1979, Arneson filed a lawsuit against Gygax and TSR in Minneapolis's U.S. district court, accusing them of violating his royalty agreement. TSR, it alleged, had published games that were copied and derived from D&D, so Arneson deserved to be credited and paid as their author. The suit also claimed that TSR falsely represented the *Monster Manual* and *Players Handbook* as the sole work of

---

*That's $100 in royalties, but some of you already knew that, because you stopped to do the math before you reached this footnote. A true nerd finds unsolved equations irresistible—they're like unopened birthday presents.

Gygax because it wanted to stop paying Arneson royalties—and that because he had been denied the "commercially and artistically valuable right" to be identified as the author of Dungeons & Dragons, Arneson's reputation had been irrevocably damaged. He requested $100,000 in damages and asked the court to order TSR not to publish any D&D rule books unless they listed him as coauthor.

In mounting their defense, Gygax and TSR claimed the books had nothing to do with Dave Arneson. "Advanced Dungeons & Dragons is a different game," Gygax wrote in his column in the June 1979 issue of *The Dragon*. "It is neither an expansion nor a revision of the old game, it is a new game . . . it is necessary that all adventure gaming fans be absolutely aware that there is no similarity (perhaps even less) between D&D and AD&D than there is between D&D and its various imitators produced by competing publishers."

In addition to arguing independent creation, the defendants also tried to get the case dismissed on a technicality: Arneson had filed the suit in Minnesota, so Wisconsin-based TSR said the court didn't have jurisdiction. But a judge denied the motion, pointing out that TSR had sold almost $12,000 worth of product to Minnesota customers. The case was set to go to trial.

But before that could happen, Arneson, Gygax, and TSR reached a settlement. On March 6, 1981, they agreed that Arneson would receive a 2.5 percent royalty on sales of all three AD&D rule books, up to a maximum payment of $1.2 million, and on "any revised edition or foreign language translation thereof." Arneson wouldn't get an authorship credit in any of the rule books, but it was still a pretty good deal: In the third quarter of 1982, he received $60,236.68 in royalties.

The detente didn't last long. In 1983, TSR published *Monster Manual II*, a follow-up to the contested bestiary. In apparent deference to the "any revised edition" language in the settlement, the company granted Arneson a 2.5 percent cut of all sales—and paid out royalties totaling $108,703.50 in the first year of its publication.

Then the checks stopped. On November 2, 1984, TSR sent a letter to Arneson saying that the payments had been a mistake because the *Monster Manual II* was not a "revised edition," and that since he'd been overpaid, the company would take the difference out of his future royalties for the other books.

Arneson sued again, alleging breach of both the settlement and his royalty agreement. The new lawsuit argued that *Monster Manual II* was substantially the same as its predecessor, so it was covered by the agreement—and that even if it wasn't, and TSR paid him the royalties by mistake, they didn't have the legal right to withhold his future earnings and had to eat the mistake. In 1985, the court ruled in his favor, and Arneson got to keep the cash.

Arneson filed five different lawsuits against TSR in the three decades after his departure, and while most of the details and settlements were kept confidential, it's clear he made a lot of money from Dungeons & Dragons. He funded his own game-publishing company, Adventure Games, and a computer-game company, 4D Interactive Systems; he also invested a lot of money in other people's game companies, never getting much in return except for the satisfaction of making good games.

Still, the relationship between Gygax & Arneson would never be repaired. "We don't hate each other," Arneson said in 2004. "We don't hang out with each other that often, though. We just kept going our own two separate ways."

10

THE SATANIC PANIC

Substance-abuse counselors sometimes describe addiction in terms of four stages. My D&D habit progressed much the same way. When I first joined Morgan's Vampire World campaign, I was only in Experimentation ("experimenting may occur once or several times as a way to 'have fun' or even to help the individual cope with a problem"), but the stuff was so good, I quickly advanced to Regular Use. By the time our characters began our journey to Las Vegas, I had moved on to Risky Use ("craving and preoccupation"); after we met the illithids and found the pyramid's treasure I was deep in Dependence ("compulsive use . . . despite severe negative consequences to his or her relationships, physical and mental health, personal finances, job security").

I could go down the list: *Negative consequences to relationships?* I saw my D&D buddies every week but neglected all my other friends. *Physical and mental health?* Forget about the freshman fifteen; I put on the D&D thirty. *Personal finances?* I spent a small fortune buying out-of-print rule books on eBay. *Job security?* Instead of completing stories for the magazine, I spent entire days browsing online role-playing game forums for interesting discussions ("If you could only take three sourcebooks to a desert island, what would they be?").

One of my favorite forums was a small section on the social news site Reddit. In April 2011, some of Reddit's users organized a Secret Santa–style gift exchange, one of those affairs where you're randomly assigned another participant and have to send them an anonymous gift. Since this swap was held online, participants were assigned a stranger—someone chosen from the entire site's user base, not just the RPG forum—and had to figure out what to get them based on what they'd written on the site. It sounded like a nice diversion from D&D, so I signed up.

I was assigned a twentysomething college student from upstate New York. I learned right away that she liked to read and was studying to be an archaeologist—more than enough information to pick out a gift. But I dug deeper into her comment history, looking for something else . . . and found it. A single post, over a year old, where she mentioned she'd played a role-playing game with some friends.

That was all I needed to hear. I ordered a few supplies, and when they arrived, I broke out my power tools and my gaming gear. A few precision-drilled holes later, I strung a purple twenty-sided die on a silver chain and attached jewelry closures to each end. It wasn't the ugliest necklace I've ever seen, but it was definitely the nerdiest. With a satisfied grin, I showed it to my wife.

Kara gave me a look that fell somewhere between amused and pitying. When I said I was going to make her a necklace, too, she seemed less than thrilled.

My sad attempt at jewelry design wasn't the first time someone tried to channel enthusiasm for role-playing into novelty products. A small

TSR licensee called Troubador Press crossed that line in 1979, when it published the *Official Advanced Dungeons & Dragons Coloring Album*; in the years that followed, other companies released a torrent of D&D-branded merchandise, including lunch boxes, beach towels, and action figures.

It seems silly, but at the time, the words "Dungeons & Dragons" could make any product a top seller. Even TSR's bigger competitors knew they had value: In 1980, TSR partnered with Mattel to release the Dungeons & Dragons Computer Labyrinth Game, which required players to move a die-cast metal hero through a molded plastic maze. An electronic sensor (the "computer") beeped and chirped every time a player moved their piece.* A September 1980 *Forbes* article described D&D as "the hottest game in the nation" and predicted explosive growth. TSR went on to post sales of $8.5 million for the year, an increase of 400 percent year over year.

In its early years, Dungeons & Dragons had been a pastime for grizzled veterans and nerdy college students. But after the success of AD&D and the Basic Set, the game went mainstream. D&D rule books and a whole universe of licensed products made it into the hands of children all across America—and it wasn't long before confused adults started freaking out.

James Dallas Egbert III was a gifted child. He graduated from high school at age fourteen, beloved by teachers—and resented by peers. Alienated and friendless, when he started college at Michigan State University he was moody and depressed, even for a teenager.

For a while, it seemed like college would provide the friends he'd

---

*In 1982, Mattel released another branded product, a D&D video game for their Intellivision console. At the time, Advanced Dungeons & Dragons was the most advanced computer game ever published, requiring over four thousand bytes of memory.

been missing. He joined a club called the Tolkien Society, where students spent time discussing *The Hobbit* and *The Lord of the Rings,* and sometimes played Dungeons & Dragons. But then on August 15, 1979, sixteen-year-old Egbert disappeared.

A few weeks passed before William Dear, a private investigator hired by Egbert's parents, developed a theory: Egbert had been playing a live-action version of Dungeons & Dragons and got lost in a labyrinth of steam tunnels located below the campus. Maybe he was still down there, wandering alone and confused—or maybe he'd been killed by a competing player.

Dear had obviously never played D&D, nor had any of the Michigan state police. But the investigators were all convinced the game was at fault, even though they didn't have any proof. Desperate for clues, officers collected several empty bulletin boards they found in Egbert's bedroom and drove them three hundred miles to TSR's headquarters. Upon their arrival, the cops asked TSR staff to analyze the placement of unused thumbtacks on each board, in case they represented some sort of secret pattern or map. Gary Gygax and Tim Kask spent three days staring at the boards before concluding—rightly—that they signified nothing.

But Dear didn't give up. The press-happy dick* gladly shared it with reporters, and the disappearance of Egbert became national news. Breathless newspaper stories pulled heartstrings with descriptions of an innocent genius led astray, a young boy tempted into a deviant world. Surely this game, they suggested, full of magic and demons, had led to his downfall.

---

*Dear pops up in the news media every few years: In 1984 he wrote a book about the Egbert case called *The Dungeon Master*; in 1995 he lent his investigative skill to a Fox television documentary called *Alien Autopsy: Fact or Fiction?* His latest effort, a 2012 book titled *O.J. Is Innocent and I Can Prove It,* argues that O. J. Simpson's son killed Nicole Simpson and Ron Goldman.

The truth was simpler. Egbert, in a fit of depression, had run away. Eventually he bought a bus ticket to New Orleans, checked into a cheap motel, and attempted to poison himself. When that didn't work, he hid out in Louisiana for a few more days before deciding to go home.*

The staff of TSR was worried about receiving so much negative attention, but only until they saw the results. "The continual press coverage of [D&D] and its 'dangers' caused sales to skyrocket," Gygax said in a 2002 interview. "We couldn't print fast enough to fill orders." Just one year after the Egbert affair, TSR posted annual revenues of $8.5 million; two years later, in fiscal 1981, revenues exceeded $12.9 million.

D&D was famous. On November 8, 1979, just six weeks after Egbert returned to his family, Gygax appeared on the late-night television show *Tomorrow with Tom Snyder* to talk about the phenomenon; to his credit, Snyder seemed to embrace D&D in the spirit in which it was intended, and even needled an unprepared Gygax to run him through an impromptu dungeon on camera. But outside of late-night, the game was treated differently. The Egbert incident had marked Dungeons & Dragons in the public eye as something dangerous. And as the 1980s began, the game became a cultural bugaboo—seen, along with satanism and heavy metal music, as a corrupter of youth.

In May of 1980, parents in the "solidly Mormon" farming town of Heber City, Utah, convinced their local school board to shut down an after-school D&D club and accused its organizers "of working with the Antichrist and of fomenting Communist subversion." Local Christian minister Norman Springer told *The New York Times* that the

---

*Sadly, Egbert couldn't shake his depression; less than a year later he died from a self-inflicted gunshot wound.

game was "very definitely" antireligious: "These books are filled with things that are not fantasy, but are actual in the real demon world and can be very dangerous for anyone involved in the game because it leaves them so open to Satanic spirits."

TSR did what it could to prevent an all-out witch hunt. A few months after the Heber City incident, the company ran a half-page ad in *The Dragon* with the banner headline "Real-life Clerics: TSR Hobbies needs you." The ad solicited players who happened to be clergy "of any organized religion" to share their stories of D&D's "helpful, positive influence."

But they were too late. In 1981, author Rona Jaffe published a novel inspired by the Egbert case. *Mazes and Monsters* told the story of Robbie Wheeling, a college student who suffers a psychotic break while playing a D&D-like game. Wheeling comes to believe he is actually his character, the cleric Pardeux, and that he must jump off one of the World Trade Center towers in order to win the game. The made-for-TV movie version, released in 1982, starred a post–*Bosom Buddies* Tom Hanks.

Mazes and Monsters is nonsensical, hysterical, and a woefully inaccurate depiction of Dungeons & Dragons. But for many Americans who knew little about the game, it cemented an idea that fantasy role-playing was the road to perdition. In the summer of 1982, officials in Oklahoma banned the game from school districts, citing its "satanic nature." In 1984, when San Diego, California, police officer Kirk Johnson was shot and killed by his own son, the boy's attorneys tried to use his obsession with Dungeons & Dragons as an explanation in an insanity defense. Later that same year, British clergymen warned that letting children play D&D was essentially handing them over to Satan: "This is indeed only a game, but it is a game of life and death!" the Reverend John Hollidge of Gold Hill Baptist Church in Buckinghamshire said in a letter to parents.

Increasingly, Dungeons & Dragons became the go-to scapegoat for teen suicides. In 1984, Bergen County, New Jersey, police blamed the deaths of two teenage brothers on D&D. "My understanding is that once you reach a certain point where you are the master, your only way out is death," the police chief told the Bergen County *Record*. Later the same year, Richmond, Virginia, mother Patricia Pulling sued Gary Gygax and TSR for $10 million, claiming that her sixteen-year-old son killed himself after his character was "cursed" by another player. The suit was dismissed, but Pulling went on to form Bothered About Dungeons and Dragons, or BADD, an advocacy group that harried D&D players for years.

In 1985, the TV news magazine *60 Minutes* dedicated an entire segment to the dangers of Dungeons & Dragons. Anchor Ed Bradley re-reported overly credulous police and local media reports as fact and relied heavily on an emotional interview with grieving mother Pulling. A psychologist interviewed for the segment, Dr. Thomas Radecki, was also highly critical of the game (a few years later, he was stripped of his medical license). After the broadcast, Gygax forwarded letters to Bradley from the mothers of two children cited in the report as D&D suicides; both letters said the game had nothing to do with their children's deaths. The show never issued a retraction.

And the criticism didn't stop. In her 1988 book *Raising PG Kids in an X-Rated Society,* co-founder of the Parents Music Resource Center (PMRC) and future second lady of the United States Tipper Gore railed against D&D, claiming it had been linked to "nearly fifty teenage suicides and homicides." After the 1988 murder of Lieth Von Stein, a North Carolina business executive, police quickly arrested his twenty-year-old stepson, Chris, as well as two of his friends, and all three men were eventually convicted of scheming to collect a $2 million inheritance. But when two competing books about the case,

Blood Games and *Cruel Doubt,* were released in 1991, both played up the fact that the friends had occasionally played D&D together.

Even the Christian pamphleteer Jack Chick piled on: In his comic-book tract *Dark Dungeons,* a young girl is inducted into a witches' coven after undergoing "intense occult training through D&D." She later learns real magic and casts a "mind bondage" spell on her father, forcing him to buy her $200 worth of D&D manuals.

D&D wasn't the first game to get this treatment. Religious extremists have attempted to ban chess repeatedly over the ages, from the prophet Muhammad's cousin Ali ibn Abu Talib, who ruled the Islamic caliphate in the seventh century, to the Afghan Taliban, who tried as recently as the twentieth century. But that must have provided little consolation to Gary Gygax, who received the brunt of the attacks. The former shoe repairman turned game designer was painted as some kind of satanic, child-corrupting madman and even received death threats. For a period in the early 1980s, Gygax had to employ a bodyguard.

Still, he tried not to take it personally. "I think I understood their motivations," he told an interviewer in 2004. "Some of them were very sincere—their ignorance was sincere. The poor woman who started BADD said in her first interview in the newspaper that she hadn't known her son was playing D&D for two years. I mean, that's a serious failure of parenting. Clearly she was transferring blame for her own failure to a game. It was sad."

Even during the worst of the satanic panic, D&D prospered. In 1980, TSR expanded its operations into a new office and warehouse, and launched a subsidiary company in the UK. New products included *World of Greyhawk,* a comprehensive guide to Gygax's home campaign that covered everything from geography to the names of days of the week.* A new spy-themed role-playing game called Top Secret even caused a panic all of its own: In the summer of 1980, the FBI showed up at TSR's headquarters after a Lake Geneva resident happened across an out-of-context TSR memo describing an assassination and turned it over to the police.

In 1981, Gygax made a distribution deal with Random House, the biggest publisher in the U.S., putting the game into tens of thousands of bookstores. TSR followed up the deal with more kid-friendly products: a revision of 1977's Basic Set, the beginner's game that covered character levels 1 through 3; and its first follow-up, the Expert Set, covering levels 4 through 14.

D&D got so popular it even appeared in an opening scene of the 1982 blockbuster *E.T. the Extra-Terrestrial*—right after the universe's most forgetful spacemen leave their long-necked buddy in the California woods. When the audience first sees the film's human protagonist, ten-year-old Elliott, he's trying to talk his way into his sixteen-year-old brother Michael's Dungeons & Dragons game. Later, one of the older kids tries to explain the game to Elliott's mom: "There's no winning. It's like life; you don't win at life."

Maybe not, but TSR seemed to be winning at business. In December 1981, *Inc.* magazine ranked TSR Hobbies number six on its annual list of the fastest-growing privately held companies in the United States. A February 1982 follow-up article crowed about TSR's surging revenues—projected at $27 million for fiscal 1982—and praised its unusual management structure:

> Perhaps most surprising about TSR's management team is its lack of relevant experience. The nine top managers—three principals (Gary Gygax and brothers Brian and Kevin Blume)

---

* Starday, Sunday, Moonday, Godsday, Waterday, Earthday, Freeday.

> and six divisional vice-presidents—represent former occupations ranging from biologist to pharmacist to plumber. Of those nine, six are currently in formal management training programs, and only in the last year has the company begun to hire people with specialized business skills. The organization operates in odd ways. Despite Gary Gygax's title of president, for instance, the company has no real chief executive. Rather it operates under the direction of a "presidential office," composed of Gygax and Brian and Kevin Blume. The company will not open the door on any new venture without a unanimous decision from these three.

To outside observers, TSR's unusual structure must have seemed innovative, even maverick. The truth was that the Blumes—backed up by three handpicked outside investors—had complete control. "I was pretty much boxed out of the running of the company because the [Blumes] . . . thought they could run the company better than I could," Gygax said.

Unable to get anything done in Lake Geneva—and in the middle of a separation from his wife—Gygax packed his bags and headed for Hollywood to start a new TSR subsidiary called Dungeons & Dragons Entertainment. "He had these ideas that in the long term, TSR should expand into visual media," says former TSR employee and Gygax adviser Frank Mentzer. "These games all take place in your head, in your imagination, and if you can transcend that and get it all onto film, that could be a big breakthrough. So he headed for the coast."

Gygax did not live the life of an exile in Los Angeles. TSR was flush with cash, so he rented a mansion on tony Summitridge Drive in Beverly Hills and played the part of Hollywood hotshot, dining with movie stars, partying with beauty queens, getting driven around in fancy cars. Before long, his expenses approached $10,000 a month—more than $20,000 in 2012 dollars. According to some accounts, he paid half a million dollars to *The Lion in Winter* screenwriter James Goldman to write a script for a D&D movie. (It was never produced, and all that ever really came out of TSR's efforts in Hollywood were twenty-seven episodes of a Dungeons & Dragons Saturday-morning cartoon.)

Back in Lake Geneva, the Blumes' management inexperience was costing the company even more. With Gygax out of the picture, TSR entered a phase of unfettered spending: In May of 1982, the company bought the long-past-its-prime pulp magazine *Amazing Stories* from Ultimate Publishing Company and acquired the games owned by a bankrupt competitor, Simulations Publishing Inc. That same year, it helped fund a salvage operation of the *Lucius Newberry,* a passenger steamship that caught fire and sank to the bottom of Lake Geneva in 1891—all they found was rusted bits of the ship's boiler. Executives procured dozens of company cars, spent millions on unnecessary office furniture, and gave high-paying jobs to relatives.

In 1983, TSR acquired several new toy and gift businesses, including Greenfield Needlewomen, a maker of needlepoint project kits; it was purchased, according to employees, to provide Kevin's wife with a hobby. D&D-branded cross-stitch patterns joined an ever-expanding list of merchandise that included Halloween costumes, wood-burning sets, wallets, flashlights, bubble blowers, flying disks, and the Official Advanced Dungeons & Dragons Cool, Cool Candles.

TSR execs even considered going into the railroad business. "There was a proposal that the company purchase the railroad line between Lake Geneva and Chicago," recalls author and designer

Tracy Hickman. "The argument went that by owning the railroad line, we would have our own railhead for product shipment, and at the same time we could run D&D game trains between Chicago and Lake Geneva. Even in the game-design department, we'd see proposals like this being considered by management and just shake our heads."

The mismanagement extended beyond overspending. At one point, Kevin Blume read a report about the amount of drug use in a typical American workplace and decided he'd tolerate no such behavior at TSR. "He got all worked up about that and wanted to go around and do surprise inspections, shining a little flashlight in employees' eyes to see if their pupils would dilate," says Frank Mentzer. "He got talked out of it by saner heads."

Despite troubles at the top, TSR still managed to put out some great game products. In 1983, the company released the third major revision of the Basic Set rules, this time edited by Frank Mentzer. Packaged in a distinctive red box with a cover illustration by fantasy artist Larry Elmore, the "Red Box" became one of the best-known and most-loved rule sets in the game's history. That same year, TSR published one of the game's all-time fan-favorite adventures, the gothic horror module Ravenloft, written by Tracy Hickman and his wife, Laura.

But none of it was enough to plug the hole created by fundamental corporate mismanagement. In the summer of 1983, TSR's financial reports showed a multimillion-dollar loss, and the company cut 15 percent of its three-hundred-person staff. Soon after, TSR Hobbies changed its name to TSR Inc. and reorganized twelve executive divisions into six. But that wasn't enough to stem the bleeding. Later in the year, the company laid off even more staff, shrinking to less than one hundred fifty employees. It contracted again in April 1984, to a staff of about one hundred.

In less than three years after *Inc.* magazine ranked TSR among the top ten fastest-growing private companies, TSR's balance sheet went from low debt and an operating profit to $1.5 million in debt and an operating loss.

Out in Los Angeles, Gygax searched for a way to save the company. He tried to arrange a merger with Ian Livingstone's UK-based Games Workshop, but Livingstone wanted to remain independent, and was wary of working with the Blumes ("I don't think they were into the games like we were . . . we felt a little bit uncomfortable," he says). Gygax also pushed Universal Pictures president Sidney Sheinberg to either write him a check to make the D&D movie or buy TSR outright—with no more success.

Finally, a five-hundred-year-old spaceman offered a chance at salvation. Gygax had been working with a writing partner, Flint Dille, on choose-your-own-adventure-style novels and to develop a fantasy film based on the world of Greyhawk. Dille's grandfather had run the National Newspaper Syndicate in the 1920s and made a fortune publishing *Buck Rogers in the 25th Century A.D.*, a comic about a World War I vet who was exposed to radioactive gas, fell into suspended animation, and woke up five hundred years later. Dille's family had a fortune to play with—and his sister, Lorraine Dille Williams, was interested in working in publishing.

Gygax returned to Lake Geneva, and at the next monthly meeting of TSR's board, he made the case to three formerly Blume-friendly directors that Kevin Blume had to go. "I fully expected to be dismissed at that time," he wrote later. "Instead, the outside directors were forced to agree, as there was no question that the corporation was in debt to the bank for about $1.5 million and there appeared to be no way to repay the loan. In the final vote, Kevin voted against my motion for his removal, Brian abstained (which speaks volumes) and the stooges voted for it, so the motion carried four to one."

But the board wasn't ready to put Gary Gygax back in control. Instead, they replaced Blume with a temporary president from the American Management Association. So in May of 1985, Gygax exercised a stock option that gave him enough voting shares to retake control of TSR. He fired the pro tem president, assumed the role of CEO, and installed Lorraine Dille Williams as TSR's new general manager.

"Shortly after this came my downfall," Gygax later said.

11

DEATH OR GLORY

When I was young, everything was simple. My friends and family were good; anyone who would hurt them was evil. I dedicated my life to protecting the things I loved and destroying the things I hated.

I haven't wavered from that commitment. But as I have grown older, I have come to understand the truth is rarely so simple. I know now that while the vampires are our captors, humanity brought about its own destruction. Vampires hid from humans for thousands of years, afraid of our strength and our numbers; they only struck when we were weak from fighting among ourselves and when our threat to the planet was too great to ignore.

I still believe in humanity's future. I know that one day we will free our brothers and sisters from the pens and deliver justice to the monsters that enslaved us. But I also know that we are imperfect beings and that we're going to need help.

When Ganubi made first contact with the residents of Las Vegas, I hoped they might be new allies. Escorting a few of them back with us to San Francisco seemed like a step in that direction. But during the long trip home, I started to worry. The four illithids who joined us were so alien and so cold. They were eager to learn about humanity but rarely willing to talk about themselves. They reminded me of predators studying their prey.

From time to time, Jhaden, Graeme, and I would walk far ahead of the group, so we could discuss what we'd do if our "friends" turned violent. Their psychic powers were a real threat, but from what we could tell, they didn't seem to have any understanding of magic or even know that it existed. As long as I avoided casting spells in front of them, they'd underestimate our defenses.

Ganubi was more trusting, but he took me seriously when I shared my concerns. So as our ragtag group traveled through the desert and back up into the mountains, Ganubi spent day after day talking to the illithids, trying to make them sympathetic to our cause. He told them about human history and our struggle with the vampires, but he also shared our values, like respect for life and protecting your friends. He even dipped into the old human religions and told them stories from scripture.

At times, he reminded me of the crazy old preachers I'd seen on street corners when I was a kid. But the illithids hung on every word. I had no way of telling if Ganubi's message was getting through to them, but they were listening, and that was a start.

When Gary Gygax decided to free TSR from the Blume brothers' rule, he knew he needed help. At first, newspaper heiress Lorraine Dille Williams seemed like the perfect ally: She was rich, she was interested in publishing, and she had experience managing midsized organizations. So he asked her to invest in the company and help him retake control.

Williams, sensing the extent of TSR's mismanagement, told Gygax that making an investment would be "money down a rat hole." Instead, she suggested a different kind of help: to go to Lake Geneva and take a position in the company where she could help rein in TSR's finances.

"I really didn't particularly have career goals," Williams says. "I took things on as individual challenges. So I went from the newspaper syndicate to a not-for-profit voluntary health agency, to a hospital, to another voluntary health agency, to a trade association."

Williams didn't know or even particularly care about fantasy role-playing, but she sensed that working for TSR would be an interesting job. "I looked upon it as another great experience," she says. "When it started out, I was going to go in and help Gary get the ship righted."

The amicable partnership lasted only a few months. Williams says that once she took on the job of TSR's general manager in the spring of 1985, she learned the true extent of the company's financial problems—and Gygax's complicity. "The whole structure of the place was that they had all sorts of offshore operations, and they had integrated profit-sharing plans that only benefited the shareholders, which were Gary, Kevin and Brian Blume, and some family members," she says. "I mean, [TSR UK] owned a house in the Isle of Man. You wouldn't have believed [Gygax's] temper tantrum when we told them that had to be sold."

According to Williams, even though the company was operating under a debt covenant that restricted its spending, Gygax wanted to keep pulling money out to fund his Hollywood projects and lifestyle. "The bank was so upset with us," she says. "We finally said, 'Gary, we can't advance a dollar. If we go in violation of the bank covenant, we have no line of credit. We're dead.' And Gary went ballistic."

Gygax remembered the falling-out differently. "I began to become uneasy about her after two incidents," he wrote in 2002. "In one she stated that she held gamers in contempt, that they were socially beneath her. In the other, when I stated that I planned to see that the employees gained share ownership when the corporate crises were passed in recognition of their loyalty, Lorraine had turned to my personal assistant Gail Carpenter (now Gail Gygax, my wife) and said: 'Over my dead body!'"

Either way, one thing is clear: Lorraine Williams got mad and decided to take over the company. "I had grown to really like the people, and I had a lot of respect for the product," she says. "I may not have understood it one hundred percent, but I understood intellectually that it was the right product for the right time."

That spring, Gygax had taken control of the company from the Blumes by exercising stock options that gave him a majority of TSR's shares. In the summer, Williams convinced Brian Blume to exercise his own options—and then she bought all of his shares. Shortly afterward, she bought all of Kevin Blume's stock too. Only a few months after arriving in Lake Geneva, Lorraine Williams was the new majority owner of TSR.

Gygax tried to fight back. He filed a lawsuit against Williams, hoping a judge would rule that the sale of stock was illegal, but the judge ruled against him. Before the year was over, Gygax gave up and sold Williams his remaining shares in TSR.

"I was so sick of the fucking company at that point, I was glad to get rid of it," Gygax said in a 2008 interview. "It was getting more and more screwed up all the time."

One night about halfway through our trip home, we made camp on a quiet hill, surrounded by forest. The journey had been blessedly quiet so far—except for Ganubi's constant chatter. I hoped he was making progress winning the illithids to our cause, but the continual preaching was getting on my nerves. I set up my bedroll at the opposite side of the fire from his nightly theology lesson and went to sleep early.

I woke abruptly a few hours later and opened my eyes to see Jhaden crouched next to me in the dark. He looked at me and held a finger in front of his lips. "There's something out in the woods," he whispered. "Smell it?"

I may not be a ranger, but this didn't require trained senses. There was a rotting stench in the air, like spoiled meat. I sat up and looked around, but by the light of our small campfire, I could only see Ganubi, Graeme, and the illithids, all asleep.

Jhaden, still crouching, moved to wake them. But he only took a few quiet steps before he drew his sword and broke into a run. As he passed Ganubi's bedroll, he gave him a kick and shouted loud enough to wake the dead: "We're under attack!"

Gary Gygax didn't give up on role-playing games after departing TSR. Immediately after leaving the business, he started another publishing company, New Infinities Productions, with TSR veterans Frank Mentzer and Kim Mohan. The company published just one full game, 1987's sci-fi-themed Cyborg Commando, and a few adventures and novels. It went out of business after an investor failed to deliver necessary funding.

Next Gygax took a job writing a new fantasy game, Dangerous Dimensions, for his old competitor Game Designers' Workshop. When it was still in development, TSR threatened a copyright-infringement lawsuit over the game's too-similar "DD" initials, so Gygax changed the name of the game to Dangerous Journeys. When it was published, TSR sued anyway. Tiny Game Designers' Workshop couldn't compete with TSR's lawyers and sold TSR the game as part of an out-of-court settlement. Dangerous Journeys disappeared into a back room somewhere in Lake Geneva, never to be seen again.

TSR wouldn't let Gary Gygax publish fantasy games, so he spent most of the next decade writing novels—fantasy potboilers with titles like *Sea of Death, Dance of Demons,* and *The Anubis Murders*. They met with a lukewarm reception. In the late nineties Gygax started work on a fantasy-themed video game called Lejendary Adventure, but that didn't work out as planned either: In 1999, Hekaforge Productions released the game as an old-fashioned pen-and-paper role-playing game. By that point, TSR had no objection.

Nothing Gary Gygax ever did after TSR approached the level of success of Dungeons & Dragons—but, of course, that's kind of like pointing out that J. D. Salinger peaked with *The Catcher in the Rye*. While he was at TSR, Gygax earned lifetime membership in the pantheon of geek gods; after departing, he enjoyed his deserved celebrity. He wrote articles, he performed interviews, he talked with fans on gaming websites. In 2000, he even voiced himself on the animated TV show *Futurama*: The plot of the episode explained that Gygax, as part of a superteam including Al Gore and Stephen Hawking, was responsible for protecting the entire universe's space-time continuum. At the end of the episode, they all sat down to play Dungeons & Dragons.

In 2003, Gygax announced that with the help of his former assistant-DM Rob Kuntz, he was compiling a massive six-volume guide to Greyhawk, using details that TSR had never published. In order to get around copyright-infringement claims, they'd call Greyhawk "Zagyg," an anagram of Gygax. But an April 2004 stroke slowed the old grognard down considerably, and only two volumes were published.

On the morning of March 4, 2008, Gary Gygax died at his home in Lake Geneva. He was sixty-nine years old.

Hideous creatures came running out of the darkness and into the light of our fire. They looked like men, but warped and terrible, with scaly skin and fingers that twisted into long, daggerlike claws. I could see three of them racing toward the center of our camp, and then Jhaden closed the distance and speared one on his sword.

Ganubi and Graeme were still waking up, so I took a step toward them, hoping to provide some cover until they could arm themselves. But then I heard a noise behind me, and when I turned, I saw another of the ghouls sprinting toward me, only seconds away. Its mouth opened impossibly wide, and a long black tongue snaked past inch-long teeth, flicking at the air.

Fads always fade, and D&D's downturn began right around the time Lorraine Williams bought the company. In the late eighties and early nineties, enthusiasm for tabletop gaming waned. While the game held on to a core group of rabid fans, demand for rule books and related products decreased: In 1989, TSR tried to inject some life into the game with the publication of *Advanced Dungeons & Dragons 2nd Edition,* but it didn't do much to excite fans—aside from removing Gary Gygax as D&D's primary author.

Instead, the attention of gamers went elsewhere. Video games and D&D had already coexisted for a decade, and TSR had made good money licensing the property to video game makers. More than a dozen different D&D video games were published between 1980 and 1990, on eight different game platforms. But by the early nineties the video game business had matured, and TSR wasn't competing against small hobby companies—it was squaring off against international giants like Sony and Nintendo.

Computer technology had also evolved to a point where video games were easier, cheaper, and better looking than any tabletop competitor. When video games were played on a computer and consisted entirely of text, they weren't much of a threat. But when you could play them on your TV and they looked like real life, companies like TSR were suddenly in deep trouble.

Video games even began to take the place of Dungeons & Dragons as the enemy of overanxious parents. By the mid-1990s, no one was blaming D&D for corrupting children—they were worried about violent video games like Doom.

New competitors also appeared in the tabletop game world. In 1993, Seattle-based game publisher Wizards of the Coast published Magic: The Gathering, a collectible card game set in a D&D-like fantasy world. The game requires players to construct a deck of cards, each one a different spell or creature, in order to wage war against a friend. Since good cards are mixed randomly with bad ones in expensive "booster packs," hard-core players might spend hundreds or even thousands of dollars to construct their perfect deck. The game fed gamers' hunger for fantasy combat and exploited the nerdy impulse to collect and complete. Magic was an instant hit; two months after its debut, Wizards of the Coast sold out the first printing of 2.5 million cards.

TSR tried to capitalize on the trend by releasing their own collectible games, including a Magic: The Gathering knockoff called Spellfire: Master the Magic and a dice game called Dragon Dice. They were both expensive to produce, and neither sold very well.

Then things got worse. TSR had increasingly come to rely on the revenues from publishing fantasy fiction books to keep the company afloat. But at the end of 1996, the market collapsed, and TSR's distributor, Random House, returned millions of dollars' worth of unsold hardcover books. On the hook to refund Random House, TSR entered 1997 over $30 million in debt, and with no cash to publish or ship new products. Operations ground to a halt.

If Dungeons & Dragons could have been represented by a character in its own game, it would have been out of spells, had only one hit point left, and been cursed with blindness. D&D was on its deathbed.

The enemy had caught us unready but not defenseless. I don't need a weapon in hand when I can channel magical energy at will. As the ghoul pounced, I hit it with a ray of searing light, and it collapsed to the ground in a sizzling pile of flesh.

There were more in the woods. Many more. As I fired off spell after spell just to keep them at bay, I heard the sounds of fighting behind me: Jhaden shouting war cries, running feet, the twang of a bow. Normally, we'd try to regroup and take a defensible position, but the ghouls were on us so quickly, it was all I could do to stand my ground, cast spell after spell, and try not to be overrun.

The melee probably lasted half a minute, but it felt like an hour. I had just dispatched my final target when I heard—well, not heard, exactly, more like felt—a voice in my head. "Save us!" it cried. "Help!"

I turned to see what was happening and found the campsite in chaos. Jhaden was fighting at least two of the ghouls at once. Graeme I couldn't see. One of the illithids was on the ground, covered in blood, while the others cowered a few feet away. A ghoul—probably the one that had killed their companion—was bearing down on them, about to attack.

I remember thinking to myself, "I guess psychic powers don't affect ghouls."

But then Ganubi was there, throwing himself between the monster and his new friends. His sword was in hand, but in his rush to get between them, he had let his guard down.

The ghoul ran into Ganubi, knocking him to the ground. Then it tore at his flesh with its terrible claws.

Morgan rolled a die and checked the results. "First attack on Ganubi is a miss," he said. "Oh, no, wait—you're on the ground. What's your armor class when you are prone?"

"I . . . I think it's a plus four or a negative four," Phil said. "Whatever. It's four in his favor."

"But what is your actual AC?"

"That would be sixteen."

"Oh boy. You are in trouble."

As soon as I saw Ganubi fall, I ran to help him. But I couldn't get there in time to stop the ghoul from attacking again.

As Ganubi struggled to get up, the ghoul stood over him and slashed with its claws, frenzied, hitting him again and again.

I watched as Ganubi collapsed to the ground. I saw the light go from his eyes. I saw my friend die.

"I feel bad about this," Morgan said. "I really do. But I play by the rules, and that's fifty-five points of damage."

"Oh wow." Phil stared at his character sheet.

We all froze, silent, waiting for him to react.

"Yeah. Well, make sure you guys tell the illithids that I was going in there to help them."

12

RESURRECTION

Adventuring is a high-risk enterprise. Characters in your campaign will die, sometimes because they were reckless and sometimes because luck was against them. Fortunately, D&D is a game, and death doesn't have to be the end.

—*DUNGEON MASTERS GUIDE,* PAGE 41

"Do we know how to preserve a body?" Alex asked. We'd finished the ghouls off without further casualties, but now had to face an even worse problem. "A week of walking around dragging Ganubi's corpse sounds like a bad idea."

"Actually, you know, I was thinking about that," Phil said. He turned to Morgan. "Would you allow me to convert one of the illithids to the Church of Ganubi and have me take them over as a player character? Because I wouldn't mind giving up Ganubi for that."

"I don't think so," Morgan said. "That would open up a great big can of worms."

Phil sighed. And then I had a flash of inspiration.

"No, Phil, wait." I pounded on the table in excitement. "Ganubi's been preaching to these guys for a week, and then he got killed trying to protect them. I'm going to spend the rest of the trip home telling the illithids, 'He died for you guys, he saved you!'"

Alex saw it coming. "Oh man, you're going to turn Ganubi into Jesus." He laughed. "Come on."

"No, seriously. If we can get some illithids to be Ganubi's followers, how awesome would that be?"

"That would be pretty cool," Alex said. "This could be the catalyst that turns their whole civilization to good instead of evil."

"He died for them, man! Every day, on the way back, I am going to cast . . . what's that spell you cast on a dead body so it doesn't decay?"

"Gentle Repose," Morgan said.

"Yes, Gentle Repose. Every day I will secretly cast that on Ganubi's body, and then I will remark on the miracle that his body is not decaying. The illithids don't know I've got these spells. I'm going to pretend to be shocked and tell them, 'Perhaps this is a sign! Perhaps Ganubi is too great to be destroyed in this manner! He may yet return to us!'"

Morgan shook his head, but he was smiling. "Make a Bluff check," he said.

I picked up my favorite d20, shook it in my hand, and tossed it onto the table. We all held our breath as it rolled to a stop.

Twenty.

Alex roared. "It was meant to be!"

"You have been remarkably convincing on this subject," Morgan deadpanned. "All right, so eventually you reach the walls of San Francisco and you have got three tentacled monsters with you. Now what are you going to do?"

We live in a dangerous world. Death lurks around every corner. But sometimes, if you have enough gold, you can tell him to take a hike.

When we got back to San Francisco, Jhaden and Graeme went to sell all the trade goods we'd brought from Las Vegas. I brought the illithids back to our docked ship and placed Ganubi's body at rest on the deck.

"This is the ship that carried Ganubi's life force across the great ocean," I told them. "Now that he's back on the vessel of his soul, we have to wait and see if he returns to us. I am praying for a miracle."

The concept of an afterlife was still confusing to the illithids, but they were perfectly familiar with the concept of death. So when we sold our trade goods and used the cash to hire a high-level cleric to secretly cast the spell True Resurrection, I knew they would be suitably impressed.*

The illithids were watching as Ganubi's motionless form stirred, sat up, and looked around.

"He has returned from the dead!" I shouted. "It's a miracle!"

Ganubi stared at me, perplexed, and then at the stunned illithids, and then back at me again. I saw a twinkle in his eye.

"Yes!" he said, standing and raising his arms toward the heavens. "I have returned!"

"Oh boy, we are all going to hell," Alex said, laughing. "See, this is the shit that they talk about when they say that D&D is the devil's game."

"I think we'll end on that note," Morgan said.

Phil laughed. "And that is how you gain a level in the evangelist class," he said.

Just like Ganubi, Dungeons & Dragons lived to fight another day. In 1997, Lorraine Williams sold TSR and all its gaming properties to Wizards of the Coast for $25 million and retired to become a full-

---

* "This spell functions like Raise Dead, except that you can resurrect a creature that has been dead for as long as 10 years per caster level . . . Upon completion of the spell, the creature is immediately restored to full hit points, vigor, and health, with no loss of level." *Player's Handbook*, page 296.

time mother. Then in 1999, Wizards was bought by gaming giant Hasbro for $325 million.

As part of the same corporate family as brands including Mr. Potato Head, G.I. Joe, Monopoly, and Scrabble, Dungeons & Dragons could have been relegated to an afterthought. But credit Wizards of the Coast for helping revive the franchise with clever marketing. In 2000, after sales of the game nearly flatlined, Wizards released *Dungeons & Dragons Third Edition,* a major revision of the rules that was well received by fans. But the third edition was more than another attempt to update the core rule books; the game was released as the centerpiece of the "d20 System," an entire universe of role-playing game rules covered by an open-source content license. Inspired by the up-and-coming Linux computer operating system, these documents were free to download, copy, distribute, and use—and they quickly found their way into the hands of players around the world.

The license also granted hobbyists the right to publish their own derivative works. In the years that followed, a rich ecosystem of homemade D&D rules began to appear, mostly online, but also in gaming and book stores. Each add-on made the game more compelling, and each drew more players back into the fold.

In 2003, when Wizards followed up the d20 System with the closed-license, $20-per-book *Dungeons & Dragons Version 3.5,* they incorporated many of the best ideas of these homegrown supplements. And since the new edition remained compatible with the open-source system, it encouraged even more hobbyist development. By 2004, the thirtieth anniversary of the creation of Dungeons & Dragons, the game was growing faster than it had in a decade.

The last update leaned heavily on tech trends to attract new players. *Dungeons & Dragons Fourth Edition,* released in June 2008, tweaked the game in ways that some critics said made it too much like a video game: A wizard, for instance, could cast the same spell over and over again, ad nauseam, like a kid mashing the "attack" button on his Xbox controller. Old-school fans were horrified, but the new edition did manage to attract some younger players.

Something happened to me after that last Vampire World game. The ridiculous, surprising awesomeness of Ganubi's death and resurrection got stuck in my head: If I'd already been addicted to D&D, now I was obsessed with it. All I could think about was making more of those stories.

The day after the game, I was leaving my office for lunch when I saw a group of students in front of the nearby Parsons School of Design filming each other with an old eight-millimeter camera. It struck me as so apt for that location that I began to wonder if it was actually planned; maybe I was a PC in someone else's role-playing game, and a cosmic DM had simply rolled up "hipsters with obsolete camera" on a random-encounters table. That night I stayed up late creating role-playing game reference tables for Manhattan: Deli, roll of 12: Homeless guy asking for change. Coffee shop, roll of 4: Unpublished novelist pretending to write on a laptop computer.

I was preoccupied with the idea even into the next morning and spent my commute into work thinking about ways to model an entire role-playing game system based on "real" life. Lost in thought, I had made it all the way to the lobby of my office, when one of my friends sidled up to me and broke my train of thought. "Hey, man," he said, "do you realize you're wearing two different shoes?"

I missed the next week's game because I was out of town for work, reporting from the annual Electronic Entertainment Expo in Los Angeles. It's the video game industry's biggest trade show, an orgy of geekdom where companies like Microsoft, Nintendo, and Electronic Arts show off the coming year's new games and hardware. There are fans around the world who would kill for the opportunity to attend—and I spent most of my time sleepwalking through each high-tech presentation, thinking about games played with paper and dice.

To keep myself interested, I started asking every video game executive and designer I met the same question: Have you ever played Dungeons & Dragons? And over and over again, I heard the same thing: They loved the game when they were a kid, and it's a big part of why they ended up making games for a living.*

"Almost everybody I know in the game-design field had that experience," says Ian Bogost, a professor of media studies and interactive computing at the Georgia Institute of Technology. "They all played Dungeons & Dragons. Some maybe not as intensely . . . but that was a touch point for all of them."

D&D had a huge influence on the development of the video game industry, Bogost says, because there was a strong overlap between players of tabletop RPG games and folks who were interested in the microcomputer in the 1970s and 1980s. "The obvious thing to do was to put those two things together, because you had a system of rules, and you had a machine capable of simulating and carrying them out." And in the same way that Tolkien's fantasy fiction inspired the first role-playing games, D&D provided a model for the first video games: The idea that you have a character that has resources, moves around, encounters obstacles, and develops over time—all that came from D&D.

---

* Even Curt Schilling, the three-time World Series champion who retired from baseball and decided to start his own video game company, told me he was "a hard-core D&D guy."

In November, I had to take a business trip to London. I took a miserable red-eye flight out of New York, sleeping only about two hours on the transatlantic leg and then not at all on a connection from Dublin. By the time I got off the Heathrow Express in Paddington Station, I was tired near the point of exhaustion, so sleepy I felt like my consciousness had become detached from my body and processed everything my body was doing—walking, talking, crossing busy streets—a few seconds after it actually happened.

So naturally I dropped off my bags, pounded down two cups of extremely strong coffee, and went straight off to play Dungeons & Dragons. Fatigue be damned; if I was going to be out of town for my regular game, I had to get my fix somewhere. As soon as I had booked my ticket—and before I even found someplace to stay—I'd located a Sunday-afternoon game at the Ship, a pub on Borough Road in Southwark.

Alistair Morgan, the DM, was a thirty-seven-year-old guy who worked as an IT manager—"possibly conforming to a stereotype or two," he admitted. But three of the five players at his table were women. "There are two females in the other game that I play in at the moment as well," he told me. "I think that video games have been driving a lot of interest in D&D, and that's brought a lot more female players."

I realized we'd come full circle. D&D helped create video games; video games almost destroyed D&D; and now video games were leading people back to Dungeons & Dragons. Everyone who plays video games—and when you take into account Facebook games, console games, and smart-phone games, that's just about all of us—has been exposed to D&D's children, absorbed their D&DNA. The stigma was falling from fantasy role-playing, because it just wasn't as strange as it used to be.

One of Alistair's players was Jodi Snow, a twenty-two-year-old visual effects artist who'd been hooked on video games since she was a kid. She tried D&D for the first time in 2011, when a friend bought the game and they all gave it a go. "You hear all kinds of geeky stories about tabletop RPGs," she said, "so we were expecting something tedious and incredibly difficult to learn. But we were really surprised."

I wondered if the other women at the table might have arrived via a more traditional route—like a boyfriend who talked them into joining his game.

Actually, Alistair told me, "Cristina has dragged her husband along to play."

After I left the game at the Ship, I walked across Waterloo Bridge and toward Cambridge Circus. I was thinking about a new generation of gamers ushering in a renaissance for fantasy role-playing—D&D night, every night! Then I spotted something at the far end of a side street and did a double take—a brightly lit orange sign with black block text, just barely legible: DUNGEONS DRAGONS.

I turned on a dime and dashed across traffic toward the light. Speed-walking down the lane, my heart raced at the prospect of discovering a new game store or hobby shop, more evidence of D&D's bright future—and then I got close enough to see that the sign actually said DVD&BOOK BARGAINS.

"We're not there yet," I thought. "And I really need to think about something other than Dungeons & Dragons."

Fortunately, the following morning was completely unscheduled and my one chance to do some sightseeing. I woke up early and looked up directions to Buckingham Palace, the Tower of London, and Saint Paul's Cathedral . . . and then ignored them, hopping on the train to Kensington to visit the Doctor Who Experience, an exhibition of props and costumes from the BBC science fiction television program. Nerds will be nerds.

13

THE INN AT WORLD'S EDGE

For a long time, Morgan had been talking up something called Otherworld, an "adventure weekend" held every fall at a 4-H camp in Connecticut. Attendees dress up like wizards and warriors and spend three days trying to complete a heroic quest; Morgan discovered the event through a friend and loved it so much he joined the staff.

I begged off. While I'd become less self-conscious about my geeky pursuits, I wasn't ready to put on a costume and run around in the woods. I could justify spending one night a week pretending to be a cleric, since it's not that different from attending a poker game or bowling night. But nobody dresses up like ten-pin legend Walter "Deadeye" Williams before they head down to Barney's Bowlarama.

Besides, Otherworld sounded awfully like something I'd grown to fear and revile: a live-action role-playing game, or LARP. The very first LARP may have been Dagorhir, a medieval battle first organized in Maryland in 1977 by a Tolkien fan named Bryan Weise. Flying high on fantasy after reading *The Lord of the Rings* and watching the Sean

Connery film *Robin and Marian*, he placed an ad on a local radio station soliciting anyone who wanted "to fight in Hobbit Wars with padded weapons."

It sounds harmless enough, but to many geeks, LARPs represent the obsessive, delusional side of fantasy role-playing—the actual freaks who make the rest of us look like freaks. There's an infamous video on YouTube of a LARPer running around in the woods, dressed up as a wizard, and shouting "Lightning bolt! Lightning bolt!" Each one of its 3.6 million views has added to the perception that D&D is weird and that I spend my Tuesdays letting grown men whack me with foam swords.

Since I'd never actually tried a LARP, this bias against LARPing was completely hypocritical and uninformed. And Morgan insisted Otherworld wasn't a LARP, anyway—the emphasis, he said, is on storytelling, not rules. He argued that many of the attendees were "normal" people, role-playing naïfs approaching the experience like some sort of Outward Bound self-improvement weekend. And he made it sound like it could be fun.

I knew I was going to have to try a LARP—or something like it—if I was truly going to understand the world of fantasy role-playing. So with the convenient excuse of "reporting" wrapped around me like a Cloak of Resistance,* I signed up.

And I started getting into it. A few weeks before Otherworld, a packet arrived in the mail containing the participant handbook and a letter printed in a faux-medieval font on parchment paper. It explained that I'd be playing a mage from Keer, "a medium-sized island in the Talian sea . . . the most wonderful and most terrible place in the whole of the kingdom." The author, the Duchess of

* "These garments offer magic protection in the form of a +1 to +5 resistance bonus on all saving throws (Fortitude, Reflex and Will)." *Dungeon Master's Guide*, page 252.

Keer, explained that the island was under attack from a sea monster, a leviathan that was sinking ships and proving beyond her means to defeat. I was to travel to the mainland, to the town of World's Edge, in order to locate the legendary "Knights of the Golden Circle" and beg them for help.

To do that, the handbook explained, I'd join five other participants in an adventuring party; we'd face a series of challenges that would be resolved through role-playing, puzzle solving, and yes, foam-sword combat. Aside from a short briefing on Friday night, we'd inhabit a fantasy world until Sunday evening; for just under forty-eight hours, I'd stop being ordinary Dave and become "a heroic version" of myself. In other words: I'd be running around in the woods, dressed up as a wizard, and shouting, "Lightning bolt! Lightning bolt!"

As self-loathing began to rise, I constructed my character. Otherworld participants aren't assigned a PC; they rely on their own attributes and skills, not numbers on a character sheet. But they are expected to integrate into the story, and that requires a costume, a character name, and a background for your heroic self.

I decided my mage was a scholar of magic, detached and intellectual—a character choice clearly driven by psychological defense mechanisms. I named my wizard Dewey, after the library classification system. The fact that I thought this indicated winking ironic detachment—instead of providing proof I was already the world's biggest nerd—shows my level of delusion.

For a costume, I'd wear brown cargo pants and a dark blue henley shirt, topped by a dramatic ankle-length black fleece cloak. At $200, the handmade item (ordered from a costume shop specializing in LARPs and historical reenactments) represented a level of financial commitment that might signify I was taking this seriously. So I told Kara and the few friends who knew where I was going that the purchase was a dodge, allowing me to wear normal clothes underneath.

(Secretly, I was pretty damn stoked: I challenge any even slightly geeky person to put on a real, high-quality cloak and not imagine they're Gandalf, Dumbledore, and/or Luke Skywalker.) A hand-bound leather journal completed the ensemble—my "spell book," doubling as reporter's notebook.

The Otherworld Adventure was held that year on the first weekend in October at the Windham-Tolland 4-H Camp in Pomfret, Connecticut. It's a lovely spot in the rolling hills about 150 miles northeast of Manhattan, a three-hour drive unless you're dumb enough to leave your Fifth Avenue office right before rush hour, in which case it takes six hours. When I finally arrived, the only light in the camp came from a two-story lodge, built into a hill so its basement opened onto the parking lot.

As I entered, I realized I was the last one there. Seven groups of six people perched on wooden benches turned, laughed, and gave me an ovation. I smiled gamely, grabbed the nearest open seat, and tried to score a 20 on my Hide roll.

Kristi Hayes, one of Otherworld's founders and its current writer and director, stood at the front of the room, giving final directions. Only rogues may disarm traps, she warned us. Stay hydrated. Don't hit people on the head with your sword.

The demographic breakdown of the participants was my first surprise of the weekend. Nearly half of them were women, and while twenty- and thirty-year-olds did constitute the single largest group, there was a decent number of adults outside that age range.

The six adventurers from Keer were no exception. Three of them, young women from Austin, Texas, had come to Otherworld as part of a thirtieth-birthday celebration. Jen, the birthday girl, would play our bard, "Kinkaid." She wore fashionable large-frame glasses, a stud in her lip, and sparkly tights under a knee-length green cloak. Summer (a rogue called "Pearl") bore a resemblance to Ally Sheedy in

The Breakfast Club; her costume included a blue and gold jacket that looked like it was designed by John Galliano for a pirate-themed fashion show, lost at the Milan airport, and rediscovered years later in a Texarkana thrift store. She got compliments on it all weekend long. Elaine (a ranger, "Merrick") was tall and thin and slightly boyish—or at least that was the effect of the overalls and flannel she wore for a costume. Charron was also female, but older, probably north of sixty. She was local and, like me, had a friend on the Otherworld staff. She'd play "Willow," our cleric. The final member of the party was comfortably familiar: Phil, from Boston, a tall thirtyish white guy, quiet and a little nerdy. He told me he'd be playing a paladin named "Sure, Swift Justice" . . . but I could call him "Justice."

There was also a fifth member of our party. Chris, a six-year veteran of the Otherworld staff, would be our companion for the weekend. A combination of a camp counselor and a fixer, a companion is charged with keeping their team from breaking anything important—including bones, the rules, and the story line. Chris grew up on Long Island and seemed familiar to me, perhaps because he fell into a common Suffolk County archetype: an upper-middle-class joe, fond of boating or lacrosse, inevitably described as "a good guy." He was slightly short, with an athletic build, a healthy tan, and hair cut close to hide where it was thinning and receding.

Chris's first duty was to lead us outside, and to our combat training. Since the ultimate goal of an event like Otherworld is to immerse yourself in fantasy, these games eschew dice-rolling in favor of actual—though carefully mediated—physical confrontation. LARP battle rules can get quite complex; at Otherworld they keep things simple. Each character gets a set number of "free hits" (hit points, basically) and each time you get touched with a sword, you lose one. When you're down to zero, a hit on a limb means you must stop using that limb; a hit to the torso knocks you unconscious. When that happens, you fall down and quietly count to fifty; if no one comes to your aid before you finish, you're dead.

As a mage, I had just one free hit, making me the weakest member of the party. I could get hit at most three times (anywhere, limb, anywhere) or as little as two times (anywhere, then torso) and be killed stone dead. Fortunately, as Ganubi has demonstrated, death is rarely permanent in fantasy role-playing games. At Otherworld, getting killed means you become a ghost, and you take a piece of cheesecloth out of your pocket and drape it over your head like a Scooby-Doo villain. You're not allowed to speak or physically interact with people, and you must remain that way until resurrected by a cleric's spell or magic potion.

A friendly staffer handed us each our "boffers"—three-foot-long swords built on a rigid core, but padded all over with thick black foam. They're light and easy to wield, and when you're hit with one, it hurts about as much as getting tagged in a pillow fight. My compatriots were all issued swords that were about three feet long; as the mage, I received a dirk, about a foot shorter but otherwise identical. I couldn't help myself: "It's not the size of the sword, but how you use it," I told them.

We then squared off against six staffers for a brief bit of sparring. I'm no fencing expert—my knowledge doesn't extend much beyond en garde and touché—but I think our performance would be classified as *manger la merde*. Sword fighting is complicated even when your health isn't on the line, and when you're in actual group combat, with enemies coming at you from all sides, it's incredibly difficult.

Once we were trained and equipped, Chris wished us good luck and pointed toward a man standing near the corner of the lodge, where a path wound uphill and around the building to its as-yet-unseen main entrance. "The Storyteller will walk you up to the tavern," he told us. "I'll see you later." He turned and walked back into the basement.

I glanced over to Jen, looking for someone to take charge, but her eyes reflected my own sudden panic. I was hoping that Chris would provide a buffer between me and *them,* that he'd be my ambassador to Otherworld and allow me to maintain emotional and intellectual distance. But now he was gone, and the members of my party seemed no more ready to commit to the fantasy than I was. I took a breath, successfully rolled an internal Will save, and walked forward.

Fortunately, the Storyteller didn't cut an imposing figure. His round body was wrapped in a professorial tweed jacket, complete with leather patches; at his neck, a faded yellow scarf was tied in an ascot knot. His thick head of brown curly hair made me think of Bilbo Baggins.

The Storyteller held a leather-bound book in front of him, and as we approached, he looked down and began to read.

"Once upon a time, in the kingdom of Lyria, six travelers embarked on a dangerous expedition," he said. "They were asked to leave their homes and families to travel all the way to World's Edge, a tiny village situated at the far border of the civilized lands. It would be a perilous journey, they knew, but the need in their homeland was very great, and so the travelers shouldered their packs and began the trip.

"They marched for days and days, not daring to tarry in any given place for very long. Every day they delayed increased the chances they would be unable to complete their mission in time, and though they spoke little of this, the knowledge weighed heavy upon them all."

He turned and began leading us up the path, still reading from his book. We left the training area behind us and stepped into the unknown.

"Upon reaching the border of Moreth, the westernmost duchy in Lyria, all the travelers looked around themselves in anticipation. Moreth was renowned as a land of strange magical energies, and inexplicable phenomena were said to be commonplace there.

"The danger they encountered on their first night in Moreth, however, was of the nonmagical variety: While the group slept, their camp was set upon by a gang of bandits. The party of travelers escaped with their lives, but the bandits absconded with most of the coins they had carried.

"Still, the adventurers' spirits were raised as they neared their destination. The autumn days were pleasant for walking, and the countryside and woodlands of Moreth were very beautiful."

At the top of the hill, all was wildness and moonlight. A lake appeared at our right, shimmering and tranquil, undisturbed but for a few wisps of fog. Beyond it, hills and forest extended to the horizon, no lights, no cars, the trees interrupted only by a few indistinct dark shadows. Cabins, probably, but perhaps something stranger.

"Night had fallen dark and silent around them by the time they reached their goal. Coming down the wooded trail, they saw lights shining from a building." To our left, the lodge had been transformed: Flickering candlelight spilled out of the windows, and the faint sounds of tavern life: a low hum of voices, clinking glasses, indecipherable fragments of conversation. The Storyteller stopped at the threshold.

"They had reached their destination at last. The six stepped up to the door and entered the Inn at World's Edge."

I recall those last few steps to the tavern in vivid detail. Self-conscious, nervous, and worried about what lay ahead, I'd been an easy target for simple theatrics and gently hypnotized by the Storyteller's tale. The other members of my party seemed similarly affected. We pushed open the doors and walked inside.

The Inn at World's Edge was a welcome sight after a long journey from Keer, warm, cozy, and safe. Small groups of strangers huddled in the dim light, dressed in simple tunics, vests, hose, and cloaks. They leaned forward and talked in low voices, as if a word spoken too loudly might wake them from a dream.

Our party took seats at a table covered with dark cloth and set with eight heavy pewter plates. A lantern and small candles flickered at the center. On the wall to our right, a royal-blue banner emblazoned with a sunburst hung above a stone fireplace—the crest of Baron Valerius, the noble who governs World's Edge.

After a few moments, a woman in a plain cloth dress with a lace-up bodice approached the table and bid us welcome. She handed us heavy ceramic mugs, stepped away for a moment, and returned with a pitcher of wine and a charger covered with grapes, cheese, and chunks of cured meat. Famished, we fell on it with gusto.

A few minutes later, we were joined by the final member of our party. A man stood at the head of our table, wearing a loose blue tunic. He seemed familiar to me . . . slightly short, with an athletic build, a healthy tan, and hair cut close to hide where it was thinning and receding.

"My name is Kint," he said, smiling. "May I join you?" He took a seat at our table. "What brings you to World's Edge?"

Otherworld is a little bit like Fight Club: There's brawling, there are secret missions, and you're not supposed to talk about it. Participants—who may only attend once—are asked to keep the plot a secret; I'm risking a boffer sword up my backside over the few details I've already shared.

The code of silence isn't a by-product of Project Mayhem–style brainwashing, despite the hugely dedicated staff. (Otherworld is run by former participants like Morgan who return year after year to share the experience; their level of devotion may border on cultlike, but it lacks any of the creepy implications.) Instead, it's all about spoilers. The Otherworld weekend is really a massive piece of interactive theater, with a script, a cast of characters, and a set of plotlines, some of which repeat year after year. Being a participant feels something like if you climbed up on the stage during the final act of *Hamlet* and kicked Laertes in the crotch . . . and the actors responded by working you into the story and reciting dialogue the Bard had written in case this sort of thing happened.

Otherworld was founded in 1991 by four members of Quest, a Connecticut-based LARPing group. Several months after completing a particularly challenging adventure, they received a letter from one of the participants.

"It was from a woman who'd attended, and she started by saying, 'You're going to think I'm crazy, but the event you ran changed my life,'" says Kristi Hayes. "She was working in a dead-end job she hated, and she was living with her boyfriend, who from the sound of it was really treating her pretty badly. She'd sort of accepted that . . . this was probably about the best she could expect from life.

"And then, she said, she came and spent the weekend having all these adventures and doing all these challenging things. She was particularly afraid of any sort of public speaking, but at one point during the event, the story line took a dark turn and she had an idea about how to fix things, so she stood up in a crowded room and told everyone about it. People listened to her and followed her idea, and as it turned out, doing so saved the day.

"She told us that for a long while after coming home from the event, she continued on with her normal less-than-stellar routine but often thought about the weekend. She thought about the person she'd been there, the one who'd stood up in front of all those people, even though she was afraid, and convinced them to listen to her. And I will never forget what she wrote about that . . . '*She* would never put up with crap like this. *She* would find a way to fix things . . . if I can do heroic things when I'm running around in the woods, why can't I do them here at home?'

"And then she did. She went out and got herself a better job and she ditched the lousy boyfriend. She'd made those changes and built herself a better life, and she felt like she needed to write to us and thank us for it. That was just amazing to me, that we'd been able to help someone reach that point. And we started thinking, 'Gosh, if this event did all that, when really our only goal going into it was for everyone to have fun, well, what would happen if we ran events where we tried to give people these opportunities?'"

Because Otherworld deliberately courts non-LARPer participants, it does away with many of the rules typically found in those games. There are no skill points or attributes, and even though you adopt a fantasy name, you remain yourself; you're not role-playing a character with its own personality.

"I'm always hesitant to use the word 'role-playing' to describe what you're doing at Otherworld, because it so often makes people think they'll be pretending to be someone other than themselves," says Hayes. "Still, having said that, we've certainly borrowed plenty of ideas from D&D and other role-playing games. We've also borrowed ideas from experience-based educational groups like Outward Bound, and then mixed them up together to make something related to both but its own separate thing."

Otherworld also simplifies the rules for activities like spell casting. In many LARPs, if you want to shoot a lightning bolt at an enemy, you have to hit them with a thrown beanbag while calling out the name of the spell ("Lightning bolt! Lightning bolt!"). At Otherworld, you blow a whistle, everyone freezes in place, and you read from a script that tells everyone exactly how to react:

"I, [name], a mage of Fire, do cast the spell of Lightning Bolt upon [select one target]. I now call down from the sky a mighty bolt of lightning, which will strike your [specify one limb of your target]."

Otherworld focuses on story, not game play; it's trying to impart an experience. In many LARPs the plot is utilitarian—"The red army and the blue army are at war" or "You've been hired to kill an evil lich."* At Otherworld, there's a fully developed narrative, a central shared conflict, and dozens of party-specific subplots.

Kint was so moved by our tale of the leviathan and Keer's desperate need for help that he offered to serve as our companion. He had a house not far from the tavern where we could spend our nights and promised to introduce us to locals who might help with our quest: Solomon, the innkeeper; Serendipity Bostwich, a scholar and scientist; and Obsidian, a cleric rumored to be among the most powerful in the kingdom.

We were discussing our first steps when the doors of the tavern opened and a man entered whose presence silenced all conversation. Tall and handsome, he was dressed in a scarlet tailcoat and wore a black top hat, which he tipped from his head and tucked in the crook of his arm.

"Ladies and gentlemen," he called to the crowd, "I am Maximilian Von Horn, ringmaster of the Circus Eternal." The troupe, he told us, had set up camp on the edge of town and for the next two weeks would hold nightly performances. We would have a chance to witness some of the finest traveling entertainers in the kingdom: acrobats, jugglers, a strongman, even a fire dancer.

The pronouncement was met with cheers from the crowd. "Do you have any clowns?" a woman yelled from a table across the room.

Von Horn scowled at the thought. "Clowns, my dear, are an unfortunate side effect of circuses."

---

* "An undead spellcaster, usually a wizard or sorcerer but sometimes a cleric or other spellcaster, who has used its magical powers to unnaturally extend its life." *Monster Manual*, page 166.

My weekend in Connecticut saw the second and final performance of *The Circus Eternal,* a story told over the entire weekend, starring most of the staff and every Otherworld participant. (Each party also has its own subplot, drawn from a pool of frequently repeated conflicts—we were not the first travelers from Keer with a nasty leviathan problem.)

Sometimes the story advanced through a form of dinner theater: When our party visited the tavern for meals, staff members (in character as residents of World's Edge) would stand to make pronouncements or act out scripted conflicts. At other times the actors used a kind of directed improvisation: while walking across town, our party might run into Bumble the Wizard or Professor Chuttlesworth, who just happened to mention a suspicious crime that had occurred the week before last.

Typically, Hayes writes a new story every two years. They're meant to entertain using elements of traditional theater (*The Circus Eternal* even included a musical number) but also to encourage participation. Each story places the village in some sort of peril and requires the participants to work toward its salvation.

It's a surprisingly effective technique. Sure, you might lose yourself in the drama if you sit in a theater and watch a play about a village in peril. But when you sit *in the village* and the actors come up to you, take your hand, and beg for your help, it's wholly engrossing.

"As a human, I think it's only natural for me to be really interested in myself," says Hayes. "So a story in which I personally play a key part? That's a story I'm going to find very compelling . . . and when I have the opportunity to do incredible things and amaze even myself with what I accomplish, seeing the story unfold is going to have a really powerful effect.

"It's like when you watch a feel-good movie and you cheer at the end, because the hero triumphs over adversity and you're left with this warm glow inside. This kind of story has all that, but the person who triumphs over adversity is you. That's really powerful."

I am not a fan of audience participation; when I'm in a theater and the performers step offstage, I tend to shrink in my chair and pray they'll pick the sucker sitting next to me. But Otherworld is designed from the ground up to pull people out of their seat and into the action, and it's so smartly scripted you can't help but be drawn in.

"Each staff handbook I write is about four hundred to four hundred fifty pages long," says Hayes. "It's not a true script, of course, in that I rarely tell our eighty-plus staff people exactly what to say. Instead, I tell them about all of their characters—each Otherworld story line has about one hundred characters, not including monsters and encounters of that sort—and the backstory and then also about the rough timeline of the weekend."

My favorite moments were when a seemingly improvised comment turned out to be a crucial element of the story. For instance, as the plot of *The Circus Eternal* played out, it became clear that Maximilian Von Horn's traveling show was more than it appeared to be. A full day after his introduction in the tavern, several parties were ambushed and killed by strange monsters in the woods—evil creatures in creepy harlequin makeup, carrying massive swords. It turned out clowns really were "an unfortunate side effect of circuses."

Successfully executing those plot twists requires tight scripting, but Otherworld also requires improvisation and flexibility, so players can make their own decisions. They need to feel like they're achieving something, instead of just watching, and that's where the companions come in.

Embedded into our party as Kint, Chris was able to gently nudge us the way we needed to go while maintaining an illusion of free will. He'd offer suggestions and advice, but since they came from a member of the group, it didn't feel like we were being railroaded.

In one task, we discovered we needed to enter the realm of Death to obtain a magic item, but the local portal to the underworld was kept closed by Bumble the Wizard, who cast a spell each morning sealing the way. Bumble—a genial but forgetful fellow, his brain lightly fried by arcane forces—wore a string tied around his finger to remind him of this responsibility. So our party decided our best plan was to wait until Bumble was alone, sneak up behind him, and bash him on the head. We'd steal the string and run off, ensuring that he'd forget his duties, the portal would open, and we'd gain access.

It was a fine plan, except for the fact that the weekend's story hinged on a totally different way to open the portal; doing so early would destroy the plot and the weekend—and we'd all be wanted criminals once Bumble woke up and reported how we'd assaulted and robbed him.

Chris initially tried to warn us off gently ("Maybe there's another way?"). When we couldn't come up with a better idea, he made an emotional appeal ("Bumble's a nice guy, do you really want to hurt him?"). When we revealed ourselves as unfeeling brutes, he succeeded through misdirection ("Since you guys can't decide, why don't we do something else and come back to this later?"). Of course, we had decided, but he was able to make his own reservations feel like they were shared. When we tried to return to our ill-considered plan later, he found ways to put us off until the situation resolved itself as planned ("Hey, who's hungry?").

Other staff members face their own challenges. Only companions play a single character over the course of a weekend; most staffers play multiple roles, hiding behind monster masks or makeup. They have to make quick changes and move rapidly from one area of the camp to another. In the staff area of the main lodge there's a massive spreadsheet hung on the walls, stretching from floor to ceiling, easily sixty feet long. It describes where each and every person needs to be at each moment, and in which costume, over the course of the entire weekend. It looks like something you might have found in George Patton's command center during the North African campaigns.

Chris also carried an iPhone in his pocket all weekend, running a staff-designed application that used the phone's GPS antenna to track our party's movements. Organizers planned to analyze the data after the fact to determine common routes around the camp and when attendees tend to do different activities. Ultimately, it will help make the weekend's planning even more precise.

The stagecraft is immensely detailed, too. Otherworld's props, sets, and costumes may be constructed by amateurs, but they're convincing enough. When I first walked into the Inn at World's Edge, I didn't see a 4-H camp mess hall—I saw something straight out of Tolkien. It might as well have been the Prancing Pony, where Frodo and his friends met the ranger Strider.

"One of my goals, and one of the ways that the stories I'm writing are different from most other authors', is that I'm really looking to create scenes we can bring to life with a reasonably high degree of realism," says Hayes. "I won't write a story that's set in a castle, because as much as I love to read novels set in castles, we don't have a castle at our disposal, and I don't want to settle for a room with cardboard rocks taped to the wall and a 'pretend this is a castle' sign. That's why, at Otherworld, you won't meet anyone who can fly."

By Saturday night, when the rising action hit a fever pitch, I'd been completely drawn into the adventure. Living in a ubiquitous fiction—one made of not just words but physical objects and real people—made me realize how stupid it was to be self-conscious, and I began to truly enjoy the adventure. When a crisis arose that required all eight parties to team up and tackle three simultaneous battles, I committed wholeheartedly—and fought tooth and nail with a dozen strangers, swinging my foam sword like it was Excalibur.

When the adventurers from Keer all returned to our shared cabin—tired, dirty, and triumphant—we were completely sold on the idea we were heroes. As we settled into bed, we swapped tales of our victories; Jen offered a well-deserved victory speech. "Other people went out drinking for their thirtieth birthday," she said. "I slayed a fucking banshee."

I had a great weekend, but something was amiss. As the event concluded on Sunday, I heard other participants describe their adventure in terms like "life-changing" and "best thing I've ever done"—and I couldn't reciprocate. Sure, it was fun . . . but not profound. I wondered why I didn't share that experience.

It's possible my initial fears and prejudices kept me from fully enjoying the event, but I doubt it. I'm sure everyone else started out nervous, but before long we were all fully engaged. Instead, I think the people affected most strongly by Otherworld lack my regular access to fantasy. Sure, they might watch *Game of Thrones* or play World of Warcraft, but that's observation, not participation. Their personal day-to-day existence is mundane: expected, explainable. We all live in the muggle world, and only a few of us are lucky enough to get a peek into Hogwarts.

I'm no wizard—but once a week, I *feel* like I am. Role-playing games allow me to experience the fantastic, and even though it's make-believe, the catharsis is real. My life isn't wanting for magic, because I've got Dungeons & Dragons.

14

D&D NEXT

A few weeks after Otherworld, I packed my dice and set out for a new adventure. I'd been sick and wasn't ready to travel—for all I knew I was patient zero in a major outbreak of Captain Trips, the Andromeda Strain, or spattergroit. But a few weeks earlier, I'd received an offer I couldn't refuse:

"Wizards of the Coast would like to invite you to our headquarters in Renton, Washington, to take part in an exclusive Dungeons & Dragons Summit. As one of our trusted press partners, and a respected member of the D&D community, you have been chosen to participate in this private meeting where we will share some exciting news."

Journalists get offers like this all the time. Companies try to get us interested in covering upcoming products by using words like "exclusive" and "exciting," and flattering us that we're "respected." It's a carnival pitch: corporate marketing manager as barker, reporter as mark. I like to think of myself, at least in professional terms, as a cynical ink-stained wretch. So I delete most of these entreaties and give them little thought.

But this one hit me hard. The people who make D&D think I'm a respected member of their community? Reading that turned me to putty; it was something like Jesus, Krishna, or Delleb* coming down from heaven and saying, "Hey, man—you're pretty cool."

Did I want to fly cross-country while exhausted and sick, sit in a conference room, and watch people read from a PowerPoint presentation? If they were the people who make D&D, hell yes I did. I also had an inkling that their "exciting news" might be a brand-new edition of Dungeons & Dragons, so forget battling the flu: For a chance to be one of the first people to see D&D 5.0, I'd fight a bugbear with a sling made from the elastic band of my own underpants.

Ground zero for the worldwide phenomenon of Dungeons & Dragons, the home of the greatest fantasy game of all time, the place where imaginations soar and adventures begin . . . is a boxy, glass-covered building in an ordinary office park. Wizards of the Coast's corporate headquarters is located in a blue-collar Seattle suburb; there's day care on the ground floor and a nice little coffee shop.

But on the fourth floor of the building, corporate normalcy fails its saving throw and dies. A twelve-foot-tall statue of a red dragon looms over the reception area; uncut sheets of Magic: The Gathering cards hang framed on the walls; conference rooms are labeled with names like "The Tomb of Horrors" and "Leomund's Tiny Hut."** A

---

* "Lesser God (Lawful Good): Delleb, an old man clutching a white book, cares only for the accumulation of knowledge . . . his clerics quote from book after book of scriptures, but the libraries in a temple of Delleb have books on all topics, not just religious matters." *The Complete Divine,* page 122.

** "When this spell is cast, the magic-user causes an opaque sphere of force to come into being around his or her person . . . The tiny hut will withstand winds up to 50 m.p.h. [but] in no way will Leomund's Tiny Hut provide protection from missiles, weapons, spells, and the like." *Advanced Dungeons & Dragons Players Handbook,* page 74.

staffer led me to a large conference room, where I joined a few other "respected members of the D&D community" in trying to sit still and avoid passing out from excitement.

Thankfully, Liz Schuh, Wizards of the Coast's head of publishing for Dungeons & Dragons, got right to the point. "We're in the midst of what a lot of people call edition wars," she told us. "We want to fix that. We don't want there to be a break in the audience. So we're here to tell you about the next edition of Dungeons & Dragons . . . a new, universally compatible set."

Here's the problem, as Wizards saw it: Dungeons & Dragons was no longer a single game. For decades, the company kept changing the rules and releasing new editions, because it was a good way to get players to keep spending money. But every time they updated the rules, they left a fraction of the customer base behind: people who preferred the old rules or couldn't afford the new. Now, half a dozen* versions later, the customer base was so fractured that only a small percentage of the people who played D&D actually paid for D&D. Most of them are still using the books they bought years—or decades—ago.

It was a big problem for players too. Every time we'd lost a player in the Vampire World game, we'd struggled to replace them, because we were looking for members of a subculture's subculture: not just D&D players, but players who knew and preferred the 3.5 edition rules. Trying to find a new player was like trying to find a needle in a haystack among a field of haystacks.

To solve the problem, Wizards had set an ambitious goal: to create a "universal rule set" that unifies all players under one single system.

---

* Even though we call the current edition of D&D "4.0," there have been many more major revisions: Original, Basic, Advanced, Advanced Second Edition, 3.0, 3.5, 4.0.

Mike Mearls, senior manager of the D&D research and development team, took the floor to explain what that meant. "We're focusing on what gets people excited about D&D and making sure we have a game that encompasses all different styles," he said. "Even if you haven't played in twenty years, we want you to be able to sit down and say, 'This is D&D.'"

Almost a year ago, Mearls explained, he sat down with his team, read through the rules, and played a few sessions of each edition of the game going back to 1974. Their goal was to look past the rules and identify the core of D&D, the experiences that define it—like exploration, combat, adventure, and story. The thinking was that if the game *feels* like D&D, the rules don't matter. Players respond to the experience and only notice the rules when they get in the way.

Of course, different people seek out different experiences. A group of old grognards that's spent the last forty years clearing out dungeons doesn't want the same thing as a clan of artsy college kids who are really into theatrical role-playing. To address that, the new edition was being conceived of as a modular, flexible system, easily customized to individual preferences.

"Just like a player makes his character, the Dungeon Master can make his rule set," Mearls said. "He might say, 'I'm going to run a military campaign, it's going to be a lot of fighting' . . . so he'd use the combat chapter, drop in miniatures rules, and include the martial arts optional rules. You can have as little or as much customization as you want. It's about letting people find their own way to play."

Mearls and Schuh weren't ready to talk about specific products. But in practice, I imagine the game will be built around a few core rule books—like the *Player's Handbook, Dungeon Master's Guide,* and *Monster Manual*—that describe the concept of D&D, its basic execution, and its fantasy setting. What rules they do contain will be simple and direct. Then, around that core, will be a whole universe of books that provide personalization to forty years of gamers. Are you an old-school gamer who wants to determine each day's weather and track the effects of temperature and precipitation on your character? Buy the new *Wilderness Survival Guide*. Do you prefer the fourth edition and want characters with powers that have push-button simplicity? Try *Heroes of Will*, a book with a long list of 4.0-style character classes.

Mearls doesn't want to tell people how to play the game—he was on the staff of designers that put together D&D 4.0 and learned first-hand why that's a bad idea. "With fourth edition, there was a huge focus on mechanics," he said. "The story was still there, but a lot of our customers were having trouble getting to it. In some ways, it was like we told people, 'The right way to play guitar is to play thrash metal.' But there's other ways to play guitar."

This time around, the idea is to make a core that everyone can agree on, provide extensions so each gaming group can customize—and then make the real money selling add-on products: campaign settings like Greyhawk; adventure modules like *The Tomb of Horrors*; accessories like miniatures; and even digital services, where you might charge gamers $9.99 a month to access tools like character-building apps, map generators, and virtual tabletops.

Mearls's biggest job is to get that core set of rule books just exactly right. It needs to feel like a fantasy role-playing game, not a video game, or a card game, or a combat simulator. It needs to be simple without being stupid, and efficient without being shallow. And it must encourage players to explore, create, and tell compelling stories. Mearls needs to capture the flavor of Dungeons & Dragons, the *feeling*. Everything else is just a distraction.

"D&D is like the wardrobe people go through to get to Narnia," he told us. "If you walk through and there's a McDonald's, it's like, 'This isn't Narnia.'"

The impending fifth edition of Dungeons & Dragons was announced on January 9, 2012. In a column posted on Wizards of the Coast's website, Mike Mearls revealed to the world that the game—now officially code-named "D&D Next"—was under development. He also announced an open-to-the-public play test, starting that spring. "By involving you in this process, we can build a set of D&D rules that incorporate the wants and desires of D&D gamers around the world," he wrote. "We want a game that rises above differences of play styles, campaign settings, and editions, one that takes the fundamental essence of D&D and brings it to the forefront."

A new edition of Scrabble or Monopoly rarely attracts the news media's attention. But D&D is embedded so deep in the heart of American pop culture that *The New York Times* covered the news on the front page of its arts section. The article's author, journalist and memoirist Ethan Gilsdorf, quoted me regarding the difficulties of playing D&D across editions: "Imagine trying to organize a basketball team, if the point guard adheres to modern league rules, but the center only knows how to play ancient Mayan handball." I'm not sure which inflated my nerd ego more: the implicit confirmation of my status as D&D expert, or successfully dropping a *tlachtli* reference in the newspaper of record.

Fan reaction to the announcement was initially skeptical, but much of their angst seemed to be connected to old grievances. "Too little, too late," one commenter wrote on the story I published online about the new edition. "The rules had better be amazing, and the marketing very apologetic to us 'grognards' if WotC is going to have any chance of drawing some of us back."

James Maliszewski, author of the role-playing games blog Grognardia, was also skeptical. "Allow me a momentary guffaw at the notion that Humpty Dumpty can ever be put back together again," he wrote. "I don't doubt for a minute WotC's sincerity in wanting to hear what D&D fans have to say about the future of the game, but I also think it's a recipe for disaster, especially given how fragmented the fanbase is these days."

The loudest dissent seemed to come from players of fourth-edition Dungeons & Dragons, who faced not only their own obsolescence but the implication that the game they loved was an embarrassing mistake. (To be fair, these players did get a raw deal; a lot of them invested serious time and money in the product, only to see it become the shortest-lived rule set in D&D's history.) Wizards tried to reassure them by saying they would continue publishing fourth-edition rule books until the fifth edition was finished, and promised that there'd still be room for "fourth edition–style play"—but I couldn't help but hear these assurances in the disdainful voice of a nerd talking to someone they think is below them: "My new computer has a six-core four-point-two megahertz processor, sixteen gigabytes of quad-channel RAM, eight terabytes of . . . yes, *Mother,* you can still play solitaire on it."

Still, most D&D fans seemed hopeful. Dedicated players may complain about changes, but ultimately they can't help but root for the game's future success; they care too much about it. One player wrote this comment on my story:

"The D&D player is a business manager that wants to take on trolls under the bridge on a Friday night . . . a chemical engineer [who] wants to rescue the gnome prince from the clutches of the evil duergar . . . a teacher who hunts for Beholders in the Underdark. The D&D fan comes in all sorts of shapes and sizes, but the hunger is unique; it is a hunger for adventure and ultimately to escape. I'm glad that [Wizards] is worried about the fans and the players. Let's just hope that they are as hungry for adventure as the players are."

Anxious D&D players got their first taste of the new edition two weeks later, when Wizards staff appeared to run play tests at the D&D Experience, a convention in Fort Wayne, Indiana. I was twitching at the prospect of another chance to play the game, so I booked a ticket—and then spent the intervening weeks complaining to friends about being forced to visit the frigid Great Lakes region in January. Fortunately, Fort Wayne International Airport provided a gentle welcome: There's a vintage Ms. Pac-Man machine right in the terminal, and when you walk outside security, a peppy gray-haired volunteer greets you with a smile and a free cookie from the bakery across the street.

The Grand Wayne Convention Center was less warm but nice enough. When I arrived, I bought one $8 ticket allowing me access to the "D&D Secret Special," Wizards of the Coast's public debut of the fifth-edition rules. Over the course of the convention, Wizards' staff and a small cadre of volunteer Dungeon Masters would lead ten four-hour play-test sessions; during each, multiple tables of gamers would run first-level pregenerated characters through the same short adventure. By Sunday afternoon, over five hundred fans would have gotten their first taste of the new D&D.

Fittingly, Wizards of the Coast set their debut game in the Caves of Chaos—the monster-filled caverns from *The Keep on the Borderlands,* a classic 1979 adventure module. It's reassuring to know future generations of gamers may first experience D&D the same way I did: killing kobolds (or getting killed by kobolds) in the twisty passages of a Gygax adventure.

By the time I found my table it was nearly full, and most of the pregenerated characters were taken. Dallas and Angela, a cute young couple, both wore identical blue T-shirts depicting Doctor Who's time machine, the TARDIS. Dallas had chosen to play a halfling rogue, Angela a half-orc fighter. John, a pale middle-aged midwestern dad, was playing an elf wizard. Mike, another fiftysomething dad, was one of the few black people at the convention. He'd chosen a dwarf cleric.

That left me with either a human female paladin or a tiefling warlord. Tieflings made their D&D debut in 1994 as a monster race in the AD&D *Planescape Campaign Setting*. They're half-demons, descendants of a human empire that made a pact with devils to gain power and territory. Tieflings appeared as a playable character race in the fourth edition *Player's Handbook*—the same time the warlord became a character class. Warlords are tactical experts, designed to increase the effectiveness of allies: Their powers include such exciting options as Commander's Strike ("With a shout, you command an ally to attack"), Viper's Strike ("You trick your adversary into making a tactical error that gives your comrade a chance to strike"), and Surprise Attack ("Despite the chaos of battle, you see a golden opportunity for an ally to make a surprising attack").

I took the paladin. Dame Eilora Arroway, a human noble, strong of heart and low on hit points. My character sheet told me she wore chain mail and carried a very big sword; I'd have to dream up any further characterization on the fly.

Our final player, Daniel, arrived shortly after I'd settled in and got stuck with the warlord. Ex-military, he wore his hair typically short, but the large earring dangling from his left lobe would have gone better with a ball gown than combat camouflage.

Our Dungeon Master, Willi, told us we'd have four hours to run a simple mission, hopefully comprising several fights and a bit of role-playing. He started our adventure in the obvious place.

A paladin swears to live by a code—to uphold the law, protect the innocent, and destroy evil. We must be paragons of virtue and, by example, inspire righteousness in those around us.

But that is not to say we cannot enjoy a few drinks with friends. I was tippling with a chosen few when a stranger approached us. He told us he had just been elected mayor and wished to serve a rare dwarven ale at his inauguration. When none could be found, he hired a merchant to ship the cask to town—but the merchant was due two days ago and had presumably been waylaid by monsters.

At this, I stood and addressed him. "Never fear, sir. I swear to you: If your man still lives, I will find him and bring him to safety. If he has been killed, I will hunt the beasts that committed the evil act and smite them."

The man waved his hand in the air between us. "If you bring back the merchant, that's all well and good," he said. "Just go and recover that cask of dwarven ale before some kobold drinks it."

John had a pile of equipment with him at the table—a respectable hoard of gaming accessories including a hand-carved wooden curio box full of dice, a pile of miniature figurines, and a bag I suspect contained a battle mat and dry-erase pens. He stopped the action to ask if they'd be needed.

"We're gonna have several encounters where we might do some fighting," Willi told us. "Some of the simpler ones, I'm gonna do the 'theater of the mind's eye' thing. I'll describe things, and you'll tell me what you're doing. We'll worry about exact distances or things like that if they become real necessary. If we start doing something that's really complicated, we'll throw out a battle mat, but for the most part we won't really worry about the details so much; we'll just get into the story of what we're doing."

We walked north from town for an entire day and saw no tracks or signs of the missing merchant. Finally, as we entered a small valley, we spotted an abandoned, broken wagon in the distance, next to a large brown-colored mound.

Fargrim, the dwarf, hefted his axe and trotted toward the cart. "I'm going to see if I can find a barrel," he rumbled. I joined him, and Zarlasa the wizard followed a few feet behind.

"As you approach, you see the wagon is tilted to one side because one of the wheels has come off," Willi said. "The mound in front is actually a dead horse, and there's no barrels in obvious view. As you're looking and poking around a little bit, three red bugs about yea long"—at this, he held up his hands about a foot apart—"with lots and lots of little legs, come scurrying out from under and inside the horse, and head toward the three of you."

Daniel chuckled. His warlord, Graben, had stayed behind with Angela's fighter, Nordik, and Dallas's rogue, Petrim. "Sucks for you guys," he said.

Willi checked the play-test rules and continued. "As they come out from under cover, please make a Wisdom [roll] for me, to see if you're surprised."

John picked a d20 from the bottom half of his dice box and rolled it into the empty top—19. Mike rolled a 16.

I picked up a black d20, a nice one with sharp corners and bright red numbers, and let it tumble from my hand to the table. It came up 1. Eilora wasn't simply surprised, she was stunned.

I'm at a loss to explain it, but I have pathetic luck when I'm not playing Weslocke. In half a dozen recent games across four time zones and two continents, I've rolled so poorly it's like I'm playing with a set of weighted dice. The logical part of my brain knows that

I'm only remembering my failures and that if I recorded every roll I made at every game, I'd see a perfectly random distribution. But the superstitious gamer knows Lady Luck is out to get me. Maybe I'm being haunted by a yugoloth, a corruptor of fate—a fiend for hire native to the plane of Gehenna that brings bad luck and enjoys causing suffering.*

In any case, getting surprised by giant centipedes turned out to be no real problem. Mike and I dispatched them in a couple of rounds; as low-level monsters, they only had 2 hit points, and a single blow was enough to squash them dead. Of course, as low-level adventurers, we didn't have many more hit points ourselves. Eilora began the game with 13, so caution was warranted.

Looking around the valley, we could see trails leading to a dozen different caves. I was ready to charge into the nearest. But Zarlasa's keen elven eyes spotted a torn scrap of lace near the mouth of a different cavern—a frippery that might have been torn from the sleeve of a wealthy merchant. So we climbed up the hillside and entered.

The cavern was little more than a shallow hole extending twenty feet into the earth. But at the back of the cave there was a stout oak door, reinforced with rusty iron. Several skulls hung from nails in the door panel, above a message that read, COME IN—WE'D LIKE TO HAVE YOU FOR SUPPER!

Petrim the rogue checked the door for traps and found nothing. So Nordik did what fighters do best: smash something. Throwing his shoulder into the door, he broke it into pieces. Chunks of oak and iron

* "A corpulent creature with sickly yellow skin [that] wears black studded leather armor. It is armed with a short sword and shortbow. As it attacks, a smell of brimstone emanates from its body and the faint sound of rolling dice can be heard." *Monster Manual IV*, page 190.

clattered onto the floor and down the tunnel on the other side. The sound echoed deep into the cavern.

"Outstanding," Zarlasa muttered. "I bet no one knows we're coming."

The fifth edition simplifies and rationalizes D&D in key ways. Breaking down a door is a great example: When Angela wanted to throw her weight around, Willi asked for her strength score—and figured it was high enough to get the job done. "The idea is if you are not rushed, and there's really no danger, we simply look at it and say anyone with a strength of fifteen or above can open it," Willi said. "If you are being chased by a horde of goblins and it's important to get in the door in a rush, then I might make you roll. But generally, it's the DM's prerogative."

Compare that to the 3.5 edition rules, which are rather more complicated. First, the player may attempt to smash the door open with a Strength check. They roll a d20 and add their strength bonus. Then the DM checks a table* that lists different kinds of doors (simple wooden, good wooden, strong wooden, stone, iron, wooden portcullis, iron portcullis) and determines the door's breaking point. If the player scored higher than that number, they're through. If not, they've got a long way to go. Next, the DM figures out the door's armor class (10, plus a modifier based on its size, and minus 2 because it's an inanimate object). Then the player has to fight the door like it's an opposing monster. They attack, and if the attack roll is higher than the door's AC, they do damage—but not before the DM goes back to his tables and figures out the door's hardness. Hardness reduces damage, so if you hit for 9 points of damage against a stone door with a hardness of 8, you really only do 1 point of damage . . . and at that

* "Table 3-10: Doors," *Dungeon Masters Guide*, page 61.

rate, you'll have to hit the door another sixty times before you eventually smash the thing to pieces. Or, more likely, you toss the stupid rule book under the couch and go play video games instead.

The inside of the cave was dark but not empty. "You hear something marching down the hall," Willi said. "It sounds like boots in cadence." We rolled for initiative, and I got to act first.

"I'm charging in," I announced, "and as I enter, I'm yelling, 'Return your stolen goods, brigands!'" It may be the worst battle cry ever uttered, but at least it was in character. Paladins are often played as uptight and humorless, and Eilora isn't that bright.

As I plunged into the darkness, our enemies stepped around the corner, and Willi described them: four tall, muscular creatures that looked like men, but with red-brown skin covered in coarse hair, and massive yellow canine teeth. Hobgoblins.

I was unable to get close enough to strike before one of them raised a crossbow and fired it. Willi rolled the dice. "His heavy crossbow pierces you for ten points of damage," he said. I groaned so loudly, it attracted the attention of gamers at nearby tables. Five steps into the actual dungeon, and I was already down to my last 3 hit points.

A second hobgoblin took a shot. I held my breath. Willi rolled his dice and gave me a tiny smile. "That hits armor class twelve." Not enough. "The bolt shatters on the wall behind you."

My fearless example inspired a few of my bolder companions to action. Fargrim charged, and with a bone-crunching thud he introduced one of the hobgoblins to his hammer. Graben followed with his axe but couldn't connect with a hit. The rest of the party dragged their feet at the cave entrance, leaving the three of us to soak up the damage. Cowards.

There were two hobgoblins left, both carrying heavy spiked clubs. Neither of them cared for my war cry, and they expressed their displeasure by attempting to crush my skull. If I took one more hit, I was finished. I held my breath, and Willi rolled two misses.

That put us back at the top of the initiative, so it was my turn again. Perhaps it was time for an honorable withdrawal. "I want to get over to our cleric for healing," I said. "So I'm gonna fight my way out. Is there a hobgoblin between me and Fargrim?"

"There is, and he just tried to hit you in the face."

"Then I'll attack." I rolled a 16.

"He runs up, attempts to hit you, and you thrust your sword right through his chest, taking him out of the fray."

That was more like it. Fargrim continued the bloodletting, and we had two hobgoblins down. Then Petrim finally made an attack. "I'm gonna move in and stab one in the gut," Dallas said. He rolled a 10.

"His gut seems to be well armored, and your blade skitters off it."

"Crap."

The foul beasts may have lacked moral fiber, but they didn't want for courage. The larger of the two dropped his crossbow, hefted a club, and charged—straight into Nordik's sword.

Only one enemy was still standing. Nordik, Fargrim, and I surrounded him, and he growled and bared his teeth. I pointed my blade at his chest and fixed him with an icy glare. "Submit, evildoer," I commanded. "Or face your final justice."

The hobgoblin dropped his mace.

Our new prisoner saved the party a whole lot of trouble. Once we bound his hands and threatened him, he told us he didn't know where the ale was, but that four humans were taken captive when it was stolen, and they were locked up not too far into the cave. He led us to their cell, where we easily dispatched a few hobgoblins and rescued the merchant, his wife, and their apparently overpaid guards.

We were hired to recover the booze, not people. But a paladin values human life over material things—and the merchant offered to pay us more than the mayor if we forgot about the ale and escorted him back to town.

So we hightailed it home. Our first mission in fifth-edition D&D was officially a failure, but nobody seemed to mind.

The following day, I returned to the conference hall for a seminar discussing fifth-edition rules and character design. Several Wizards of the Coast designers sat on a flimsy stage and answered questions from a few dozen fans about paladins and warlords and rogues.

I was only half listening when I noticed Mike Mearls sitting alone at a table in the play-test area. He was reading a piece of paper, and I watched as he studied it. After a few minutes, he put it aside, reached into a cardboard box on the table, and pulled out another paper. He was reading play-test documents, short surveys each player completed after their trip to the Caves of Chaos. He looked fascinated.

After a decade writing about businesses for a living, I'm fairly cynical. When Wizards of the Coast announced the fifth edition, they put "listening to the needs of the D&D community" up front and center—and I knew it was hype. Disaffected players had become a market liability, so Wizards needed to make them feel engaged. Play tests and customer surveys were, at some level, set decoration.

But watching Mike Mearls pore over those surveys, I knew they mattered to him—and even though the play tests may solve a marketing problem, they'll also help shape the game. Guys like Mearls are part of the tribe; they grew up playing D&D, and the game means more to them than just some job. They want to do right by the community.

The first time I met Mearls, he talked about the responsibility he feels as a steward of D&D's direction. "When you are in this position, you are affecting people's lives," he said. "It's entertainment, so it's not like healing the sick. But it's something that's really important to fans.

"We're the caretaker of something people have put passion and energy into. You know, they could just sit and watch TV or do something passive, but they choose not to, they choose to be engaged. And the game is filling something in their lives that they can't get somewhere else."

15

THE SONG OF MARV AND HARRY

On my final night at the D&D Experience, I had a ticket to play another game—an old AD&D module, *Dwellers of the Forbidden City.* It's a tournament game, first run at the Origins Game Fair in 1980; author Zeb Cook earned his TSR hire in part due to the strength of the adventure. The final module, published in 1981, is considered a classic.

I skipped it. Instead, I hit the convention center snack machine and stocked up on Mountain Dew and candy. I went back to my hotel room, plopped on the couch, and pushed everything off the tiny coffee table. Then I laid out two mechanical pencils, a highlighter, and an unused leather-bound graph-paper notebook I'd been carrying around for months.

I cracked the spine, skipped a few pages in, and sketched a map: a deep valley, a forest, and a tower at the edge of the tree line. This would be the home of Mad Marv, a powerful wizard who would serve as the antagonist for a new D&D campaign—*my* D&D campaign, the one I'd run for my friends using fifth-edition rules. My first campaign, my first serious attempt at being a Dungeon Master, the apex of my art. It was time. I was ready.

I flipped the page and wrote "TOWER MAP" across the top line, and then "FLOOR ONE" below. An attempt to sketch a circle freehand failed miserably, so I jumped from the tatty hotel couch and ransacked the room looking for something to trace. A plastic coffee cup lid and an empty can of salt-and-vinegar Pringles were too big and too small, but the water glass from the bathroom was just the right size: precisely seventeen graph-paper squares across, or at five-foot scale, a tower eighty-five feet in diameter.

With the external walls in place, I erased a bit to open up the bottom of the circle and closed it with a straight horizontal line, three squares long. I erased the line's center and drew in a rectangle, and then bisected that with another line—map code for double doors, each seven and a half feet wide.

The first floor should be majestic, I figured. Anyone who entered needed to know they were facing someone powerful, not just a random encounter. So I drew a solid horizontal line across the map a few squares above center, creating a grand hall forty feet deep. Another wavy line just below that indicated a tapestry—perhaps this would depict some allegorical scene, a way to reward observant adventurers with information about the perils that lay ahead. On either end of the tapestry I drew a circle with a star in it, the symbol for a statue. Maybe they were previous "guests," turned to stone by the mad wizard?

Behind the wall, I sketched in a tiny guardroom, two squares by three, and a storeroom with a locked door. Inside that, a rectangle marked with a letter *C*, to indicate a locked chest: treasure, perhaps . . . or better yet, a trap. A box full of poisoned darts ready to pincushion a careless thief.

Steps led to the second floor: a lounge area, with couches and tables; a small study; and a few hidden passages, so servants could pop in and out unnoticed. On the third floor, guest rooms and kitchens. I hesitated, worried that it might be dumb to put the kitchens aboveground, and then left it.

The fourth floor started as more bedrooms, but then I had an idea. Marv built this tower before he was Mad—sure, he intended to host guests and live like a noble, but as his power grew he became alienated from society and increasingly obsessed with his studies. I imagined consecutive floors in disarray, expensive furniture piled up haphazardly to make room for inscrutable experiments.

Or maybe one big experiment? What if Marv became obsessed with astronomy, and at some point he'd gone through the tower and hacked holes in each floor with an axe, creating a multistory space where he could hang a Foucault pendulum, an apparatus that demonstrates Earth's rotation?

I flipped back through the notebook and carefully erased the same spot on each floor of the tower. I got on the Internet, studied Foucault's design, and calculated how much room a pendulum would require to swing freely if it hung on an eighty-four-foot cable.* Then, on each level of the map, I drew a hole just big enough to fit the width of the pendulum's swing—14.9 feet at the second floor, 12.8 feet at the third, and so on.

Non-nerds may find this attention to detail confounding. Calculating the correct geometries for a piece of set decoration is unlikely to affect the player's enjoyment of the game, so why bother?

I got the pendulum right for one of the same reasons I play D&D in the first place. The prime mover in a nerd brain is the need to

* Multiplying the height of the pendulum by the tangent of the angle of maximum swing, of course.

understand how things are put together. My mood-regulating neurotransmitters do the tango when I find a way to impose order on chaos. Biochemically, it's no different than the pleasure a jock gets sinking a free throw.

Every rule, every chart, every geeky statistic in a game book or module feeds into this impulse. All those details allow us to take apart existence, look at the individual parts, figure out how they work, and put them back together. Some people relieve stress by getting drunk or high and losing control; nerds find comfort by taking control and applying structure. Logic is like a warm blanket.

This is also the reason why I started designing a world by making maps, instead of addressing the story. Most folks would come up with a plot before they worried about where the bad guy eats his dinner. But I find the structure of hallways and rooms inspiring, as well as reassuring. The parts speak to the function of the whole: By creating Marv's physical world, I illuminate his character and, in turn, how he will move the story. It had already told me one important detail. Even in madness, Marv's the kind of guy who remembers to multiply the length of a pendulum's cable by the tangent of its maximum angle of swing *before* he takes an axe to his floor. His intellect will be dangerous.

I pushed ahead with the campaign design in this manner—like painting a landscape starting with the leaves, intending to fill in the trees and the sky later. The sixth floor of Marv's tower was a library. I jotted down a few names of books, in case any of the players looked closely—*Principia Mathemagica, The Voyage of the Bullywug, Goblins in the Mist*—and made a note to come up with more later. The seventh floor became an alchemical laboratory, then the eighth a blacksmith's forge—no, a machine shop. Why not make Marv an inventor? In addition to being a wizard, he's an accomplished engineer, combining steam-powered mechanics with magical items. Intruders in his tower will face clockwork guardians and traps far more complex than pits full of spikes. I can also populate the tower with lots of strange inventions . . . how about a sphere of annihilation (like the one Graeme jumped into in the Tomb of Horrors) inside a wooden box with a hole in it? D&D commode!

On the ninth and top floor, I sketched a giant telescope. It fit in with the pendulum, and I liked the image of a tower topped by an observatory dome. It also suggested something about Marv's motivations. Maybe he was obsessed with astronomy because he was looking for something—a sign from the gods, or a distant source of power?

Before I could answer, I needed to understand the world Marv lived in. Was this a traditional D&D campaign based in Greyhawk, or a unique homebrew setting, like Morgan's postapocalyptic Earth? Set your game in Gygax's world, and you can draw on decades of work by D&D's most talented designers. Go homebrew and you're on your own—but without limits and preconceptions.

It was not a hard choice. Sitting on a couch in a hotel in Fort Wayne, Indiana, I realized that a year of playing and studying and thinking nonstop about D&D hadn't gotten it out of my system, as intended—instead, it had intensified my desire to slip into fantasy, to make it and shape it. After a quarter of a century spent wandering other people's landscapes, I wanted to explore my own.

I flipped to a clean page in the notebook.

Ardhi is an ancient continent. For countless millennia, nomadic tribes of elves and orcs lived in harmony with the land. Clans crossed swords and great chiefs snatched power, but all that rose soon fell and was forgotten. Ardhi's rich mountains and fertile valleys were enough for all her children to share. It was an epoch of peace.

Then came the age of empires. The two great races, human and dwarf, overran their homelands and spilled onto Ardhi's shores. They saw her riches and waged war to consume them, trading blood and land in a hundred years of war.

When the great war ended, the empires drew maps and divided Ardhi between them. War machines gave way to mechanized industry; mercenaries turned merchants.

In the region called Tanz, near the foothills of Ardhi's highest peak, the human empire built an outpost, Simon's Town, a home for the mining guilds. It prospered and grew. Dwarven laborers lived alongside human bureaucrats, elven servants, and fortune seekers from lands beyond even imperial reach—halflings, tieflings, and gnomes. A royal charter even established a wizard's college and attracted students from around the known world.

In the fifty years following the great war, Ardhi saw more change than in the ten thousand years that preceded it. But all that would pale compared to what followed—the chaos caused by just two men.

The campaigns I admire the most take place in unique worlds. Greyhawk's great, but it's cool to see a DM put together his own universe. I think they're more invested in the material and passionate about its development, so the game is more interesting. This is not to say that a detailed world requires a detailed plot: Good games often allow the players to start exploring, go anywhere and do anything. I find that openness hugely appealing, and I'm excited that the new edition of D&D seems to encourage those sprawling, epic campaigns.

But I'm intimidated by a completely open world—it seems awfully hard to DM. For my freshman excursion, I decided to create antagonists, rising conflict, and all the plot elements that keep a party within certain bounds. Making an interesting story has its own difficulties, but they're more familiar to me than total improvisation.

Marv and Harry were raised in Agon, the heart of the human imperium.

They were boys when they met, at one of the royal schools of magic. Singled out for their gifts and torn from their families, they found like souls in each other. Both possessed great arcane power, were fascinated by science, were entranced by the arts of blacksmithing and engineering—and were full of disdain for the academic life of an imperial mage.

When the two young wizards came of age, they took their required residencies together, in the most distant place imaginable: the first college on the dark continent of Ardhi, in a place on the edge of civilization.

Marv and Harry came to Tanz with noble intentions. It's true that they hoped to escape imperial control, study forbidden disciplines, and learn the magic of Ardhi's natives. But their pursuit was for the sake of knowledge, not power, and they bore no ill will toward others.

While most wizards rarely left the college, Marv and Harry explored the wilderness. They made friends among a small tribe of elves in the west, in a village called Forest Edge, and won their trust with supplies from the college's stores. The grateful elves shared their magic and their secrets—including the location of their holiest site, the Fracture, a cave in the heart of the ancient Kigeni crater.

Kigeni was wild then, a deep valley that took a day to cross, dense with jungle and home to dangerous animals. The elves of Forest Edge believed the crater was formed when a dying god fell from the sky and that the Fracture led to the deity's final resting place.

Marv and Harry didn't believe the legend, but they knew the place was special. It radiated strange energy and was full of rare ores. Creatures like they'd never seen before haunted its depths. Exploration was hazardous, but the lure of discovery was too great to resist: The two mages swore to learn the Fracture's secrets. They would combine their imperial science with local magic, use all their knowledge and every resource available, and penetrate deep into the earth.

Marv remained in the crater and, working with the people of Forest Edge, constructed a tower—a place to study and protect the site. Harry returned to the college and applied his wiles to gain influence. As he climbed through its ranks, he secretly diverted resources to the project.

Together, they dug deep. But they weren't ready for what they would find.

Marv and Harry will provide enough structure to keep my game moving—each time we sit down at the table, I'll have a good idea what's going to happen, so I can plan ahead and prepare myself. It will require more prep work but make the job of running a game much easier.

Besides, I think I've come up with a plot that will allow greater freedom and increased improvisation as the game goes on. What Marv and Harry discovered deep inside the Fracture is that the Kigeni crater was created by something falling out of the sky—not a god, but a spacecraft. Ardhi doesn't exist in an alternate fictional reality; it's a planet in our universe, and the game takes place thousands of years from now, in what would be our future. A long time from now in a galaxy far, far away.

After the people of Earth first stepped on their moon, they hesitated. Humans didn't return to colonize Luna until sixty years later. But from there, they moved quickly. By the dawn of the twenty-second century, Homo sapiens *lived on Mars, Venus, and the moons of Titan and Europa . . . and began setting their sights on the stars.*

In the year 2134, the government of Earth launched a fleet of "arks," spacecraft designed to make the long journey to worlds around faraway stars and prepare them for human colonization. Each unmanned ark was piloted by an artificial intelligence and equipped with a terraforming system. When it arrived at a new planet, the AI would land the ship and release billions of microscopic robots into the alien environment; each nanobot would start disassembling matter into its component atoms and reassembling it into something else. Over time, the alien atmosphere would turn to breathable air and its land to water and soil. When the job was done, the AI would send a message back to humankind: Your new home is ready.

Of course, something went wrong. The arks were only supposed to transform barren planets—if they found evidence of life, they were programmed to send the news back to Earth and shut down. But for all their scientific advances, humans had no understanding of magic. When an ark entered Ardhi's atmosphere, the planet's strange magical energies disrupted its systems, and the spacecraft crashed.

The crash created the Kigeni crater, and the ark embedded itself far below the surface—damaged, but not completely destroyed. Terraforming nanobots leaked out into the caves and tried to begin work, but magical energy continued to disrupt their computer brains. They behaved erratically, and shut down entirely if they moved too far from the ship.

For thousands of years, the nanobots wrote and rewrote the matter around them. They created a huge network of caverns, a subterranean world full of breathable air and drinkable water, but also full of hazards; when the crippled nanobots encountered life, they rewrote that too, giving birth to strange half-alien monsters.

When Marv and his elven laborers dug into the Fracture, they disturbed this bizarre ecosystem. For the first time, the nanobots had direct exposure to surface life. They tore into it, warping its DNA in unpredictable ways. Marv lost most of his crew—and much of his sanity—before he found a way to protect himself with magic.

Marv came to understand he had discovered a technology of nearly immeasurable power. But he knew it was dangerous to push farther into the caves, to find the ark itself. So he sent a message to his partner Harry—now dean of the College of Magic—to find some adventurers to do the job for them.

I'll introduce Alex, Morgan, R. C., and Phil to Ardhi with simple, classic D&D adventures. The mage college will hire them to clear a tribe of kobolds out of the forest or recover stolen supplies from a gang of bandits. They won't realize that they're being auditioned for a bigger job . . . and when the dean of the college asks them to investigate a crazed wizard in the wilderness, they won't know he's part of a secret plan to send them into the Fracture.

It's a long-term plot, designed around a new game system, with potential for an epic campaign. The players will start out tentatively, with familiar goals, so they can learn their way around the rules. As they level-up their characters and become more comfortable, they'll find out about Marv and the Fracture. And as exploring the caves becomes the main focus of the game, they'll grow in power as the threats become greater—until they reach the ark itself.

There's one more twist. Humanity launched its ark fleet in the year 2134—the year of scientist Carl Sagan's two hundredth birthday. He's one of my heroes, so I decided the ark should carry something like the "golden records" Sagan helped install on the *Voyager* probes NASA sent into space in 1977. Included as a symbolic gesture, the records were a statement of who we were and how we lived: They bore digitized photographs of Earth, audio recordings of greetings in fifty-five human languages, and music including Beethoven's Fifth Symphony and Chuck Berry's "Johnny B. Goode." Each ark carries a small computer memory bank, a complete archive of all human media. Nonfiction and fiction, art and camp . . . every bit of music, literature, and film preserved in digital form. So when the terraforming nanobots went rogue, they found the data bank and processed its information. It became part of their collective memory and will influence the world they build around them—sometimes subtly, sometimes not.

When the adventurers penetrate deep into the caves, they might find strange cities carved out of the bedrock or weird runes in unknown Earth languages. Or since the nanobots can also take apart and rebuild living matter, they might twist it in interesting ways. Maybe the party will encounter monsters from human legend—the Sphinx, Grendel's mother, or, for that matter, Optimus Prime. They could even find themselves thrust into the plot of a novel, its characters played by genetically engineered mutants or robot automatons. Imagine our heroes spending one week fighting cave trolls and the next tackling the mystery of the Maltese Falcon.

I'm cheating, of course. Including a crew of culture-savvy robots in my game lets me swap genres at a whim to keep things interesting.* It'd be harder to make a good game that sticks religiously to the fantasy genre. But I like the idea of introducing these elements slowly, and only when the players start to tire of cave after cave. It will allow me to keep things interesting and to mix together different kinds of role-playing.

I filled nearly thirty pages of my graph-paper notebook that night in Fort Wayne. Maps gave birth to characters, which suggested plots and eventually worlds. By two or three in the morning, wired on caffeine, sticky with vending machine junk food, and damp with nerd sweat, I had outlined an entire campaign.

---

* It's also admittedly similar to a *Star Trek: The Next Generation* episode called "The Royale," where the crew of the *Enterprise* discovers a cheesy Earth casino in outer space, faithfully reconstructed by aliens based on a novel they found in a wrecked human spacecraft.

But it wasn't ready to play just yet. Over the last year, I had leveled myself to the prestige class of Expert Player, but I was still a Dungeon newbie, not a Master. Before I could walk that path, I needed to consult with my elders. I had to go to the place where the game was born and show my respect.

I had to go to Lake Geneva, Wisconsin.

16

PILGRIMAGE

When I studied anthropology in college, I developed a minor obsession with funerary customs, the rituals that allow the living to celebrate and say good-bye to the dead. They're a constant in human society, present in every culture dating back to the birth of *Homo sapiens,* something shared by every person who has ever lived.

Yet, despite their ubiquity, death rites vary wildly between cultures. Hindus practice cremation; Islam forbids it. Jews sit shiva; Irish Catholics pass the whiskey at wakes. Some Tibetan Buddhists practice *jhator,* or sky burial, where a body is left on a mountaintop to be consumed by birds. Others save the meat for themselves—until the 1950s, the Fore people of Papua New Guinea consumed the brains of their beloved deceased.

When Gary Gygax died in 2008, gamers developed their own ritual. In the hours after Gygax's funeral service, his friends and family headed over to the American Legion Hall on Henry Street in Lake Geneva for an impromptu gaming session. Four decades' worth of

D&D designers and players crowded around tables to roll dice and tell stories. Afterward, a few referred to the event as "Gary Con."

A year later, Gary's kids made the name official. Gary Con I (the postfuneral session is now known as "Gary Con 0") returned to the American Legion Hall as a free two-day "mini-con," a living memorial to Gygax's legacy. About a hundred friends, family, and fans attended, some traveling there from around the world.

The convention has kept growing. Gary Con IV was held in late March 2012, at the Lodge at Geneva Ridge, a hotel resort in Lake Geneva. It's a paid event now, to support its size: five hundred fifty attendees playing more than two hundred organized games over four days, from D&D to Star Frontiers to Shadowrun to Call of Cthulhu.

Obviously, I had to go. I was so excited about the chance to play D&D in Lake Geneva, I reserved a hotel room six months ahead of time—but as the date drew near, Gary Con came to mean more to me than just fun and games. My headlong leap into the deep end of D&D gave the trip an almost religious significance: I started to think of it as my version of the hajj, the Islamic pilgrimage to Mecca. An expression of devotion; a chance to seek wisdom; a time to show unity with my brethren.

The bard had walked for many moons and across many kingdoms. His pack was heavy on his back, and his feet ached, but he persisted. There wasn't much farther to go.

As he walked, the bard thought of what he'd left behind. He'd been raised in a village outside a great city. His parents loved him and worked hard so that he would want for nothing. When he came of age, he studied at an academy and apprenticed himself to kind masters. They worked hard so that he would want for nothing. He made a name for himself, found some success, and found a wife. She was loving and worked hard so that he would want for nothing.

Then one day, as men do, he found himself wanting. He wanted the one thing he'd always been denied: He wanted danger, he wanted risk, he wanted adventure.

But the bard was no warrior. So he left his homeland and walked from town to town, collecting stories of the great heroes of old. With each new tale he grew stronger as he learned from their triumphs and failures. It had been a long journey, and he was nearly ready to begin his own adventure. But not yet.

The bard broke his reverie and stopped in the road. He adjusted his pack and tapped his boots against a rock, shaking loose the dust of many miles. He raised a hand to shade his eyes from the sun and gazed into the distance.

Ahead, he could see the city of the gods, the place where the world began. Inside its walls, he would seek out the great elders and learn from their wisdom. Only then would he be ready for whatever adventure lay ahead.

David, the wandering bard, member of the tribe Jor-na-lizt, scribe in the court of Lord Forbes, tightened his pack on his shoulder and entered the holy city.

"We're gonna start off with a whole lot of blood and guts." Frank Mentzer sat at the head of the table and smiled at his new players. "You're headed to the most wretched, dangerous place in the entire realm."

Mentzer, sixty-one, was the perfect person to run my first game at Gary Con: a close friend of Gygax, one of the most experienced Dungeon Masters on the planet, author of the legendary 1983 Basic D&D "Red Box" and the subsequent Expert, Companion, Master, and Immortals sets. He looked the part, too: gray hair pulled back in a long ponytail, bushy arched eyebrows, a full beard, and an overgrown mustache twisted to points just a centimeter short of handlebar status. He couldn't have looked more like a wizard if he spat fireballs and wore a pointy hat.

He was clearly pleased with our choice of adventure. Once all eight ticketed players had gathered, Mentzer passed around a piece of paper describing several game modules he was play-testing and asked which we'd like to play. *The Witches of Chell* was described as "minimal combat . . . fatality rating 15 percent," while *Death in Wretched Swamp* was "very dangerous . . . fatality rating 75 percent or more." Wary of looking like wimps to one of the godfathers of gaming, we chose the latter.

Mentzer was developing *Death in Wretched Swamp* for his new game company, Eldritch Enterprises. After leaving TSR in October 1986, he helped Gygax start the ill-fated New Infinities Productions; when it was sued out of existence, he left the game business entirely and opened several bakeries. But old grognards die hard. In 2010, Mentzer formed Eldritch Enterprises with game designer Chris Clark and fellow TSR alumni Tim Kask and Jim Ward. The company planned to debut their first products at Gary Con and to play-test future adventures; *Death in Wretched Swamp* was slated for release in 2013.

"Most previous groups that have gone to the Wretched Swamp have gotten bogged down in the first hundred yards," Mentzer told us. "I have plenty of ways to kill you, no matter what you do."

As the players readied themselves, a courier arrived at the table with a taped-up cardboard mailing box and handed it to Mentzer. He opened it, removed something that looked like a magazine, and held it up so we could see the title: *Frank Mentzer's Lich Dungeon, Level One.* "This is my first published dungeon level in twenty-seven years," he said. I had the urge to start clapping but suppressed it when everyone else at the table just smiled and nodded. The cover featured a gray-bearded mage in a brown cloak and floppy pointed hat. He looked an awful lot like Mentzer himself.

Eldritch's modules are old-school adventures, with rich settings and sometimes incredible odds. They're written in what Mentzer describes as "gamer common," using generic terms for specific game mechanics and rules. The idea is that fans of different role-playing games can use the story and setting and consult their own rule books to figure out what it takes to pick a lock or knock down a door. It's not too different from what Wizards of the Coast hopes to do with the fifth edition of D&D.

"The root of our philosophy is whatever system you are using, whatever mechanics are being used to resolve the variables—it's story and interaction that is the core of the game," Mentzer said. "That's the part that really means something. The rest is details."

Mentzer hopes to build a twenty-first-century game company, small and adaptable, that won't build up the piles of unsold inventory that killed TSR. Eldritch doesn't make any physical product, they just design books, and their retail partners—like a website called DriveThruRPG—primarily sell digital downloads. If a customer wants a physical copy, they can print, bind, and ship a single book.

Operating on demand frees up Eldritch's founders to do what they do best: make games. It also makes it easy to expand around the world. To sell French gamers a copy of *Mort dans Marais Damné,* all the company has to do is arrange for a translation and then farm out production to a local printer. There's no risk of piles of unsold *livres de règles*—and little or even no cost to the company.

"There are all of these gamers all over the world who got their start in D&D on my creation, who look at me as one of the fathers of their role-playing culture," Mentzer said. "I can call people and say, 'Hey, would you do the German or Norwegian or Spanish translation of Eldritch's new game product?' Because they got their start on my stuff, they'll work at lower rates, as a labor of love."

Death in Wretched Swamp has what it takes to be a hit—or at least what counts as one among the tiny world of independent role-playing game publishers. It's full of memorable action (one fight sets the party against a cloud of hundreds of tiny flying demons) and strange creatures (the catalepus, essentially an elephant with a face on the end of its trunk, which can kill you by looking at you). It's fast paced, funny, and deadly: Our team of adventurers played for four hours, and while we did get past the first hundred yards, we had to leave our horses behind, and most of our gear with them. Chances are good that if we had more time to play, we'd have exceeded that 75 percent fatality rating.

After it was over, I took Mentzer out to dinner. I wanted to get him away from the crowd and pry away his secrets. After we ate, I laid out my problem. "I've been playing D&D since I was a kid," I told him. "But I've hardly ever run the game, and the few times I have, I've used prewritten modules. Now I'm planning my first original campaign, and it's scary."

He smiled, and I paused for a moment, grateful for the kindness. Then I asked my question. "What's the secret to being a good Dungeon Master?"

He twisted the end of his mustache and thought. "Emphasize priorities with your players," he said. "We all have, especially in this day and age, a very limited amount of time. So when you sit down at a gaming table, don't waste time on trivialities. Don't get bogged down in rule arguments. Resolve them equitably and quickly and keep things moving.

"Whether you are a teenager playing with friends or you are fifty or sixty years old like me, you must communicate. Talk between the players and the game master. Find out what they want from the game, what rules, what level of granularity, what level of interaction, what type of interaction.

"You must have your sensors out, find out what grabs people, and cater to it. The ideal game is a player-driven game. They are not acting in a play that you wrote. You are presenting a setting, you are doing the stage dressing and letting *them* come up with the play. And when they come up with a plot twist, you should be able to go that way full force, because that is what they want to do. Some of the worst games are when somebody has a great, grand, and glorious vision, and they want victims to walk out and play their roles with no input in what happens."

I knew he was right. As a player, I delight in the freedom of role-playing games and love when my party surprises our DM with unexpected solutions to problems. But as a DM, that's my biggest fear.

"What if my players come up with a great idea, and I have no idea how to respond?" I asked. "I can't plan for every path they might take ahead of time. Isn't that impossible?"

Mentzer shook his head. A good DM doesn't need to counter every clever idea with a clever rebuttal, he explained. Instead, they collaborate with players to find common ground, a place where both can be comfortable.

"Remember, the game master is part of the group," he said. "It is not an adversarial situation, though plenty of game masters run it that way. The game master has to be able to transcend his own desires and evolve. All the members of the gaming group—and that includes the game master—have to feel like they're winning."

The old wizard had advised great kings and seen empires rise and fall. He was renowned for his wisdom, so many desired his counsel. But few succeeded—for while the wizard was benevolent, his time was valuable, and the demands on it were great.

David was not yet a hero, but he was not without skill. So he brought the wizard to a tavern and showered the innkeeper with silver. After a warm bowl of tortellini, the old sage spun a tale; the lesson, he said, was one of cooperation. Lone heroes are for storybooks; real heroes work together, to make sure everyone wins.

David heard the words and knew they were true. He bade the wizard farewell and returned to his bunkhouse, where he changed out of his tunic, for it had become stained with diavolo *sauce.*

Then he set out again, into the heart of a walled castle, to receive the blessing of a prince.

Paul Erdős understood the value of cooperation. During his six-decade career, the Hungarian mathematician published more than 1,500 papers with 511 coauthors—an astonishing level of output. Today, his colleagues celebrate the feat by calculating their Erdős number, a measure of collaborative distance. Share credit on a paper with the man himself, and your Erdős number is 1. Write with someone who wrote with Erdős, and your number is 2. It's a nerdy in-joke, but it serves a purpose, reminding mathematicians that they belong to a worldwide community.

Similarly, D&D fanatics have been known to track their Gygax number—the number of players between them and the world's most famous DM. When I began playing the game, my Gygax number was effectively incalculable: I played only with my friends, and they played only with me. I shot up to a 2 when I played with Frank Mentzer. Sadly, I'll never climb higher. But after visiting Gary Con I feel like my number should have a footnote or notation after it: David Ewalt, Gygax number 2, played D&D with Ernest Gary Gygax Jr.

"Ernie" Gygax, Gary's oldest son, was present for the world's first session of Dungeons & Dragons. He and his sister, Elise Gygax, were the only participants in their father's initial play test; they didn't just play the game, they contributed to its creation. When I saw Ernie was going to DM an "Old School Dungeon Crawl" at Gary Con, I had to be there. It felt like an apotheosis, something that would elevate my game, making me part of the D&D pantheon. Before tickets for the game were scheduled to go on sale online, I sat in front of my computer for hours, checking and rechecking my Internet connection. I scored one of only six spots at the table a few seconds after the event went live.

The day of the game, I arrived at the assigned room early. But Ernie was already there, at the head of a large playing area—two long rectangular tables, set side by side, with a round table at the top, like a fat lowercase *i*. He was perched on the tittle* behind an unfolded four-panel Dungeon Master's screen, and I recognized him instantly. Like his father, he had a paunch, wore wire-rim spectacles, and had long gray hair pulled back in a ponytail. Four other eager gamers had arrived even earlier, so I took an open seat near the far end of the table.

When all the players had gathered and Ernie handed out blank character sheets, I began to remember some of the reasons I once fled from the arms of Dungeons & Dragons into other role-playing games: First-edition AD&D is ridiculously complicated.

Ernie wanted us to make our own characters. I decided to be a thief, and marked the class on my sheet. But then I rolled my ability scores, got a 6 for dexterity, and discovered the rules set the minimum for a thief at 9. I erased and started over. My highest stat, a 13, was wisdom. So I decided to be a cleric instead. But then I started talking to the other players, and we realized we didn't have a dwarf in the party—a crucial ingredient due to their ability to find their way underground. I erased and started over. A slow but strong dwarf cleric. I liked the idea, but then I realized the rules forbade dwarves from becoming clerics. I erased and started over.

---

* That's what the dot in a lowercase letter is called. Stop snickering.

And so my human thief became a half-elf cleric, and the first ninety minutes of a four-hour game were wasted as we repeatedly tried and failed to create first-level characters. I erased my character sheet so many times that by the time I'd finished, I was surrounded by a cloud of dirty bits of rubber. It was like the Michelin Man had sneezed on the table.

Finally, the game got started, and Ernie explained that our characters were headed toward a walled castle, with a goal of penetrating the fortification and exploring the passageways below. He quickly expedited our entrance (we found a shack outside the walls with a trapdoor in the floor) and the party set itself to dungeon crawling.

Surprisingly, that's just what the game was—a crawl. We'd enter a room and find it empty. Ernie would describe its dimensions and the location of the exits. Then we'd move on. No combat, no role-playing, just exploration. The players fell into repetitive execution of the same few actions: The thief listens at the door. The fighter and ranger smash down the door. The ranger and cleric, both half-elves, search the room for secret doors.* Finding nothing, the party approaches an exit. The process repeats.

Room after room, hallway after hallway, we discovered nothing, or next to it—like an abandoned holding cell with manacles chained to the wall but no prisoners. We even found a privy. Eventually, Ernie described the approach of another group of adventurers, mostly armored humans, and I got my hopes up for some action. But the other party passed without incident. One of them even called out a warning to look out for kobolds.

Our only challenge was not getting lost. Once we were in the dun-

---

*"Secret or concealed doors are difficult to hide from elves. Merely passing within 10' of the latter makes an elven character 16 2/3% (1 in 6) likely to notice it. If actively searching for such doors, elven characters are 33 1/3% (2 in 6) likely to find a secret door." *Advanced Dungeons & Dragons Players Handbook*, page 16.

geons, one player was pressed into mapping our travels on a whiteboard, drawing rooms and hallways with a dry-erase marker. But because Ernie's dungeon was so sprawling—and so empty that we moved through it quickly—it wasn't long before the map spilled over the edge of the board and had to be continued on pieces of paper.

For many players, this is the point of a dungeon crawl. These old-school adventures offer exploration and path finding; it's the thrill of spelunking, without getting bat poop in your hair. The challenge is to find your way and see how much you can discover, not to role-play your way through a narrative. Killing monsters and finding treasure is part of the fun but not the point of it.

Ernie's a talented DM. Great skill is required to manage a complex map and accurately describe the players' surroundings; I know because I lack it. Every time I have tried to run an adventure, I've given incorrect dimensions or described doors on the wrong side of the room. But I get away with it, because in my sort of games, those navigational details aren't that important. I'd crash and burn in an old-school dungeon crawl, getting hopelessly lost and driving my players insane with frustration.

Eventually, with less than an hour to go in the session, we opened yet another door and finally found something different: four humans wearing plate mail and shields, and a man in long robes and a peaked cap. Frustrated by the slow pace of the adventure, our party's not-too-bright barbarian came out swinging, and we began the game's first and only combat. But before I could even get a spell off, the pointy-hatted wizard cast Sleep and knocked me out—as well as most of my party.

As the game's four-hour time limit drew close, I couldn't help but feel disappointed. In my head, I'd built playing D&D with Ernie Gygax into the apex of gaming: I expected to be not only entertained but enlightened. I thought I would somehow become more skillful, as if mere exposure to a legendary DM could bestow his special powers. But playing D&D with Ernie Gygax isn't a magical act; it's just playing a game. And not every game is for me.

D&D means different things to different people: Some folks want action, others want drama. I want problem solving, a sense of achievement, and an interesting narrative. To be a successful DM, I have to remember that. If I'm not having fun, neither will my players.

I also must know my strengths and weaknesses, what kinds of games I can and cannot run proficiently. I won't succeed through gross osmosis, reading every book on the subject and playing every edition. Play what you know, and love what you play.

Strangely, the key to role-playing mastery has little to do with understanding a character. It's knowing yourself.

Every hero needs a quest, and every kingdom has one. A kidnapped princess, a missing treasure, maybe a dragon terrorizing the countryside. David was sure the prince would give him purpose and grant him the powers necessary to deliver the king's justice.

He arrived at the royal palace early, eager to begin a great adventure. But he did not find it there. "You want to be a hero," the prince told him, "but I cannot tell you where to go. You won't find fortune and glory following footsteps others have trod.

"Know yourself, and you'll find your own path."

David thanked the prince and left the castle.

On the second day of Gary Con I ran into Tavis Allison, one of the designers of a new role-playing game called Adventurer Conqueror King, and his son, Javi. Tavis was at the show selling copies of his game, and playing D&D whenever possible. Javi had just come from one of the convention's kid-friendly game sessions, D&D for preteen players, run by a twelve-year-old DM.

"I played a wizard, and I named him Gandalf," Javi said, shaking my hand up and down with exaggerated fervor, until Tavis told him to stop. When the adventure concluded early, he explained, the DM let the players fight each other for fun, and it came down to Javi versus one other kid. "I hit him with a web and then a magic missile, and then I hit him with my staff, until . . . *ka-pssh!*" He mimed something exploding with his hands.

Tavis and I had both signed up to play a game of Dungeon!, the 1975 TSR board game. Its creator, David Megarry, had driven from Minneapolis to teach the game to curious fans. As Tavis and I talked, we watched him set up four different editions of the game on top of a beat-up old Ping-Pong table; the original 1975 version, with its floppy vinyl board and generic Parcheesi-style tokens, looked comparatively ancient next to 1992's Classic Dungeon, which had a hard-backed board and molded plastic pieces shaped like wizards and warriors.

Megarry looked a bit out of his era as well. His chestnut-colored hair and ubiquitous grognard beard were well on their way to white, and he wore simple wire-frame glasses and a straw boater hat with a black ribbon band. A member of La Compagnie des Hivernants la Rivière Saint Pierre, a nonprofit organization that creates historical reenactments from the seventeenth- and eighteenth-century Midwest, Megarry looked like he could have come directly from a fur trading post.

I get a weird sense of cognitive dissonance when I think about David Megarry reenacting eighteenth-century history, because he was a first-person witness to events that have their own historic importance. Megarry grew up in the Twin Cities and got involved in the war-gaming community when he was still a teenager. He played in some of Dave Wesely's earliest Braunstein games and delved into the depths of Dave Arneson's pioneering dungeon crawls.

"In fact," Megarry told the dozen or so players who had gathered around the table to play his board game, "this was the original table that was in David Arneson's basement. We played Napoleonic miniatures on it, and we came down one Saturday morning, and there was this medieval castle on it."

Suddenly, the beat-up Ping-Pong table seemed to grow in my vision. I felt my heart pound and the hair on my arms stand up, a physical reaction to a sudden realization: This is where Dave Arneson ran Castle Blackmoor. In a very real way, this was the birthplace of fantasy role-playing.

The thought made my head swim—to play a game on Arneson's table is to literally touch the history of D&D, to share a physical and psychological connection with its creators. I experienced something like what devout Christians must feel upon entering the Church of the Nativity in Bethlehem, or, less sacrilegiously, what a baseball fanatic would experience if he got the chance to hit a few balls in Yankee Stadium using Babe Ruth's bat. I thought I'd purchased tickets to play an out-of-print board game, a fun diversion; instead, I was performing an act of devotion.

I took out my camera and started taking pictures of the table: a close-up of the wood grain, visible through fading green paint; a piece of yellowed masking tape, peeling off on a corner; little nicks and scratches; even a tiny pencil mark, potentially dating back to Blackmoor itself. After a minute I looked over at Tavis. "It's amazing," he agreed. "My son, of course, is totally uninterested and went off to play video games."

Had he stayed, Javi probably would have enjoyed himself. Dungeon! is still a lot of fun. The game simulates exploration of a series of rooms filled with monsters and treasure. Each player takes a premade character, heads out into the dungeon, kills the creatures, grabs their loot, and repeats. Since the monsters and treasures are printed on small cards and placed facedown on the board, players don't know what sort of peril is in a room until they enter it—or how big the reward. Color-coded numbers on each monster identify what you must roll on a 2d6 to kill them: My character, Flennetar the Paladin, attacked using the red numbers, so I needed only a 2 to kill a goblin, whereas Longbranch the Elf attacked on white and would need a 3. Miss your target number by a point or two, and you could lose one of your 2 hit points. Miss by a bigger margin, and you're dead. In addition to providing my combat details, Flennetar's matchbook-sized character card explained I could move five spaces per turn and needed thirty thousand gold to win. It also detailed a paladin's unique power—that I could take a turn to heal myself or another player.

If this all sounds familiar, it's not a coincidence. Dungeon! is a direct relative of D&D, born out of the same gaming sessions that inspired Arneson and Gygax. After a few months of playing Arneson's Blackmoor games, Megarry began to notice the toll it took on his friend. "I was watching Arneson just be completely drained by the whole process," he said. "It was an incredible amount of work. He couldn't play his own game. It seemed unfair." Megarry began to wonder: Could he make a dungeon crawl that didn't require a referee, so everyone at the table could have fun?

The game came together in October of 1972, after Megarry broke up with a girlfriend. "After an argument with her, I just went home and sort of sulked," he said. "But as part of that, I said, 'Well, I'll work on this game idea.' And the minute I started working on it, I couldn't stop." He drew the dungeon outline on nine 10" by 13" pieces of poster board taped together at the edges, and glued on squares of colored paper to represent individual rooms. Monsters and treasures were described on tiny chits half the size of a business card. When laid out, the completed prototype—a white background covered with yellow and orange shapes—looks like a Mondrian painting.

His friends loved it, and mixed in a few sessions of Dungeon! between their Blackmoor adventures. Megarry decided to try to get the game published: "I sent a letter to Parker Brothers asking if they would like to look at it, then I got my first rejection letter," he said. "So Arneson and I went down to see Gary Gygax to show off our stuff."

Today, we remember Arneson and Megarry's 1972 trip to Lake Geneva as the occasion when Gygax first saw Blackmoor, the "you got your peanut butter in my chocolate" moment when D&D was born. But Megarry was there too—and his board game must have helped inspire Gygax's work. David Megarry's contribution to the origin of role-playing games may not be as fundamental as that of Arneson and Gygax, but it's still significant. He might not be one of the fathers of Dungeons & Dragons, but he's at least a favorite uncle.

In 1975—when TSR was flush with cash from the newly released Dungeons & Dragons—Megarry's board game was finally published. But even though Dungeon! eventually sold half a million copies, Megarry never got rich or famous from the game, or for his part in the history of D&D. His relationship with TSR ended in a series of disappointments.* But Megarry isn't bitter—he made the game to entertain people, and he's happy knowing he did.

"You can second-guess all you want. But I can come away knowing that I made a fun game that people like, to this day," said Megarry. "I'm satisfied with that."

This was the wisdom I'd been searching for. I had spent so much time learning about where D&D came from, about the controver-

---

* Including spelling his name incorrectly on the Dungeon! rule book. "They had a 'Gary' in the room all the time, so they dropped an *r*," Megarry said. "I figured, 'They'll get it right on the next printing.'" But when the first three thousand games sold out, TSR—knowing they had dropped a letter in "Megarry"—corrected it by adding a second *g*. "David Meggary" had to tell his editors they'd gotten his name wrong again. "Tim Kask was crestfallen," he said.

sies, the management errors, the lawsuits, and the edition wars, that I nearly forgot the most important thing about the game: It's supposed to be fun.

I won't master the game by memorizing obscure historical arcana. I won't find the key to a successful campaign in rule books or in obsessively detailed homemade maps. I just have to think about my friends and make sure they're having fun.

As he departed the temple of the creator, David thought back on what he'd left at home—family and friends, people he cared about but left behind.

With a grimace, he realized his error. He wouldn't find happiness choosing his own adventure; he'd find it sharing adventures with friends.

He needed to think, to figure out where to go next. He wandered the city aimlessly, unsure where his feet were taking him.

After the game, I got in my rental car and drove a few miles east into downtown Lake Geneva. During the summer, the resort town is flooded with tourists. But in the third week of March it was half-empty, with only a handful of locals on the sidewalks, quietly strolling and enjoying unusually warm weather.

I parked on the street next to the public library, a one-story brick building on the north shore of Lake Geneva. The back side of the library faces the lake, and floor-to-ceiling windows look out onto a small park. I followed a neat walkway past the building and down the shoreline for about a half mile. It's a nice walk—the thick grass of the park slopes up on one side of the path, and the placid lake sits just a few feet away on the other.

Halfway down the path, I sat on a park bench and looked out on the water. There were two men fishing on a rowboat a few hundred feet from shore, but I could see them only in silhouette against the rippling water. Birds chirped and sang in the trees. An older couple walked past, hand in hand, quietly talking.

Someday soon, Library Park might be home to the Gary Gygax Memorial. Gary's widow, Gail, has been working on the project for several years. Eventually, she hopes there will be a small statue here, perhaps a bust of Gary surrounded by the tools of his trade: a fantasy castle, a coiled dragon, some polyhedral dice.

The city government has tentatively approved the location, but there are years of planning and permits and approvals before the memorial becomes reality. Fund-raising, too—although with Gary's rabid fan base, coming up with the cash shouldn't be a problem. Wizards of the Coast has already promised to donate the proceeds from a special-edition reprint of the original AD&D core rule books.

After a while, I walked out of the park and past the library to the Riviera, a banquet hall built back in 1932, when Lake Geneva was a swinging summer party destination for Chicago's rich and famous. In front of the old building, there's a fountain surrounded by a memorial walkway—one of those things where local businesses and families make donations to get their names or a short message carved on bricks in a path. There's one inscribed "to the world's best husband," one for "The Birkenheier Family," another with the logo of a local bank. Then, near the base of the fountain, directly in front of the doors of the Riviera, there's a large square brick depicting a dragon sleeping on top of a twenty-sided die. "In loving memory of E. Gary Gygax," it reads. "Creator of Dungeons & Dragons. Donated by his family, friends, and fans."

I stood there for a while, thinking. Then I walked a little farther along the shoreline and turned left on Center Street, heading away from the lake and uphill into town. Four blocks in, on the corner of Wisconsin Street, is the house Gary lived in when he created Dungeons & Dragons. It's a little white house with a gray roof, set back from the road behind a small garden. Since it was March, nothing was growing. But there was a small plaque in the dirt, resting against a wall of rocks: "If tears could build a stairway and memories a lane, I'd walk right up to heaven and bring you home again."

I lingered on the corner and imagined Gary sitting on the porch, smoking a cigar and thinking about wizards. Then I crossed the street and walked a few blocks to Sage Street.

Don Kaye's house on Sage Street is where TSR got its start. It's gone now, bulldozed to make room for an elementary school. As I walked past, I saw a mom and dad leading their kids into the school for some after-hours event. The dad was wearing a tuxedo T-shirt, and I laughed at his silliness, but then remembered I was wearing a shirt with a picture of the Ghostbusters chasing the Pac-Man ghosts, Inky, Blinky, Pinky, and Clyde.

I kept walking. A lady gave me a wave and a smile as I walked past her house on Marshall Street. A little farther on, I stopped to consider a house on the corner of Williams Street—the original home of the Dungeon game shop. Now it's someone's home, just slightly gray and faded. It's next door to a Laundromat, and on the opposite corners there's a Pizza Hut and a gas station.

I turned on Williams Street and headed back downtown, toward the final destination of my pilgrimage. As I got closer to the lake, there were fewer houses and more storefronts, and then, in the last few blocks before Main Street, nothing but commercial space—a crepe restaurant, an antiques store, and lots of stores with beach towels and sunblock in the windows, waiting for summer and crowds of strangers.

My final stop was the corner of Main Street and Broad. The building is currently called the Landmark Center, but back in 1873, it was the Hotel Clair. A hundred years later, it became the headquarters of TSR—the rickety old building where AD&D and the Red Box were born.

Today, the residents of the Landmark Center include a jeweler, a bank, and an architecture firm. The main storefront—once the second home of the Dungeon—is a candy store called Kilwin's Chocolates. A sign outside promises "Mackinac Island Fudge & Homemade Ice Cream."

I went inside. It smelled like caramel, a sweet, burnt aroma. Rows of glass-fronted bakery counters showed fresh-made fudge and candies. A few display tables had gift boxes of treats. I picked out a box of dark-chocolate cherry cordials—my favorite—and an assortment of truffles to bring home to Kara.

There were two teenage girls behind the counter, neither older than sixteen. As one of them rang up my purchase, I casually asked a question.

"Do you guys know the history of this building?"

She looked at me, a little startled, but friendly. "No, I don't think so."

"There used to be a game store here."

In the corner of the room, an older woman had been cleaning the marble table used for cooling fudge. She stopped what she was doing and walked toward the register.

"Oh yeah, I know that," she said. She pointed a finger at the ceiling. "Up there. Dungeons and Dragons."

"Yeah. Their offices were up there, back in the 1980s."

"I know that was there. I don't know anything else, though."

"How long has the candy store been here?"

"Oh, she's been here sixteen years. I just work here, I don't know much."

The young girl fished my change out of a drawer. I took it and turned back to the woman. "Thanks," I said. "I was just curious."

"The building's got a lot of history, I don't know what. But if these walls could talk, you know . . ." She trailed off and smiled. I smiled back.

There was a park bench on the sidewalk just outside the store. I sat down and watched the traffic. A couple walked by, perhaps on their way to dinner. An old lady shuffled past with a walker, followed by her tiny dog. A kid with Spider-Man sneakers rode his bike up the sidewalk. None of them even glanced at the old brick building, the place where countless adventures began.

I opened up the bag from the candy store and ate a cherry cordial. It was fantastic.

Fortified in mind and body, David strode from the city. It hadn't been what he'd expected, but he did find wisdom there: Build something together. Know yourself. Have fun.

With the sun at his back, he surveyed the road ahead. A few dozen yards away, the path split and continued in different directions. Farther in the distance, he could see each path split again, and again, dozens of roads, headed to all corners of the globe.

He had no map and no idea which path to take. So he reached into his pocket and pulled out a lucky token, something he'd carried since childhood—a small geometric figure, almost a sphere, but flattened to show twenty identical faces, each one numbered sequentially.

He threw it high in the air, caught it on the way down, and opened his hand so it rested flat on his palm. He read the number on top and then laughed to himself. He stuffed the die back in his pocket and walked on with purpose.

He was ready for adventure.

When I returned to Brooklyn and met with the guys for our next game session, I left Weslocke at home. I'd scored our group an invite to Wizards of the Coast's private play test of the fifth edition of Dungeons & Dragons, so it was time to start a new campaign, with new characters, in a new world of adventure.

Once everyone had arrived, I reached into my bag and produced a fat folder of paper: five copies of an in-progress *Player's Handbook,* collated and bound, hot off the laser printer in my office. One for each of us.

We sat at Alex's dining room table and read through the packets. Every few minutes someone would tut-tut or chuckle and point out a particularly controversial or exciting change in the rules. After half an hour we told ourselves we knew enough to begin and started to roll up new player characters.

Alex decided he'd play an elven rogue named Kilën, after a beloved grandfather. The fifth-edition rules ask players to choose one of several themes that describe their character's identity; Alex said Kilën would be an "adventurer." Later, he told me he'd really chosen "spy" but decided to keep that a secret from the other players.

Phil rolled up a wizard and named him Tealeaf. Because he's Phil, he made him an acrobatic gnome. In my mind's eye, I pictured Yoda doing backflips and shooting bolts of Force lightning from his fingers.

R. C. made a dwarf fighter, a nobleman named Beauteponce. When he rolled his intelligence score, it came up seven, not much smarter than a troll. It would be fun to have him in the party. And aggravating.

Morgan would play a human cleric. He chose the theme of "pub crawler," which grants the character an advantage to find information, since everybody knows his name in all the local bars. He called the character Norm.

When they were done, I glanced over each character sheet, then returned them to their owners. I had brought several of my own characters with me, along with a few maps—winding caves, an unexplored countryside, a strange wizard's tower. I also brought a few pages of notes—nothing too detailed, just an outline. Set decoration for a simple story, a quest to find a box of lost books. There'd be plenty of room for the players to fill in the details.

I took a breath and surveyed the table, looking each of my friends in the eyes. "You have all gathered at a tavern," I said, "in search of adventure and glory."

AFTERWORD

Ten Years Later

WEDNESDAY

I had my noise-canceling headphones on and was watching a movie on my iPad, oblivious to what was happening on the airplane around me, so I jumped when the stranger in the window seat tapped my arm.

I looked over and pulled down my headphones. "Sorry," he said, flashing an apologetic grin. "I need to go to the bathroom."

"Oh, sure!" I said. I paused the movie, undid my seatbelt, and stepped into the aisle, dropping the tablet on my seat. It landed screen-up, showing a close-up of Chris Pine playing a lute for two guards wearing plate armor. I'd been watching the final act of the recent release *Dungeons & Dragons: Honor Among Thieves*.

The man glanced down at the screen as he crouch-walked past my seat. He straightened as he stepped into the aisle and smiled at me with an excited look. "I loved that scene," he said. "I can't believe they made a good D&D movie."

"I know, right?" I smiled back, and he made his way toward the rear of the plane.

Over the decade since the launch of the fifth edition of Dungeons & Dragons, the world had turned into a very different place.

In December 2013, four months after the hardcover edition of this book was originally published, Wizards of the Coast announced that it had completed its public play test of the fifth edition of Dungeons & Dragons. More than 175,000 people signed up and downloaded the draft rules during the eighteen-month-long test, so perhaps as many as a million people around the world had played "D&D Next."

Dungeons & Dragons Fifth Edition made its official debut on July 3, 2014, with the release of a free, downloadable Basic Rules booklet. The 110-page document contained nearly complete rules for playing, including details of four races, four classes, and lots of equipment and spells; it wasn't just a teaser or an excerpt, it was the finalized game, ready to play.

Twelve days later, the first paid product hit shelves. The $19.99 *Starter Set* consisted of a thirty-two-page rule book with full rules for creating characters and advancing them up to level five, a sixty-four-page adventure module called *Lost Mine of Phandelver*, five pregenerated characters, and a set of polyhedral dice.

"Stores put in orders for triple the quantities they normally order for something like this, and still sold out on the first day," Nathan Stewart, brand director for Dungeons & Dragons at Wizards of the Coast, told me a few weeks after the boxed set's release. "It landed really, really well. I don't have any sales numbers yet, but the early indicators are that we're going to have one of the biggest box launches that we've ever seen."

A month later, on August 14, Wizards of the Coast debuted the $49.95 hardcover *Player's Handbook*, and within hours of the official release, it was Amazon's number one best-selling book. The *Monster*

Manual and the *Dungeon Master's Guide* followed in September and December, at the same price, and to the same quick success.

The new version of Dungeons & Dragons was a critical hit.* The rules were simplified in a way that handed power back to the Dungeon Master and helped everyone at the table move through a story without getting lost in minute details; but at the same time, they contained enough complexity to satisfy nerdier players. It wasn't dumbed down, and it didn't feel like a video game. It felt like Dungeons & Dragons.

In the four and a half months between the release of the new *Player's Handbook* and the end of 2014, Wizards of the Coast sold 156,556 copies of the three core fifth edition rule books, according to NPD BookScan. In 2015, that number increased by 23 percent; in 2016, by 31 percent; in 2017, by 35 percent; and in 2018, by 53 percent. Five years after fifth edition hit shelves, the game's growth was still accelerating. By that point in the lifetime of fourth edition, Wizards of the Coast already considered the rules obsolete and had started the D&D Next play tests.

So what happened? Consider the guy next to me on the airplane, who, for the sake of moving this narrative along, has finished up in the restroom and come back to his seat. He was young, maybe in his mid twenties, and a fan of genre entertainment,** judging by the cartoon Jolly Roger symbol on his T-shirt, a reference to the Japanese manga series *One Piece*. He was probably a teenager when fifth

---

* "When you score a critical hit, you get to roll extra dice for the attack's damage against the target. Roll all of the attack's damage dice twice and add them together. Then add any relevant modifiers as normal." *Player's Handbook*, page 196. By the way, we're using fifth edition rules in the footnotes now. Deal with it, grognards.

** No, I didn't ask him if any of this was true. Ten years may have passed, but I'm still a nerd, and there's no way I'm making the wisdom save to overcome social anxiety and start up a conversation with a stranger on a plane.

edition came out, and awash in stories that weren't just heavily influenced by Dungeons & Dragons but actively featured it.

From 2007 to 2019, the protagonists of the highest-rated comedy on television, *The Big Bang Theory*, were depicted as enthusiastic D&D players. Another series, *Community*, featured two episodes in which its ensemble cast attempts to cheer up and help people by inviting them to a session of Advanced Dungeons & Dragons. And when the hugely popular Netflix series *Stranger Things* debuted in 2016, it was structured around a group of kids who played D&D, and used their fantasy adventures as a central element of its storytelling. D&D is so important to the main characters' worldview that they dub their supernatural nemesis "the Demogorgon."* Kids growing up surrounded by this kind of media weren't brainwashed to think D&D was satanic or unforgivably nerdy; it was a mainstream game, and cool people played it. Seeing a young Finn Wolfhard or Millie Bobby Brown roll polyhedral dice was a formative moment for many Gen Z D&D players.**

The Internet, naturally, also helped boost the game's popularity. In 2017, Wizards of the Coast collaborated with an Alabama-based computer game company called Curse to release D&D Beyond, the official digital tool set for fifth edition.*** The website (and, later, app) functioned as a compendium of the game's rules and supplements,

---

* "Prince of Demons, the Sibilant Beast, and Master of the Spiraling Depths, Demogorgon is the embodiment of chaos, madness, and destruction, seeking to corrupt all that is good and undermine order in the multiverse, to see everything dragged howling into the infinite depths of the Abyss." *Out of the Abyss*, page 236.

** The causal link between watching *Stranger Things* and wanting to play Dungeons & Dragons was so strong that in 2019 Wizards of the Coast published a licensed *Stranger Things* D&D starter set. It included basic instructions, character sheets, dice, and an adventure called *The Hunt for the Thessalhydra*, based on the campaign the kids play in the show's first season.

*** It's worth nothing that D&D Beyond wasn't Wizards of the Coast's first attempt to move the game onto the Internet. In 2008, the company launched an online service called D&D Insider that had rules, character sheets, and even a primitive virtual tabletop. But much like the fourth edition rules it was built on, the site had relatively few users.

and included interactive character sheets; not long after, I started keeping my all my characters digitally and carrying an iPad to game nights instead of a pile of loose papers and rulebooks.

But the Internet's biggest influence on the game didn't come through official channels. The Venn diagram between computer nerds and D&D players has always been close to a circle, so when podcasts emerged as a new medium in the early 2000s, shows about role-playing games were among the first examples available; a short while after, players started recording their game sessions and releasing them as episodic adventures.

These "actual-play" recordings function as a kind of metatextual fantasy epic. They're part improvisational theater, part directed storytelling, and part behind-the-scenes banter among friends; when done well, they're entertaining but also instructive, the perfect vehicle to drive new players into the D&D hobby.

By 2007, there were enough role-playing game podcasts—and a few video series, thanks to a two-year-old website called YouTube—that the annual ENNIE awards, a fan-driven recognition of excellence in role-playing games, added a "Best Pod/VidCast" category. The first winner, *Have Games, Will Travel*, was hosted by freelance writer Paul Tevis and featured news and reviews of tabletop games.

Game publishers were quick to realize the potential of the new medium. In 2008, following the release of fourth edition D&D, Wizards of the Coast hired the creators of the *Penny Arcade* web comic to appear in an actual-play podcast to help demonstrate and teach the new rule set. Their campaign, which followed the employees of an adventuring company called Acquisitions Incorporated, proved so popular that it later transitioned to live performances at game conventions in front of thousands of fans.*

---

*Jerry Holkins and Mike Krahulik's creation even got its own fifth edition Wizards of the Coast–published supplement, 2019's *Acquisitions Incorporated*.

Various actual-play campaigns would follow their lead, including, most notably, a 2015 streaming video series called *Critical Role*, in which the players and the Dungeon Master were all professional stage, screen, and voice actors. The quality of their character performances—and the exceptional storytelling skills of their Dungeon Master, Matthew Mercer, made it stand out among the rest.

Even though *Critical Role* episodes starred actors, they weren't dramatized; they were live recordings of actual D&D games. So they ran long—usually two to four hours per session. The entirety of *Critical Role*'s first campaign, which told the story of an adventuring group known as Vox Machina, ran for 115 episodes, or more than 447 hours in total.* But the fans of the series couldn't get enough.

D&D players loved *Critical Role* because it was well written and entertainingly performed, but a huge portion of the audience had never even picked up a die. They discovered the series on YouTube or the Amazon-owned streaming platform Twitch and then decided to try the game later; this drove a massive wave of new, mostly young players into the hobby.**

Critical Role campaign two started in January 2018, and was equally popular. Then in March of 2019, the team launched a crowdfunding campaign on the website Kickstarter to fund a twenty-two-minute animated *Critical Role* special. The campaign raised $11,385,449 from 88,887 backers, making it one of the biggest and fastest-funded projects in the site's history. In November of that year, Amazon announced that it would fund an additional fourteen episodes for its Prime Video platform.

At the time of this writing, *Critical Role* has produced 394 episodes across three main campaigns and a handful of limited series and one-

---

* *The Simpsons*, which ran 752 episodes in its first thirty-five years, only totals about 300 hours.

** It also created a genuine problem for many D&D groups, which saw an influx of new players who expected each session to reach the dramatic highs of *Critical Role*. This disparity between performed D&D and real-world gaming has come to be known as the Matt Mercer Effect, and continues to be an issue for many home campaigns.

shots; that's about 1,500 hours, or two months straight of uninterrupted content. In October 2021, when an anonymous hacker released 125 gigabytes of Twitch's internal data, it revealed that *Critical Role* was paid almost $10 million for subscriptions and advertising in the previous two years on that platform alone—a figure that suggests it wasn't just one of the biggest franchises in fantasy role-playing but also one of the most profitable in the entire world of streaming video.

Back in 2023, I had finished watching my movie, and the guy next to me was dozing. He was right about the scene with Chris Pine—it's a highlight of the film. In it, the half-elf sorcerer Simon creates an illusion of Pine's character, Edgin, in order to distract some guards and sneak past them. Simon gets his foot stuck in a hole and loses his concentration on the spell, so the illusion glitches, and Edgin's illusory head melts and sinks into his torso.

It was still hard to believe that four months earlier, a D&D movie had reached number one at the box office on its opening weekend, with ticket sales of $71.5 million. And it was even harder to believe that everyone seemed to like it, including critics.

"Even if you've never once rolled the dice in the role-playing game, there's a solid chance you'll enjoy the whiz-bang fantasy adventure that is *Dungeons & Dragons: Honor Among Thieves*," *Chicago Sun-Times* reviewer Richard Roeper wrote in his review. The aggregation website Rotten Tomatoes reported critical reviews at 91 percent positive—shockingly high when you consider that the game's last cinematic adaptation, the December 2000 flop *Dungeons & Dragons*, has an aggregate score of just 9 percent.*

---

*There were also two direct-to-video sequels in the twenty-three-year interim, the 2005 miscarriage *Wrath of the Dragon God* and the 2012 excretion *The Book of Vile Darkness*. But their language is that of Mordor, which I will not utter here.

Honor Among Thieves had been in development, in one form or another, for almost exactly as long as D&D's fifth edition. Warner Bros. Pictures announced in May 2013 that it had a D&D film in development; two days later, Hasbro issued a lawsuit saying they had the rights to the game's cinematic adaptations and were working on their own production. The film languished in development hell and legal battles for the better part of a decade, moving from studio to studio and director to director, never getting made but never actually dying, perhaps in part due to the tantalizing success of related properties like *Stranger Things* and *Critical Role*. Finally, in January 2020, writers/directors Jonathan Goldstein and John Francis Daley announced that they had completed a new draft of the script for Hasbro-owned studio Entertainment One, and it was ready to go into production.

Then a novel coronavirus initially identified in Wuhan, China, kicked off a global pandemic.

The history of the Covid-19 era is better told in more serious books than this volume, and by authors who have more interesting tales to tell than my own experience of never changing out of pajamas and playing approximately sixteen thousand hours of the video game Animal Crossing. But the subsequent shutdown matters to this story, because all of the United States—all of the world, basically*—was stuck at home. No more in-person socializing at school or after-school hangouts for kids; no more workplace watercooler chat, bar visits, or weekly game nights for adults.

Isolated at home with few options for social connection besides each other and the Internet, families everywhere turned to games, either played in person among members of their virus-safe social "pods" or online using newly popular video conferencing solutions

* Except for idyllic and apparently better-governed places like New Zealand, which escaped the worst of it. As if being home to the *Lord of the Rings* movies wasn't enough to make an American jealous.

like Zoom or Google Meet. And what game does an entire generation of parents who grew up in the 1980s and '90s think of when they're faced with school-aged kids who are both desperately in need of a creative outlet and starved for social interaction?

Dungeons & Dragons spread nearly as fast as the actual Covid virus. Because they were stuck at home, kids had lots of time to stream D&D-adjacent content like *Stranger Things* or actual-play sessions on YouTube, priming them to want their own role-playing game experience. Gen X and Millennial parents who grew up loving the game finally had a captive audience and time at home to sit down and teach their children. And countless people, young and old, who couldn't see their friends in person realized there was a game that could be played via video conferencing, at little to no expense, exploiting the theater of their minds.

During the pandemic, widespread lockdowns and a lack of in-person social interaction boosted US toy sales by 16 percent to $25 billion, and a whole lot of that went to Dungeons & Dragons. A year into the pandemic, Wizards of the Coast posted revenue of $816 million for the previous year, up 24 percent from the year before the virus. D&D and Wizards' other big brand, Magic: The Gathering, were doing so well that corporate owner Hasbro even reorganized its structure to emphasize those products, dividing the company into three units: consumer products (toys like Transformers action figures and classic board games like Monopoly), entertainment (licensing, distribution, and production of film and television content), and Wizards & digital (housing the assets of Wizards of the Coast and focusing on expanding the existing tabletop games and creating new ones).

When I spoke to then Wizards of the Coast CEO Chris Cocks in February 2021 for a *Wall Street Journal* article, he told me the D&D business alone was five times bigger than it had been before the debut of fifth edition. "It's been a tremendous growth rate, but what really fueled our growth in 2020 was a hunger for authentic social connections that the game really helped to foster," he said. "It meant so much to connect with each other on Zoom and be silly for three or four hours and tell some stories . . . and D&D was fantastic for that."

My own D&D stories changed significantly during the pandemic, but they'd already moved on from Vampire World and the initial plans for my own campaign in Tanz.

After the original publication of this book, Alex, Morgan, Phil, R. C., and I continued to meet in person for our weekly D&D fix. After Weslocke, Jhaden, Graeme, and Ganubi finished their business in San Francisco, we sailed south, made contact with a free human city in Mazatlan, Mexico, and secured their trust by vanquishing a giant that had been harassing the citizens. Then we returned to Las Vegas, and with the help of Ganubi's new religious followers, won over its illithid leaders.

After that, Morgan warned us that the story was close to coming to an end, and told us he had a new campaign world he was excited to try out. We knew it was nearly time to rally our forces around the world for a final attack to liberate the vampire-occupied cities, so we made one more voyage—this time to Australia, where we met and befriended a creature the size of a city, a kind of living island that we saved from monstrous parasites. We also added two new characters to the team, Nigel and Sheila, played by our old pal "Deuce" and Jennifer, his wife.

After the final session, Morgan wrote an epilogue of sorts and sent it to each of us as an email. I'm sharing it here with his permission.

> *It was Liberation Day in the city of Seoul, and the boys and girls of the Weslocke and Abel Memorial School of Magic were very excited. Partly because it was the anniversary of the Battle of Seoul, the first battle in the War of the New Dawn that eventually freed humanity from the tyranny of the vampires, but mostly because it meant a half day of class.*

Mrs. Park had decided to use the half day to take her class to see the war memorial in the center of town. They had learned all about the battle in school, and this would be a nice way to finish off the unit.

As they walked toward the memorial, Mrs. Park's students chattered with each other. Two of them, a larger boy and a smaller one, were involved in a highly intellectual conversation.

"Nuh-UH," said the smaller boy.

"Uh-HUH," said the larger one.

"Nuh-UH. There aren't any vampires anymore. The Jade Squadrons killed the last ones like a hundred years ago. Teacher SAID."

"That's Jhaden Squadrons, dumbass," said the larger boy. "And Teacher doesn't know everything. I'm telling you, I saw one. Maybe there's one under your bed right now."

"Stop it! Stop it or I'm telling Teacher."

"Quiet, both of you," said Mrs. Park. "We're almost at the memorial."

The memorial was a massive statue. The heroes who led the battle to liberate Seoul—Ganubi, Jhaden, Weslocke, Graeme, Nigel, and Sheila—were at the center of it, striking outsize poses. Around them were representatives of all the armies that had joined in the battle: the mighty army from Kyoto, the heroic forces from Beijing, the street fighters from San Francisco, the sailors of Mazatlan, and the underground fighters from Seoul and New Seoul. Even the nonhuman forces, once called "monsters," had their representatives in the statue: the formian sailors, the illithids of Las Vegas, and the enigmatic living island. And around the base, weak, tiny vampires fled the mighty heroes.

The two boys gazed silently at the statue. They thought about the incredible sacrifices those heroes must have made to ensure freedom for the world. They thought about how difficult the struggle must have been, and how the warriors never gave up despite seemingly impossible odds. Then, being boys, they thought about how badass the battle must have been, and wished they could have been there to see it.

"All right," called Mrs. Park. "Enjoy the rest of your day."

"Let's go to the ganubies," said the smaller boy. "I hear Count of Monte Cristo *is playing."*

"Nah," said the larger one. "Let's see if there's anything new at Graeme's Toy Store."

"No, let's . . ." The smaller boy's voice faded as they wandered off happily, filled with the excitement of a perfect day.

When Vampire World concluded, Morgan started a new campaign. Before the first session, he had us dream up characters who, like us, lived in modern New York City. My character, Raymond Todd, was an NYU dropout who worked as a carnival performer at the Sideshows by the Seashore Theater in Coney Island.

We began the game as a group of friends at a tavern, of course; this time it was a Lower East Side dive. But a little too much refreshment led to our stumbling insensibly out of the bar, taking a wrong turn somewhere, and getting so lost that when we sobered up, we found ourselves in an entirely new world—The City, a seemingly endless urban sprawl that operated under the rules of Dungeons & Dragons and was full of magic, monsters, and heroes. Raymond is now a seventh-level rogue who calls himself "Stingray" and, unlike his friends, has absolutely no desire to find the way home.

Today we're alternating playing in The City with sessions of my own D&D campaign—that story about a mad wizard in a tower at the base of an ancient crater. It's hard to believe the adventure is a decade old, and that I was once extremely nervous about being a Dungeon Master, when now the role fits like an old pair of Living Gloves.* I feel

* "These symbiotic gloves—made of thin chitin and sinew—pulse with a life of their own. . . . While attuned to these gloves, you gain one of the following proficiencies: sleight of hand, thieves' tools, one kind of artisan's tools of your choice, [or] one kind of musical instrument of your choice." *Eberron: Rising from the Last War,* page 278.

confident as a Dungeon Master, able to roll with the many, many surprises this particular group of gamers is so fond of producing. I've learned how to hold their attention and keep the story moving, even when they callously destroy my meticulously crafted plans.

One time I designed a complex trap around a magic mirror that would lead the player characters into an essential area of the plot. R. C.'s impulsive dwarf fighter Beauteponce smashed it to pieces a few seconds after entering the room. On another occasion I planned for them to spend hours clearing monsters out of a cavern—and they hired different monsters to do the work for them, forcing me to improvise the game for the rest of the night.

The biggest change to the campaign has been to discard my initial vision of the Tower of Marv. I had designed that wizard's keep before the game even started, and then when it did, I allowed the players so much leeway to wander the world of Tanz that by the time they finally received orders to find the tower, the hardcover edition of this book had been published, and all of them knew what and where it was.

So I changed things. When the players arrived at the center of Kigeni crater, expecting to ascend a wizard's tower, I surprised them with a small lake full of a strange gray goo—a pool of self-replicating nanobots that had escaped from the Fracture and destroyed the tower, and that were now slowly consuming the entire crater. If unchecked, they would destroy the entire world. Kilën, Tealeaf, Beauteponce, and Norm had to play through a series of seven quests to secure divine intervention and end the blight.

After they did that, their frequent employer Harry, the dean of the magic college, sent them on a mission into the Fracture itself, to find the source of the blight. I used this as an opportunity to introduce elements of D&D's Underdark setting to the campaign, and new character races like the Drow. R. C. took the opportunity to retire poor, dumb Beauteponce and rolled up a new character, a scholarly Githzerai monk named Arrkharr.

And after the source had been located and temporarily contained—with the assistance of a suspiciously helpful and apparently not at all mad Marv—I sent the players on a long sea voyage to find a lost race of beings whose unique techno-magic could seal it away forever. In the process, they added a new player to the table, Morgan's wife, Christina, who plays the Dragonborn ranger pirate Altos Rashazar, the captain of their ship.

The pandemic affected both Tanz and The City, of course. The characters in my campaign got on that boat more than three years ago, when the world was just starting to hear about Covid-19. We've played almost every single session since then virtually, using D&D Beyond, Discord voice chat, and a virtual tabletop called Roll20. It's not the same as playing face-to-face, but it's much easier to schedule, especially as players get older and have more responsibilities, including kids. For instance, Alex moved out of the city, and it's easier for him to find four hours to play online than the six hours it becomes if he has to commute.

Being a virtual Dungeon Master changes some fundamental things about the process. For one thing, sites like Roll20 allow you to prepare complex maps that all the players can see on their computers and interact with, moving tokens that represent their characters, like in a top-down perspective video game. You can even build light sources, create fog of war, or add music or sound effects.*

Rewriting, reinventing, and expanding a world on the fly has been challenging, but it's my favorite thing about running a D&D game. I love improvising and riffing off my players, building a story together like jazz musicians working on a tune. Our game sessions are a highlight of my week, and I feel like I'm part of a special community—

---

* *I* don't, because I'm finally becoming an old, crusty grognard, but *you* can.

not just here in Brooklyn but one that includes D&D fans around the world. The game is more than just a pastime; it's part of who I am.

And finally, I realized, as I watched a full airplane's worth of people disembark into the Indianapolis International Airport, I'm not in the minority. D&D is mainstream. That's why seventy thousand people like me traveled to Indiana for the Gen Con gaming convention—the fifty-fifth annual gathering of gamers, and the same event where David Arneson and Gary Gygax began their legendary collaboration.

Back in 1968, the first official "Geneva Convention" barely attracted enough interest to fill Lake Geneva's Horticultural Hall. But more than half a century later, Gen Con sprawls across the massive Indianapolis convention center and spills out into the conference rooms of a dozen nearby hotels. The four-day event would see record attendance, even in the shadow of a still-receding pandemic; more than 570 game publishers and vendors; and more than twenty thousand ticketed events ranging from board games to role playing games to comedy shows and concerts. According to the Indianapolis convention and tourism agency, Gen Con accounted for more than $75 million in economic impact to the city, more than the Indianapolis 500 auto race and only just surpassed by the Super Bowl.

I practically floated with excitement out of the airport and into a cab. They don't call it "The Best Four Days in Gaming" without good reason.

THURSDAY

Things are different at Gen Con.

When I got onto the hotel elevator in the morning, there were already three people on board: two men, probably in their thirties, both wearing gamer-themed T-shirts over the soft physiques that often result from a sedentary hobby, and an older woman, slight, with short white hair. They all greeted me with smiles as I stepped into the car.

The doors closed, and then there was silence, and then the doors opened again on a lower floor. The woman stepped off and walked away around the corner.

As soon as she was out of sight, one of the men elbowed the other. "That was so cool!" he said.

His friend seemed confused. "What was?" he asked.

"That was Margaret Weis!"

"No fuckin' way!"

There's a different order of celebrity at Gen Con, one where a seventy-five-year-old author of fantasy and science fiction novels is practically a movie star. I can't imagine Ms. Weis gets recognized like that when she's not at a convention, even though she's responsible for multiple beloved, bestselling series like the Dragonlance Chronicles, which she cowrote with fellow TSR vet Tracy Hickman. She's like a superhero with a secret identity: At home in Wisconsin, she's an unassuming mother of two with a degree in creative writing; at Gen Con she's a mythical figure, a midwestern Calliope, author of the stories a whole culture of people grew up reading, loving, and playing.

I got out of the elevator on the second floor and headed through the warren of hallways and sky bridges that connect downtown Indy's hotels to the convention center. They were already crowded, even though it was a weekday morning and Gen Con had just barely started, packed with happy faces young and old, masculine and feminine, white and of color, all positively vibrating with anticipatory excitement.

And it's a good thing everyone was in a fine mood, because the first lesson a new attendee learns at Gen Con is that it is *crowded*, and there are lines *everywhere*. At nine in the morning, the line to pick up attendance badges and event tickets stretched about a quarter of a mile, from one end of the massive building to the other, and even outside onto South West Street, where a staffer stood on the sidewalk holding a sign that said LINE ENDS HERE. But the gamers took the wait in stride and seemed utterly unbothered. This wasn't a long queue—it was the first big event of the convention, a chance to commune with like-minded people.

I eavesdropped on a few conversations as I stood in the line and occasionally shuffled forward. A tall, round guy with a bushy beard, wearing a black newsboy cap, was having an animated conversation with a skinny fellow in a Green Lantern T-shirt. "That's the point of the open gaming license," he said. "It's supposed to encourage innovation!" A young woman wearing pink cat ears chatted with a mom struggling to hold a toddler. "We just drove in from Kentucky," she said. "I love your T-shirt!" It was blue with line drawings of two twenty-sided dice across the chest, each one showing a 20, and the caption "Yes, they're natural."

The line crawled forward, down a wide hallway full of people either waiting to check in or already on their way to the day's first activities. Some of them wore cosplay, even though the annual costume parade and contest wouldn't be held until Saturday. I spotted a woman dressed as the Scarlet Witch (comic book–accurate, not movies). A young boy in a Minecraft creeper costume. Half a dozen different elves of both High and Wood varieties. Countless unidentifiable wizards and warriors, probably those attendees' characters from their home D&D campaigns. And two men wearing a kind of knee-length tartan skirt with pockets I've only ever seen at conventions, known as a "utilikilt."

The line kept moving up the West Concourse, past some of the convention center's smaller meeting rooms. ICC-120 was decked out in the rainbow colors of the Tabletop Gaymers, a nonprofit organization whose mission is promoting diversity, equity, and inclusion in the hobby. A few doors away, the Latine Lounge offered a space celebrating games made by people with cultural ties to Latin America. There was an old-school video arcade with machines that took quarters, and a Kid Zone with activities for little children—and soft chairs for their exhausted parents.

The line wound past the merchandise booth, which had its own line, and then across Crossroads Corridor, where a man was playing Filk music* on a zither as we finally neared the Will Call desks. When I got my tickets, I had a song from the sci-fi TV show *Firefly* stuck in my head:

He robbed from the rich and he gave to the poor.
Stood up to the Man and he gave him what for.
Our love for him now ain't hard to explain,
The Hero of Canton, the man they call Jayne.

Tickets procured, I headed to the day's first event, a new, live onstage D&D game that was part long-form theatrical improv and part anthology television series—kind of the Harold meets *The Twilight Zone*.

It was fronted and cocreated by Matthew Lillard, a prolific actor probably best known for his performance as one of the Ghostface killers in the 1996 horror classic *Scream*, or for his multiple turns as Shaggy in the *Scooby-Doo* live-action and animated movies, TV shows, and video games. Here at Gen Con, Lillard would also be recognized as one of our own; the crowd lined up to get inside the Westin hotel's Grand 5 ballroom surely knew him as a frequent player on D&D live plays, and as the co-owner of Beadle & Grimm's Pandemonium

---

* That's not a typo. Filk music is a self-aware genre that grew out of comic book and science fiction fandoms and features songs about everything from Bilbo Baggins to computer programming.

Warehouse, a company that sold limited editions of products licensed from Wizards of the Coast, like a $399 "Legendary Edition" boxed set of the 2016 adventure *Curse of Strahd* that included everything from faux-leather canvas maps to actual versions of jewelry found in the game.

Like many of his Hollywood contemporaries, Lillard had grown up in the golden age of D&D, first discovered the game as a kid, and then returned to it as an adult. He cofounded Beadle & Grimm's in 2018 with four of his gaming buddies as part of a self-described "midlife crisis"—and then a year later, he took it to Gen Con.

"One of the big moments for us was when we went to go see *Critical Role* play in a live theater," Lillard told me after the show. "We knew they were good. We knew they were talented. We knew that people loved them. But in that moment, we saw a full theater, tens of thousands of people, and we were like 'Oh my god.' "

The Beadle & Grimm's team was inspired, and started thinking about how to make their own live-play game.

"When *Critical Role* first got famous, there were a lot of groups that looked at them and said, 'Oh, people love to watch games for three hours,' " said Lillard's Beadle & Grimm's partner Bill Rehor. "But I think actually they're just great at it, and for most people a three-hour program is too tough a hill to climb. So we tried to think about it in terms of, 'How do you create a meaningful D&D experience for both the players and the audience, but keep it to an hour?' And our answer was: 'How about if we kill everyone?' "

And thus was born *Faster, Purple Worm! Kill! Kill!*, a live-play game series performed by four actors and improvisers who each control a first-level D&D character. Every session of the series has a new plot with new heroes, each with their own unique hopes and dreams of glory—and at the end of each sixty-minute episode, they've all been brutally murdered, and the next episode starts with new characters.

Faster, Purple Worm was developed with an eye toward becoming a TV series, so its deadly conceit was a smart way to keep the stories fresh and to allow for a revolving cast of special guests and celebrities. It also meant the game could be more improvisational and go off on wild flights of fantasy, since there were no long-term storylines to worry about or characters with destinies that gave them impenetrable plot armor.

Shorter games also meant that episodes could be performed not just live but live in front of an audience—a tough thing to pull off if you're planning a four-hour game. "Having an audience made a huge difference in the journey of the show, because you start playing to them, you start raising the energy, and performers start playing at a different level," Lillard said.

And like an improv show, each episode could also be shaped by the audience, who were encouraged to offer plot suggestions or even come up on stage to play minor characters. When the team pitched the show to executives at Hasbro's Entertainment One film and TV studio, their pitch line was "D&D meets *Whose Line Is It Anyway?*."

"D&D is an improv show anyway," Rehor said. "Everyone is making up the story as they go, so we wanted to lean into that."

For Gen Con, Rehor served as the game's host and Lillard was one of the players, joined onstage by actors Gabe Hicks, Luis Carazo, and Kelen Coleman.* Dungeon Master John Ciccolini was also an actor, as well as another Beadle & Grimm's cofounder. And just offstage, musician Scott Passarella sat at a keyboard to provide a live, improvised soundtrack.

The game itself was a raucous affair, an unusual but still entertaining mix of bawdy comedy, bad puns, and improvised songs crammed

* Coleman is instantly recognizable for a small part she played in the insanely popular sitcom *The Office* as Pam's friend Isabel, who sleeps with Dwight Schrute at Jim and Pam's wedding.

into a short adventure about a family of dwarves trying to protect their ancestral forge against an invasion by the Red Wizards of Thay, a clan of notoriously powerful and evil D&D villains. And there was audience participation—in fact, the biggest laugh of the show was when Lillard pulled a random guy onstage to play a minor NPC representing another dwarven family. When the players begged him for assistance, he listened quietly to the request and then growled, "Did you say Red Wizards? You're fucked," and walked off the stage to an ovation.

Before they arrived at Gen Con, Lillard and his team had already produced and recorded an entire season of *Faster, Purple Worm! Kill! Kill!* episodes for a new free, ad-supported streaming television channel owned by Entertainment One and completely dedicated to Dungeons & Dragons. When it launched, *Purple Worm* would run alongside content like a video version of the live-play podcast *Encounter Party*, a cooking show called *Heroes' Feast*, and episodes of the animated *Dungeons & Dragons* cartoon produced by TSR Entertainment in the 1980s.

After the show I went to play D&D with a few other game journalists, and after that to a party hosted by Wizards of the Coast at a nearby bar that had several dozen classic video game arcade cabinets. As I stumbled back toward my bed sometime around midnight, I stopped at one of the convention center–adjacent hotels to peek in on what I thought was going to be a D&D-themed live comedy show but turned out to be one of the performers from *Sesame Street* reading bedtime stories to a bunny puppet.

When I hesitated at the doorway, confused about what was happening, she guided me into a comfortable chair, put a fuzzy blanket over me, and returned to her stories.

Yep, things are different at Gen Con.

FRIDAY

Back in the days of Gygax and Arneson, when Gen Con was a wargaming convention, one of its primary functions was to allow far-flung members of the hobby to meet in person and share their new projects. Usually that meant new game rules, and that's how Gary and Dave began their partnership: bonding over naval warfare simulations and figuring out how to make their rules better.

Fifty-five years later, Gen Con had more games based on television than Trafalgar, but rules still mattered, and the biggest set of rules to hit in a decade was just around the corner: Wizards of the Coast's 2024 rules revision to Dungeons & Dragons.

Careful readers may note here that the phrase "rules revisions" has not previously appeared in this book, the vast majority of which is devoted to detailing at some length a pattern of D&D's various publishers releasing entirely new editions of the game every five to eight years in a nakedly capitalist scheme to persuade fans to buy the books over and over again, even if they're happy with the old ones.

That pattern hasn't ended, exactly. But as I keep saying—things are different.

Back in 2011, when I traveled to Wizards of the Coast's headquarters for the very first briefing about the fifth edition of Dungeons & Dragons, the company's messaging was already changing: They were ending the edition wars and designing the platonic ideal of D&D, a system that unified all players under a single rule set. D&D Fifth Edition would also be the Final Edition, and the future of the business would be driven by adventures and supplements, not reinventing the wheel once a decade.

Of course, that was mostly marketing, and nobody really expected them not to change the core rules again. But the idea of ending edition wars was sound, and the game's designers were serious about it.

The fifth edition, to their credit, lived up to many of those promises. It felt like classic D&D, and enabled different styles of gaming; it allowed for an easy transition to the new rules, whether you were a player who started in the 1970s playing a wargame with wizards or one who picked it up in the twenty-first century with the video-game inspired fourth edition.

But over time, cracks started to appear in the system. Take, for example, the fundamental D&D concept of player character races. In the 1970s, Gygax used the word "race" to describe whether a player character was an elf, a dwarf, or a human; a better word for that might have been "species," but "race" worked, too, if you relied on a slightly archaic definition—a group of living things considered as a category. But culture changes and language moves with it, and five decades later "race" was a loaded word, particularly in the years following the Black Lives Matter movement.

And then what about the D&D concept of player alignment, a way to describe whether your character was innately good or evil? Twenty-first-century morality has largely moved past the idea that anyone is born inherently rotten, favoring the belief that we're all products of our environment and upbringing and capable of making both good and bad decisions.

Now consider the two concepts together. From the birth of D&D all the way up to the fifth edition, the game included races of sentient creatures that were inherently evil, and thus lesser than other beings. It was okay for players to kill goblins because they were evil; hell, it was okay to commit *genocide* and kill entire villages. Encouraged, even.

The 2014 *Monster Manual* described goblins as "black-hearted, selfish humanoids that . . . crave power and regularly abuse whatever authority they obtain." That's the same sort of language that real-world racists and fascists have used to justify their hatred of ethnic and religious minorities for centuries.

It was clear there had to be changes.

My first session at Gen Con on Friday morning, the "D&D 2024 Rules Revision Update," was initially scheduled for a room in the convention center, but sometime between ticketing and the start of the event, it got moved to a larger room, the Grand Hall of Indianapolis Union Station, an attractive Romanesque space more suited to ballroom dancing than an extremely nerdy discussion of tabletop gaming mechanics. I didn't realize it had been moved, though, so I arrived at the convention center right on time, and then had to run, according to my smart watch, 0.46 miles to the station. Gen Con is big.

Inside, the seminar had already started, and Jeremy Crawford and Christopher Perkins, the lead game designers for D&D at Wizards of the Coast, were leading the audience through an overview of upcoming rule changes.

In 2024, coinciding with the tenth anniversary of the fifth edition and the fiftieth anniversary of the game itself, Wizards of the Coast would release new versions of the *Player's Handbook*, the *Monster Manual*, and the *Dungeon Master's Guide*. These products, Crawford and Perkins were quick to disclaim, did not represent a new edition of the game but rather an updated version, meant to address cultural changes, add new features, and fix broken ones.

"We are indeed now moving toward a revision of the 2014 core books," Crawford told the crowd. "Those of you who have been with fifth edition for its entire life are very familiar with our process. . . . We don't have any agenda as to what changes or what stays the same until we have spoken to the community and gotten their feedback through surveys. That informs the game; that's what transforms the game."

Crawford explained that in addition to more editorial, language-focused changes, like the move from "race" to "species," the updated rules would include a host of tweaks and new features that had already been tested through periodical "Unearthed Arcana" rule releases on the D&D website and then evaluated using survey data from thousands of real-life players.

"Thanks to the ongoing conversation that our team has had with the D&D community for the past decade, we have an amazing amount of feedback from you here, and from the hundreds of thousands of people outside this room who also enthusiastically play," he said. "So we want to optimize the best elements of the game, and then the other main goal for this process is to turn the unsatisfactory satisfactory."

For instance, Crawford explained, in 2021 the company performed a detailed survey on the entire 2014 *Player's Handbook* and found that one particular character option, the "Path of the Berserker"* feature of the barbarian player class, was incredibly unpopular and very rarely played.

"The berserker subclass of the barbarian had only a 29 percent satisfaction score," Crawford said. "We consider 70 and above to be the target number. So we thought it could absolutely be better." In the following months, the design team reworked the rules, updated the Path of the Berserker, and then released their new ideas as part of a fifty-four-page play test document that included changes to five classes, two new subclasses, new spells, new weapons, new feats, and adjusted ability score rules. And then they surveyed the thousands of players who had tried out the draft rules.

"When we introduced the new version of the berserker, it went from 29 percent satisfaction to 84 percent satisfaction," Crawford explained. "That is exactly the arc that we want to see from this process."

Testing out rules before you publish them isn't a new idea—that's

---

* "For some barbarians, rage is a means to an end—that end being violence. The Path of the Berserker is a path of untrammeled fury, slick with blood. As you enter the berserker's rage, you thrill in the chaos of battle, heedless of your own health or well-being." *Player's Handbook*, page 49.

why Gary Gygax ran all those games in his basement during the early days of TSR. But Wizards of the Coast has a huge advantage over TSR because they can release draft rules on the Internet and then survey the players the same way. The line of players waiting to get into the Gygax basement would have stretched halfway to Chicago if he'd tried to obtain those numbers.

The designers spent the first two-thirds of the session running through more rules changes, including a new "weapon mastery" system that lets martial characters perform tricks like cleaving through multiple enemies with one swing or pushing an opponent away with their sword—the idea being not to fundamentally change the way the game is played but to offer someone playing a fighter exciting new options, rather than just slash, slash, slash.

Then came questions from the audience—mostly softballs, all an easy yes. Can we expect more support for wilderness exploration in the new *Dungeon Master's Guide*? Will the new books be compatible with old adventures? Are the D&D panel locations for the rest of the weekend still where the program says they will be?

And then came a question that actually got the heretofore relaxed crowd suddenly sitting up in their folding chairs. Will the new rule set be compatible with the open gaming license or Creative Commons? A low grumble rolled through the room.

Let's take a moment to jump way back in time to 1999 (and to page 180 of this book, if you're feeling metatextual), shortly after Lorraine Williams sold TSR and all of its intellectual property to Wizards of the Coast, and then Hasbro bought that company for $325 million.

Dungeons & Dragons was still a popular game among a subculture that had never stopped playing, but there were way too few *new* players, and sales of the game were woefully tiny. Designers at Wizards of the Coast knew they had to do something to revive the property, so naturally they planned for a new edition. But *this* one would be the centerpiece of an entire ecosystem that could be bigger than just D&D.

The "d20 System" was the brainchild of Ryan Dancey, a vice president at Wizards of the Coast who was in charge of Dungeons & Dragons. He believed that the real value of the game was in its massive community of dedicated fans, not in any single edition of the rule set: People loved the game because their DM invented, for example, a story set on a future Earth ruled by vampires. They loved sharing ideas at conventions, cribbing ideas from one another, and using magical items they'd read about in fantasy novels.

So, during the development of the game's third edition, Dancey advocated for a system in which the basic game would be legally available for other people—whether they were lone DMs or competing companies—to use as a basis to make their own stuff. (If any of this sounds familiar, it's because the idea was directly inspired and heavily influenced by the open-source software movement, which came to prominence in the late 1990s and has now been embraced by even the biggest tech giants, including Google and Microsoft.)

"I think there's a very, very strong business case that can be made for . . . embracing the ideas at the heart of the Open-Source movement and finding a place for them in gaming," Dancey said in an interview at the time. "Wizards can establish a clear policy on what it will and will not allow people to do with its copyrighted materials. . . . Just that alone should spur a huge surge in independent content creation that will feed into the D&D network."

The result was the Open Gaming License, or OGL, a public copyright issued by Wizards of the Coast in 2000 that made it legal for other people and companies to use some of the core elements of D&D to make and sell their own products. And it worked. Lots of independent authors wrote adventures for the new third edition of Dungeons & Dragons, which in turn encouraged more gamers to buy Wizards of the Coast's rule books. Others took the open rules and reworked them into different games entirely, including what became D&D's biggest competitor, Paizo Inc.'s Pathfinder Roleplaying Game. Even so, the OGL was considered a massive success: A rising tide lifts all boats.

The OGL remained popular, and enabled a prosperous environment of small and midsize game publishers for the next two decades. It got tweaked here and there, and during the release of fourth edition D&D, Wizards tried to a supplant it with the more restrictive "Game System License," but the OGL survived. And in January of 2016, the company released the system documents for the fifth edition of D&D under the good old tried-and-true open game license.

In September 2021, Wizards of the Coast announced that it was working on updating fifth edition for the rule set's tenth anniversary and the fiftieth anniversary of the game—what we now know as the 2024 "Rules Revision." And a few months afterward, leaks started dripping out of the company that it was also making changes to the beloved Open Game License, rendering the original "unauthorized" and replacing it with a new version.

Lin Codega, a reporter at Gizmodo (where I was editor in chief at the time) got their hands on a leaked copy of the proposed "OGL 1.1" and found that it included many radical changes, including a 25 percent royalty payout for anyone publishing OGL content with revenues over $750,000 and a copyright clause that would cede ownership of some content to Wizards of the Coast entirely.

The D&D community collectively reacted as if they'd all taken the Path of the Berserker. They raged on social media and in the comments of articles about the OGL changes; they swore oaths to boycott the new version of the game and said they'd switch to other systems. A number of major third-party publishers promised to stop making content for the D&D game entirely.

Within a week, Wizards buckled, announcing that they would make the original OGL "irrevocable" and place the game's core rules under an open Creative Common license. It was a positive conclusion, and one that should have made gamers happy. But by considering messing with the OGL in the first place, the company lost a lot of goodwill—and reminded customers that even though Wizards of the Coast may be staffed by D&D fans, it was run as a for-profit company and owned by an *intensely* for-profit multinational conglomerate holding company.

So now, returning to the Rules Revision Update panel and the question of whether the new set would be compatible with the OGL or Creative Commons, one might understand why a look of anxiety flashed across the designers' faces. Crawford turned to a member of the Wizards of the Coast marketing team on the side of the stage. "I have to ask over here, because we just focus on making the game itself," he said.

"We are very much making sure that there will be compatible rules, and that everything is updated so that folks can create moving forward," came the answer.

"Okay, cool, we're doing that!" Crawford said, laughing.

SATURDAY

The nineteenth-century French author Stendhal wrote that upon his first visit to Florence, the sublime beauty of the place was so affecting that he was "seized with a fierce palpitation of the heart . . . and walked in constant fear of falling to the ground." In 1979, psychiatrist Graziella Magherini named this psychosomatic condition "Stendhal Syndrome."

I experienced a similar sensation upon entering the Gen Con Exhibit Hall, home to nearly six hundred different vendors across three hundred thousand square feet of convention center space. That's a solid six acres of commerce, or three hectares of gaming merchandise. Faced with such overwhelming geekiness—perhaps the highest density of nerd on earth—my knees went weak and my head started to swim.*

To be fair, maybe the effect was exacerbated by the tens of thousands of people pushing their way through the floor, practically shoulder to shoulder. But either way, the Gen Con exhibit hall was a glorious thing, unlike just about any other place on the planet. Picture the biggest room you can think of—an airplane hangar, a Walmart Supercenter—and double or triple it in size, then cram it *full* of people who are both desperate to see everything and absolutely delighted to be there. It's a unique kind of good-natured frenzy I've never seen anywhere else. There's a brief ceremony on the morning of the first day, when Gen Con chairman and owner Peter Adkison** welcomes back gamers and then they throw open the doors. The subsequent surge of people makes those Black Friday doorbuster deal videos you see on the local news after every Thanksgiving look like a few old ladies walking into church, only somehow much friendlier.

Don't think that everyone's good mood and the depths of fandom present mean this isn't all about money. Gen Con is an expensive proposition. First, all the attendees have already made significant investments: $135 for a four-day badge, or $85 just to go on Saturday. There's even a $700 "Very Important Gamer" badge that gets you benefits such as access to a special VIG lounge area and your own entry doors to the exhibit hall; it sells out every year. Finding housing is a complicated and costly venture; on a very stressful weekend in February, attendees have to enter an online queue that then gives

---

* I've been working on a name for the phenomenon, something less ominous than "Stendhal Syndrome." Should we call the geek equivalent a "Congasm"? Or maybe a "Fan attack"?

** Peter was the founder and first CEO of Wizards of the Coast; one of the places he put all that Hasbro acquisition money was into purchasing Gen Con, and he's made it significantly bigger over the years.

them a randomly assigned housing registration access time; when they come back to the site during that window, they can choose from whatever rooms are still left. A four-day stay near the convention center can easily run to thousands of dollars.

And then there are the vendors, some of whom have made their biggest expenditure of the year to make it to the convention. In addition to the cost of travel and transporting all their products, the exhibit hall space itself costs a small fortune: $2,174 for the tiniest ten-foot-by-ten-foot booth, located somewhere on the inside of a long row; expect to pay five figures if you'd prefer to have room for more than one customer at a time, and six if you want space to do something audacious like set up multiple tables so people can actually try playing your game before they buy it. Then there are advertising costs—$5,500 to put your graphics on stairs in prominent lobby locations, or $1,450 for two promoted posts on Gen Con's social media accounts in the month leading up to the convention—plus insurance and power, staffing, branded T-shirts for your staff, meals for your staff, rooms for your staff, promotional swag for customers . . . The bottom line is, commerce is king, and the vendors are *very* motivated to get your attention.

Stepping into that environment as an attendee is overwhelming. I didn't know where to start or what to look at; the games, the accessories, the craft goods, or even the people—lots of convention-goers put on their cosplay before hitting the expo floor, which is fun to look at but can make it even trickier to navigate when there's a non-zero chance of catching a tiefling's horn in your face.

So, like a good nerd, I instinctively gravitated to a bookseller right near the doors where I'd entered and whiled away a few minutes hunting through a spinner rack with vintage sci-fi and fantasy paperbacks like Fred Saberhagen's *Ardneh's Sword*, L. Sprague de Camp's *The Unbeheaded King*, and Edgar Rice Burroughs's *Tarzan and the Lion Man*.

Then further in I went, adopting the convention shuffle to navigate through the thick crowd: a few inches forward, a one-foot sidestep, another few inches forward, nodding gamely when I made inadvertent eye contact with one of the dealers trying to lure a minnow out of the massive school of gamers.

So many board games, and so many I'd never heard of, much less played before. Racoon Tycoon, a Monopoly-style property game in which all the players are cute animals. Heroes of Barcadia, a party game in which players place tiles to track down a band of monsters who stole their drinks and hoarded them in a dungeon; each player's health is tracked through a plastic cup with hit point markers on the side, and they drink when they take damage. Cult of the Deep, a worker placement game where you play as cultists competing to establish your faction's rise to power.

And so many media tie-ins! The trading card company Upper Deck had a huge booth decorated with life-size cardboard cutouts of the superpowered cast of the Amazon Prime series *The Boys*. Its "Vs. System" card game had expansion packs available for dozens of different media properties, from James Bond to Disney's *Loki* series to *The X-Files*. At another booth, Dark Souls, a board game based on the blockbuster FromSoftware video game series. Even American Psycho: A Killer Game, which features Christian Bale's blood-spattered face as Patrick Bateman screaming at you from the box top.

There were lots of role-playing games, too, of course—long bookshelves full of current and archival D&D content, Pathfinder, and dozens of cool indies. Hasbro had obviously decided to try to replicate the success of D&D with some of its other big brands, judging by the presence of RPGs based on *My Little Pony*, *Transformers*, and *G.I. Joe*. (I admit it, I almost bought the *Cobra Codex* sourcebook.)

At the end of every aisle, it seemed, there were dice. So many dice. The big two manufacturers had multiple locations—Chessex had four booths, Crystal Caste had three—so if you passed by something you liked at booth 315, you could reconsider when you hit 2419. And a whole cottage industry of artisans had their own booths selling dice made of unique materials. Clear poly dice with sharp edges; opaque sanded dice with smooth ones. Sixteen-dollar sets in the rainbow Pride colors, the Transgender flag colors, or the Polyamorous flag colors. There were sixty-dollar sets made of obsidian, bloodstone, or aventurine. A ninety-dollar one made of amethyst. Or $125 for some kind of speckled black-and-green composite called "Troll's Blood." Can't decide on one style? Take a thirty-two-ounce beer pitcher and dip it into a huge box full of random dice, then take home the entire scoop for fifty dollars.

There were accessories, like a forty-nine-dollar handmade leather dice bag, custom dividers for your board game boxes, or fifteen-dollar wooden tokens to replace the cardboard ones. A balsawood World War II tank manufacturing warehouse kit for sprucing up the battlefield in a wargame. A box of thousands of "non-holo rare" Pokemon cards, twenty-five cents each or five for one dollar.

T-shirts with pictures of unicorns, dragons, mummies, eagles, wolf packs, or phoenixes; bootlegs of branded characters ranging from Mario and Luigi to the Teenage Mutant Ninja Turtles, Jack Skellington, and Link and Zelda; gamer in-jokes like "It's dangerous to go alone," "The cake is a lie," and "It's never sunny in Barovia." Even a shirt featuring the long, drawn face of legendary horror author and insane racist H. P. Lovecraft, whose stories I may love, but I have a very hard time imagining celebrating on my clothing.

I kept my spending relatively modest: A Gen Con 2023 T-shirt (thirty dollars) and pin for my backpack (ten dollars). A reprint of one of my favorite RPG adventures ever, *The Yellow Clearance Black Box Blues* for the Paranoia role playing game (fifty dollars), a set of precision-milled aluminum dice (sixty dollars), and a handmade stainless steel chain mail dice bag to hold them (thirty dollars).

Later that night, at 1:42 a.m., I walked through the still-lively Indianapolis Convention Center. Gen Con is a twenty-four-hour event, with games constantly scheduled; the convention center stays open, as do the common areas of the hotels, so even if you haven't claimed one of the tickets to a 3:00 a.m. session of a party game like Are You a Werewolf or Blood on the Clocktower, there's room to set up a pickup session of whatever excites you.

Earlier in the evening, there had been a wealth of entertainment events in addition to the countless game options. An audience of five hundred filled the historic Indiana Roof Ballroom on Washington Street to watch a live D&D game DMed by Brennan Lee Mulligan, an actor and comedian who runs the popular actual-play web series *Dimension 20*. In the ICC, a thousand people crammed into the main ballroom for D20 Burlesque's Nerdlesque Extravaganza, an annual favorite featuring striptease and go-go dancing based on game, movie, and comic book characters. Another thousand filled the Grand Hall at Indianapolis Union Station for the official Gen Con Dance, boogying the night away to a mix of nerd classics and pop hits. And all over the city, in conference rooms, event spaces, hotel suites, and bars, seventy thousand gamers sat down with old friends or made new ones for sessions of every game imaginable.

I'd elected to start the evening with my own set of friends, an eclectic group of D&D historians and collectors at Gen Con's annual charity auction, and then I'd wandered the convention center for a while, peeking over people's shoulders to get a look at games I'd never seen in action. Everyone was friendly and happy to explain what they were doing; more than a few tables offered to make room for me to join in, even when they were halfway through playing. I took one group up on the offer, two men and two women from Chicago who were just setting up a game of Wingspan, the 2019 winner of the prestigious Kennerspiel des Jahres award,* that I'd always meant to learn. I can confirm that the game is excellent, and the company was delightful.

Wandering further, I met a woman from Milwaukee who'd just finished her first session of D&D ever. She told me she'd started watching *Critical Role* and it made her want to come to a convention. "It was fun!" she said. "We got to kill this serpent thing. I grasped it and I head-butted it and I threw it over the side of a boat."

In the Hoosier Concourse, the main hallway outside the closed exhibit hall, I chatted with some of the people camped out in line overnight. They planned to get to the Ravensburger booth first thing in the morning when the doors opened and get their hands on the new collectable card game Disney Lorcana, which was making its world debut at the convention and wouldn't appear in stores until two weeks later. There were lines upon lines all weekend, because if you bought the game, you also received a Gen Con–exclusive card of Mickey Mouse in Three Musketeers garb. "The game's actually really fun," one of the people in line told me, but he was going to sell his Mickey on eBay, not play with it. (In the months following Gen Con, copies of the card sold for anywhere from $100 to $500, depending on condition.)

Later, I wandered over to the corner of the convention center where attendees had spent all weekend constructing the annual Cardhalla, a sprawling city of card houses made of old, donated stock from games like Magic: The Gathering. Construction starts Wednesday morning and is open to anyone who wants to sit on the floor and start building; by Saturday night, the city fills a space larger than a commuter bus, and has numerous towers stretching six feet or

* The Germans take their board games very seriously.

higher. For twenty-four years, on the last night of the convention, a crowd has gathered and destroyed the whole thing in a glorious fusillade of pocket change. After it's done, someone collects all the cash and donates it to charity. Between all those coins—and a frenzied bidding war for the right to the first throw—Cardhalla raised well over $4,000 for Game Pathways, which supports diversity in the tabletop game industry, and Indy Reads, a local literacy charity. After it was over and my pockets were empty, I met a friend at a nearby brewery that makes custom brews every year for the convention, with names like Twenty Sided Rye, Froth of Khan, and Flagon Slayer.

And that is why I found myself walking through the convention center again at nearly two in the morning, tired but happy, smiling at a group of people sitting in a circle with their eyes closed playing Werewolf; at two guys at a table in front of a closed concession stand locked in a heated game of Lost Cities; at a young woman in a fairy costume dozing as she leaned against a boy in a jester hat who was intently reading a worn old rule book; and at everyone else I came across.

Things are different at Gen Con, as I've already said. And it's big, and it's complicated, and it's noisy, and it's expensive, and it's sometimes smelly, and it's very special, just like the entire family of gamers I've come to know and love over the past decade or so. I love that so many people have found a culture where they can feel at home—a place that has always been safe for outcasts and weirdos, but that has now grown to include basically everyone. I love that games bring people together and create such special bonds. I love that there once was a culture war, but the geeks won.

And I love that you read all the way to the end of this story. Thanks for joining me. I hope we get to play a game together sometime.

David M. Ewalt
October 12, 2023

NOTES

Like a beholder, my eyes are bigger than my stomach. While researching this book I consumed far more information than I could possibly fit into the final printed product, from books, newspaper and magazine articles, websites, panel discussions, seminars, and podcasts to more than a hundred original interviews with past and present D&D designers, executives, and players. You can read some of what couldn't fit here on my website, davidmewalt.com.

And the story of Dungeons & Dragons doesn't end there. To learn more about the history of the game, I recommend that readers take a look at the following sources.

First and foremost, anyone who's serious about understanding role-playing games and where they came from needs to read the various works of Jon Peterson, our hobby's preeminent thinker and historian:

Playing at the World: A History of Simulating Wars, People and Fantastic Adventures, from Chess to Role-Playing Games (Unreason Press, 2012)
The Elusive Shift: How Role-Playing Games Forged Their Identity (MIT Press, 2020)
Game Wizards: The Epic Battle for Dungeons & Dragons (MIT Press, 2021)

Also of note are Michael Witwer's biography *Empire of Imagination: Gary Gygax and the Birth of Dungeons & Dragons* (Bloomsbury, 2015) and Ben Riggs's deep dive into the history of TSR, *Slaying the Dragon: A Secret History of Dungeons & Dragons* (St. Martin's Press, 2022).

Michael Witwer, Kyle Newman, Jon Peterson, and Sam Witwer have also collaborated on two gorgeous art books that tell the story of D&D through its art and illustrations and contain hundreds of images from the archives of Wizards of the Coast and private collectors: *Dungeons & Dragons Art & Arcana: A Visual History* (Ten Speed Press, 2018) and *Lore & Legends: A Visual Celebration of the Fifth Edition of the World's Greatest Roleplaying Game* (Ten Speed Press, 2023).

Some other books worth your attention include the following:

Peter Archer, ed., *30 Years of Adventure: A Celebration of Dungeons & Dragons* (Wizards of the Coast, 2006).

Jennifer Grouling Cover, *The Creation of Narrative in Tabletop Role-Playing Games* (McFarland, 2010).

Gary Alan Fine, *Shared Fantasy: Role-Playing Games as Social Worlds* (University of Chicago Press, 1983).

Paul Hughes, ed., *Cheers, Gary: Celebrating a Legend* (Gygax Memorial Fund, 2011).

Robert J. Kuntz, *Dave Arneson's True Genius* (Three Line Studio, 2017).

Robin D. Laws, *40 Years of Gen Con* (Atlas Games, 2007).

Daniel Mackay, *The Fantasy Role-Playing Game: A New Performing Art* (McFarland, 2001).

Lawrence Schick, *Heroic Worlds: A History and Guide to Role-Playing Games* (Prometheus Books, 1991).

Michael J. Tresca, *The Evolution of Fantasy Role-Playing Games* (McFarland, 2010).

J. Patrick Williams, Sean Q. Hendricks, and W. Keith Winkler, eds., *Gaming as Culture: Essays on Reality, Identity and Experience in Fantasy Games* (McFarland, 2006).

The sources for unique facts or uncited quotes in the text of this volume are as follows:

Archer, Peter, ed. *30 Years of Adventure: A Celebration of Dungeons & Dragons.* Wizards of the Coast, 2004.

Cover, Jennifer Grouling. *The Creation of Narrative in Tabletop Role-Playing Games.* McFarland, 2010.

Fine, Gary Alan. *Shared Fantasy: Role-Playing Games as Social Worlds.* The University of Chicago Press, 1983.

Hughes, Paul, ed. *Cheers, Gary: Celebrating a Lejend.* Gygax Memorial Fund, 2011.

Laws, Robin D. *40 Years of Gen Con.* Atlas Games, 2007.

Mackay, Daniel. *The Fantasy Role-Playing Game: A New Performing Art.* McFarland, 2001.

Schick, Lawrence. *Heroic Worlds: A History and Guide to Roleplaying Games.* Prometheus Books, 1991.

Tresca, Michael J. *The Evolution of Fantasy Role-Playing Games.* McFarland, 2011.

Williams, J. Patrick, Sean O. Hendricks, and W. Keith Winkler, eds. *Gaming as Culture.* McFarland, 2006.

The sources for unique facts or uncited quotes are as follows:

2: Little Wars

33 archaeologist Gary O. Rollefson: "A Neolithic Game Board from 'Ain Ghazal, Jordan," *Bulletin of the American Schools of Oriental Research* 286, May 1992.

34 carved stone dice and an ebony board: "World's Oldest Backgammon Discovered in Burnt City," Payvand.com, December 4, 2004, http://www.payvand.com/news/04/dec/1029.html.

34 The Bronze Age settlement of Mohenjo-daro: "Play Was Important—Even 4,000 Years Ago," *ScienceDaily,* February 8, 2011.

35 the ancient folk tale about a queen: H. J. R. Murray, *A History of Chess* (Oxford University Press, 1913).

40 couldn't afford a set: Jon Peterson, *Playing at the World* (Unreason Press, 2012), 223.

3: Grognards

43 Steve Jobs was a Kriegsspiel fan: Walter Isaacson, *Steve Jobs* (Simon & Schuster, 2011).

4: Druids with Phaser Guns

55 To be conversant with the Principles of War: Charles S. Roberts, "Charles S. Roberts: In His Own Words," 1983, http://www.alanemrich.com/CSR_pages/Articles/CSRspeaks.htm. Last accessed April 23, 2012.

59 I'd given the defending brigands: Gary Alan Fine, *Shared Fantasy: Role-Playing Games as Social Worlds* (The University of Chicago Press, 1983).

59 a medieval Braunstein: Jon Peterson, *Playing at the World* (Unreason Press, 2012), 65.

60 Frankly, the boys in my club were bored: Douglas Alger, "The Keepers of the Realm: Fantasy Fans Still Game for Dungeons & Dragons," *Los Angeles Times*, August 21, 1995.

62 That sealed my fate: Ciro Alessandro Sacco, "The Ultimate Interview with Gary Gygax," *Dungeons.it*, undated, retrieved from http://www.thekyngdoms.com/interviews/garygygax.php.

62 the *Magazine of Fantasy*: Jon Peterson, *Playing at the World* (Unreason Press, 2012), 101.

62 Even now I vividly recall my first perusal: Gary Gygax, "The Influence of J. R. R. Tolkien on the D&D and AD&D Games," *The Dragon*, March 1985.

63 Since we're only talking a couple hundred people: Allen Rausch, "Dave Arneson Interview," GameSpy, August 19, 2004, http://pc.gamespy.com/articles/540/540395p1.html.

65 I asked Dave to please send me: Gary Gygax, "Gary Gygax on Dungeons & Dragons: Origins of the Game," *The Dragon* 2, no. 1 (June 1977).

65 a slightly concave, circular plane of force: *Dungeons & Dragons Player's Handbook, Core Rulebook I, Version 3.5* (Wizards of the Coast, 2003).

66 The reaction . . . was instant enthusiasm: Gary Gygax, "Gary Gygax on Dungeons & Dragons: Origins of the Game," *The Dragon* 2, no. 1 (June 1977).

70 The reaction was so intense: Ciro Alessandro Sacco, "The Ultimate Interview with Gary Gygax," *Dungeons.it*, undated, retrieved from http://www.thekyngdoms.com/interviews/garygygax.php.

71 They laughed at the idea: Ibid.

71 One fellow had gone so far: Gary Gygax, "View from the Telescope Wondering Which End Is Which," *The Dragon* 2, no. 5 (December 1977).

71 a security guard who couldn't afford shoes: Allen Rausch, "Dave Arneson Interview," GameSpy, August 19, 2004, http://pc.gamespy.com/articles/540/540395p1.html.

71 Don Kaye saw the turnout: "The Story of TSR," in *TSR Silver Anniversary Collector's Edition* (Wizards of the Coast, 1999).

72 We published Cavaliers & Roundheads: Paul Hughes, ed., *Cheers, Gary: Celebrating a Lejend* (Gygax Memorial Fund, 2011).

72 badgered Gary into letting [him] in: Timothy J. Kask, "In the Cauldron," *The Strategic Review* 1, no. 5 (December 1975).

5: Strength of Character

88 This spell functions like Summon Monster I: *Dungeons & Dragons Player's Handbook, Core Rulebook I, Version 3.5* (Wizards of the Coast, 2003), p. 286.

6: Temple of the Frog

92 Sales are really quite good: Gary Gygax to Dave Megarry, letter, June 2, 1974.

92 Counting all of the illicit photocopies: "The Story of TSR," in *TSR Silver Anniversary Collector's Edition* (Wizards of the Coast, 1999).

93 Although this was not exactly a 'hot' reception: Gary Gygax, "View from the Telescope Wondering Which End Is Which," *The Dragon* 2, no. 5 (December 1977).

93 We will never allow TSR to become: Gary Gygax to Dave Megarry, letter, March 6, 1975.

94 A magic-user can use a given spell: "Questions Most Frequently Asked about Dungeons & Dragons Rules," *The Strategic Review* 1, no. 2 (Summer 1975).

94 This is a super-intelligent, man-shaped creature: "Creature Features," *The Strategic Review* 1, no. 1 (Spring 1975).

95 Greyhawk had a fountain: Gary Gygax and Robert Kuntz, *Dungeons & Dragons Supplement I: Greyhawk* (TSR, 1975).

95 Ours is known as the 'Living Room': Ibid.

98 Tactical Studies Rules is not a giant company: Brian J. Blume, "TSR—Why We Do What We Do," *The Strategic Review* 1, no. 2 (Summer 1975).

98 impossible to work with: "AD&D and My Leaving TSR," Gygax.org FAQ, archived April 21, 1999, at http://web.archive.org/web/19990421153255/http://www.gygax.com/gygaxfaq.html.

99 There is no question in my mind: Ciro Alessandro Sacco, "The Ultimate Interview with Gary Gygax," *Dungeons.it,* undated, retrieved from http://www.thekyngdoms.com/interviews/garygygax.php.

101 Deep in the primaeval [*sic*] swamps: Dave Arneson, *Blackmoor* (TSR, 1975).

101 Pool of the Frog: A downward sloping area: Ibid.

102 like a grist mill: Gary Gygax, "TSR News & Editorial," *The Strategic Review* 1, no. 4 (Winter 1975).

102 It started out being fun: Jeremy L. C. Jones, "Interview with Dave Arneson," *Kobold Quarterly,* April 9, 2009, http://www.koboldpress.com/k/front-page460.php.

7: The Breaking of the Fellowship

104 This is the last issue: Timothy J. Kask, "In the Cauldron," *The Strategic Review* 2, no. 2 (April 1976).

105 Somewhere along the line, D&D lost: Gary Gygax and Brian Blume, *Dungeons & Dragons Supplement III: Eldritch Wizardry* (TSR, 1976).

107 gaming, variants, discussion, fiction by authors: Timothy J. Kask, "Dragon Rumbles," *Dragon* 1, no. 1 (June 1976).

108 TSR had its lawyers: Jon Peterson, *Playing at the World* (Unreason Press, 2012), 555.

108 TSR had sent a cease-and-desist: Ibid., 552.

110 a heavily muscled dark skinned man: Robert Kuntz and James Ward, *Dungeons & Dragons Supplement IV: Gods, Demi-Gods & Heroes* (TSR, 1976).

110 a lotus flower capable of restoring all lost hit points: Ibid.

110 Perhaps now some of the 'giveaway' campaigns: Ibid.

110 We've told you just about everything: Ibid.

111 Gygax told a war-gaming newsletter: Jon Peterson, *Playing at the World* (Unreason Press, 2012), 536.

111 *Blackmoor* is finally done: Timothy J. Kask, "In the Cauldron," *The Strategic Review* 1, no. 5 (December 1975).

111 My first assignment, fresh out of college: Robert Kuntz and James Ward, *Dungeons & Dragons Supplement IV: Gods, Demi-Gods & Heroes* (TSR, 1976).

111 contradictory, confusing, incomplete: James Maliszewski, "Interview: Tim Kask (Part I)," *Grognardia,* September 18, 2008, http://grognardia.blogspot.com/2008/09/interview-tim-kask-part-i.html.

112 His function will be to help us co-ordinate: Gary Gygax, "TSR News & Editorial," *Strategic Review* 1, no. 4 (Winter 1975).

112 July issue of *Little Wars*: Jon Peterson, *Playing at the World* (Unreason Press, 2012), 571.

112 the introduction to *Valley Forge*: Ibid., 572.

112 a credit for "special effort" in Lankhmar: Ibid.

113 even less in promoting the game: Ibid.

113 Perhaps Arneson simply preferred: Ibid.

8: Why We Play

114 Everything around me takes the shape of the Knight: David Shenk, *The Immortal Game: A History of Chess* (Anchor, 2007), xvii.

115 Duchamp's wife, Lydie Sarazin-Levassor: Ibid.

116 As we wandered around, uncertain: Clifford Geertz, "Notes on the Balinese Cockfight," in Clifford Geertz, *The Interpretation of Cultures* (Basic Books, 1973).

119 A play community generally tends to become permanent: Johan Huizinga, *Homo Ludens: A Study of the Play-Element in Culture* (Beacon Press, 1971).

121 American culture has some nuances: Michael J. Tresca, *The Evolution of Fantasy Role-Playing Games* (McFarland, 2010), 13.

121 A hero ventures forth: Joseph Campbell, *The Hero with a Thousand Faces*, 2nd ed. (Princeton University Press, 1968), 23.

122 I see role-playing as an opportunity: Leonard H. Kanterman, MD, "My Life and Role-Playing," *Different Worlds: The Magazine of Game Role-Playing* 1, no. 1 (1979).

122 a 2011 study of middle and high school students: G. E. Harrison and J. P. Van Haneghan, "The Gifted and the Shadow of the Night," *Journal for the Education of the Gifted* 34, no. 4 (2011), 669–97.

125 Comeliness reflects physical attractiveness: Gary Gygax, *Advanced Dungeons & Dragons Unearthed Arcana* (TSR, 1985).

9: Arneson vs. Gygax

132 Before the third supplement: Gary Gygax, "D&D Relationships: The Parts and the Whole," *The Dragon* 2, no. 8 (May 1978).

134 The 'Basic Set' of D&D is aimed: Ibid.

135 an imaginative game: Gary Gygax, "View from the Telescope Wondering Which End Is Which," *The Dragon* 2, no. 5 (December 1977).

136 the same notes: Jon Peterson, *Playing at the World* (Unreason Press, 2012), 583.

136 approximately 1,000 Peasants, 100 Soldiers and Nobles: David Arneson, *The First Fantasy Campaign* (Judges Guild, 1977).

136 the main livestock: Ibid.

137 there is some evidence that the company considered: Jon Peterson, *Playing at the World* (Unreason Press, 2012), 582.

137 California gamer Steve Perrin: Ibid., 589.

137 killing the project: Ibid.

137 embarassing Gygax into action: Ibid.

137 hateful, aggressive, and avaricious: Gary Gygax, *Advanced Dungeons & Dragons Monster Manual* (TSR, 1977).

138 the molecular vibrations of the displacer beast: Ibid.

138 is loathsome beyond description: Ibid.

138 ideal for cleaning: Ibid.

138 they roam such: Ibid.

139 Imitation is claimed to be the sincerest: Gary Gygax, "View from the Telescope Wondering Which End Is Which," *The Dragon* 2, no. 5 (December 1977).

140 Gandalf is quite ineffectual: Gary Gygax, "The Influence of J. R. R. Tolkien on the D&D and AD&D Games," *The Dragon* 9, no. 95 (March 1985).

140 The seeming parallels and inspirations: Ibid.

143 Giants have been raiding the lands of men: Gary Gygax, *Steading of the Hill Giant Chief* (TSR, 1978).

146 diligent prayers and deeds: Gary Gygax, *Advanced Dungeons & Dragons Players Handbook* (TSR, 1978), 20.

147 There is one dweeb-like chap on the back cover: Col_Pladoh (Gary Gygax), "Gary Gygax Q&A Part VIII," EN World message board thread, comment #359, March 22, 2005, http://www.enworld.org/forum/archive-threads/121380-gary-gygax-q-part-viii-36.html.

147 TSR sold ten thousand copies: Gary Alan Fine, *Shared Fantasy: Role-Playing Games as Social Worlds* (The University of Chicago Press, 1983), 27.

147 inspires the sort of fanatic devotion: Liam Lacey, "Dungeons and Dragons: An Underground Game Is Ready to Surface," *The Globe and Mail,* November 29, 1978.

148 the J. R. R. Tolkien of the games world: Ibid.

148 Only the most severe critic could: Don Turnbull, "Open Box," *White Dwarf* 16 (December 1979/January 1980), 15.

149 Our once lonely pastime has arrived: Timothy J. Kask, "Dragon Rumbles," *The Dragon* 4, no. 9 (March 1980).

149 The course of TSR Hobbies' development: Gary Gygax, "What's Ahead for TSR?" *The Dragon* 4, no. 9 (March 1980).

151 commercially and artistically valuable right: Plaintiff's Memorandum, Arneson v. Gygax, 473 F. Supp. 759 (D. Minn. 1979), May 7, 1979.

151 Advanced Dungeons & Dragons is a different game: Gary Gygax, "D&D, AD&D and Gaming," *The Dragon* 3, no. 12 (June 1979).

151 any revised edition or foreign language translation: Arneson v. TSR Hobbies, Inc., US Dist. LEXIS 21340 (D. Minn. 1985), March 27, 1985.

152 We don't hate each other: Allen Rausch, "Dave Arneson Interview," GameSpy, August 19, 2004, http://pc.gamespy.com/articles/540/540395p1.html.

10: The Satanic Panic

153 experimenting may occur . . . craving and preoccupation . . . compulsive use: "Stages of Addiction," Intercept Interventions, http://www.interceptinterventions.com/stages-of-addiction/.

155 the hottest game in the nation: Geoffrey Smith, "Dungeons & Dollars," *Forbes,* September 1980.

157 The continual press coverage: Ciro Alessandro Sacco, "The Ultimate Interview with Gary Gygax," *Dungeons.it,* undated, retrieved from http://www.thekyngdoms.com/interviews/garygygax.php.

157 of working with the Antichrist: Molly Ivins, "Utah Parents Exorcize 'Devilish' Game; Fomenting Communist Subversion Complaints Began Right Away," *New York Times,* May 3, 1980.

158 very definitely . . . These books: Ibid.

158 Real-life Clerics: TSR Hobbies needs you: *The Dragon* 5, no. 2 (August 1980), 49.

158 This is indeed only a game: Martin Wainwright, "Child's Play for Satan," *Guardian,* April 6, 1984.

159 My understanding is that once you reach a certain point: "Dual Deaths Are Linked to Fantasy Game," United Press International, November 4, 1984.

159 nearly fifty teenage suicides and homicides: Tipper Gore, *Raising PG Kids in an X-Rated Society* (Abingdon Press, 1987).

160 intense occult training through D&D: Jack Chick, *Dark Dungeons* (Jack T. Chick LLC, 1984).

160 I think I understood their motivations: Allen Rausch, "Gary Gygax Interview—Part I," GameSpy, August 15, 2004, http://pc.GameSpy.com/articles/538/538817p1.html.

161 Perhaps most surprising about TSR's management: Stewart Alsop II, "TSR Hobbies Mixes Fact and Fantasy," *Inc.*, February 1, 1982.

162 I was pretty much boxed out: Allen Rausch, "Gary Gygax Interview—Part I," GameSpy, August 15, 2004, http://pc.GameSpy.com/articles/538/538817p1.html.

163 paid half a million dollars: Paul La Farge, "Destroy All Monsters," *Believer*, September 2006.

165 I fully expected to be dismissed: Ciro Alessandro Sacco, "The Ultimate Interview with Gary Gygax," *Dungeons.it*, undated, retrieved from http://www.thekyngdoms.com/interviews/garygygax.php.

11: Death or Glory

169 I began to become uneasy: Ciro Alessandro Sacco, "The Ultimate Interview with Gary Gygax," *Dungeons.it*, undated, retrieved from http://www.thekyngdoms.com/interviews/garygygax.php.

170 I was so sick of the fucking company: David Kushner, "Dungeon Master: The Life and Legacy of Gary Gygax," Wired.com, March 10, 2008.

13: The Inn at World's Edge

185 The very first LARP: "The Pre-History of Dagorhir," Dagorhir.com, http://www.dagorhir.com/dagorhir/history.htm.

14: D&D Next

207 By involving you in this process: Mike Mearls, "Charting the Course for D&D," Wizards of the Coast website, January 9, 2012, http://www.wizards.com/dnd/Article.aspx?x=dnd/4ll/20120109.

207 Imagine trying to organize a basketball team: Ethan Gilsdorf, "Players Roll the Dice for Dungeons & Dragons Remake," *New York Times*, January 1, 2012.

207 Too little, too late: Houstonderek, comment on David M. Ewalt, "'Wizards' Announce New Dungeons & Dragons," *Forbes*, January 9, 2012, http://www.forbes.com/sites/davidewalt/2012/01/09/wizards-announce-new-dungeons-and-dragons-an-inside-look-at-the-game/.

207 Allow me a momentary guffaw: James Maliszewski, "Quelle Surprise," *Grognardia,* January 9, 2012, http://grognardia.blogspot.com/2012/01/quelle-surprise.html.

208 The D&D player is a business manager: Khaver, comment on David M. Ewalt, "'Wizards' Announce New Dungeons & Dragons," *Forbes,* January 9, 2012, http://www.forbes.com/sites/davidewalt/2012/01/09/wizards-announce-new-dungeons-and-dragons-an-inside-look-at-the-game/.

ACKNOWLEDGMENTS

To learn the story of Dungeons & Dragons, I interviewed hundreds of designers, players, and executives who made the game what it is today. They gave up valuable time to share their memories, and I'm grateful to all of them.

First and foremost, thanks to the guys in my weekly game night: Alex Agius, Brandon Bryant, R. C. Robbins, Phillip Gerba, and Morgan Harris-Warrick. They're good friends, and I'm grateful for the time they've shared. They are also, in a very real sense, coauthors of the Vampire World sections of this book. We wove those stories together, so I'm lucky they're all so clever. My old gaming buddies deserve recognition, too, particularly Michael Bagnulo, Ray Cuadro, and Everett Meyer.

Special thanks are due to Peter Adkison, Tavis Allison, Rich Burlew, Monte Cook, Cory Doctorow, Jeff Gomez, Eric Hautemont, Kristi Hayes, Jerry Holkins, Mike Krahulik, Mary Kirchoff, Ian Livingstone, James Lowder, David Megarry, Frank Mentzer, Michael Mornard, R. A. Salvatore, Lorraine Williams, Skip Williams, and Tracy Hickman.

And thanks to everyone at Wizards of the Coast, including Greg Leeds, Jerome Lalin, Shelly Mazzanoble, Mike Mearls, Chris Perkins, Liz Schuh, Rodney Thompson, Laura Tommervik, and especially Marcella Kallmann and Tolena Thorburn.

It would have been impossible to complete this project without the support and forbearance of my editors at Forbes, especially Randall Lane, Bruce Upbin, Eric Savitz, and Lewis DVorkin.

Thanks to all the people who helped get this book started: Jessica Stockton Bagnulo, good friend and world's greatest bookseller, provided my first introduction to a publisher. Elisabeth Eaves and Michael Noer gave invaluable edits and advice on my first attempted chapters. My agent, Chris Parris-Lamb, helped craft a half-baked idea into something with value, and I appreciate his counsel, intelligence, and hard work. Amelia Mularz did a brilliant job fact-checking the final manuscript, and John Sellers read it and provided great advice. Jon Peterson provided additional notes and critiques, and I'm grateful for his expertise.

Thanks to everyone at Scribner, especially Susan Moldow and Nan Graham, for taking a chance on a weird idea and showing great patience during its production. I would also like to tell them that whatever they're paying my editor, Brant Rumble, it's not enough. He's insightful, funny, talented, and understanding. I can't imagine a better editor, and I'm in his debt.

Thanks to my parents, Larry and Barbara Ewalt, and my sister, Elissa Ewalt Ghosh. Thanks to my nieces and nephew—Casey, Maddie, Sophia, and Sid—for being awesome. And all my love and thanks to my wife, Kara, who was incredibly supportive and understanding while I worked on this project. I would have to write a hundred books to describe how amazing she is.

Finally, thanks to Gary Gygax and Dave Arneson for the good times.

ADDENDUM, OCTOBER 2023

I'll reiterate the thanks to all above, unless there is, hypothetically, someone I've deleted since the first publication of the book, in which case, I don't like you anymore.

The crew at Wizards of the Coast continues to be immensely generous with their time, and I'm especially grateful to Sheila Hughes and Greg Tito for all their hard work and camaraderie over the years.

Michael Witwer is a gentleman, a scholar, and a valued friend. Joe Manganiello maxed out all his ability scores, yet remains humble and kind. Thank you both.

Sabrina Pyun is my amazing editor at Scribner, and the person who had the idea to update and rerelease this tome after a decade. She is awesome, and I think they should change the name of the company to Simon & Sabrina. Thanks as well to Nan Graham, Katie Monaghan, Brianna Yamashita, Jaya Miceli, Stu Smith, Annie Craig, and the whole Scribner team.

I want to thank my niblings Casey, Maddie, Sophia, and Sid again, because it won me significant cool uncle points last time, and also because I can use this space to shout out Sid and Sophia's D&D characters, Zek Eko and Ula Broccolini, who will now be remembered forever in some dusty Library of Congress warehouse.

Thank you to composer Howard Shore, the London Philharmonic Orchestra, the New Zealand Symphony Orchestra, the London Voices, and the London Oratory School choir, who all perform on the soundtrack to Peter Jackson's *Lord of the Rings* trilogy, which I have probably listened to at least five hundred times while writing versions of this book.

And, finally, I would like to recognize the small group of extremely nerdy readers who read the first sentence of this addendum and then dug out an old hardcover copy of this book to see who I was snubbing. I hope they weren't too disappointed to realize it was a feint, meant to self-identify some of the people who've read this book multiple times over the last decade and then said very nice things to me. Thank you to them, and to everyone who has spent their valuable time with one of my books. For the record, I love hearing from readers at davidmewalt@gmail.com, but please don't be offended if it takes me a long time to respond to your email.

THE WALL OF HEROES

Inscribed on this page are the names of the members of the "Dice Army" who selflessly gave their time and labor to help spread the word about this book. We are grateful for their service.

COLONELS

Anthony Franchini

Greg Gilbraith

Garrison Hoffman

Eric Owens

Lori Richards

David Tinker

Fernando P. Tirado

Keith York

MAJORS

Ernest Decoteau

Tim L. Foster

Victor Johnson

Rodrigo Morales

Donald Toner

CAPTAINS

Andrew Bush
Bradley Daniels
Laurent Daubas
Drew Fleisher
Brian Forster
Mike Langdale
Michael Maiello
Cena Mayo
Amanda Moreau
Jeffrey Noffz
Curtis Obert
Mark Rojewski
David Schweizer
Joshua Starr
Haralambos Syristatides

ADMIRAL OF THE DICE NAVY

H. Murphey McCloy III

INDEX